Praise for One-Car Caravan

"This is a terrific book, at once wise and hilarious, about my favorite part of presidential politics—the campaign that takes place before the primaries, before the public gets interested and, sometimes, before the candidates themselves know what they're doing. Walter Shapiro never takes the easy cynical path; he appreciates the lovely intricacies of politics—and he manages to provide a belly-laugh (sometimes at his own expense) on just about every page."—**Joe Klein, *Time* magazine columnist and author of *Primary Colors***

"[T]hese are moments of candidates unplugged, musing, philosophical—and much harder to come by later in a campaign."
—***Washington Post Book World***

"Walter Shapiro ... was among the first to grasp the fact that 2004 would be a radically different presidential contest... [*One-Car Caravan*] astutely characterizes several '04 contenders."
—***Baltimore Sun***

"The great strength of the book, in addition to the author's brilliant, fair, and uproarious journalistic style, is its focus on describing the campaign process as it evolves, uninfluenced by the conclusion. Shapiro cleverly showcases the realities, complexities, and intensity of not only the candidates but also the political process itself.... He demonstrates that the political process, much like the candidates that operate within it, is flawed, imprecise, and more intimate than we may have imagined...."—***Political Science Quarterly***

"Walter Shapiro knows pols, and loves them enough to show how funny they are."—**Richard Ben Cramer, author of *What It Takes***

"Shapiro... has both the perspective and the wit to analyze the 2004 crop of Democrats... The book is studded with telling insights and offers an amusing yet astute assessment of those who would be president."—***Hartford Courant***

"[Shapiro] isn't interested in the predictable answers candidates offer to the question, 'Why me for president?' He is going after deeper insights, and his active mind looks for clues everywhere: in private conversations with the candidates, in whom they hire to run their campaigns and how they make the crucial decisions, small and large, about their futures.... Shapiro succeeds in offering a commentary that is mature, witty, entertaining and marked by political and emotional intelligence."—*Publishers Weekly*

"Shapiro combines seasoned political savvy with a keen eye for the absurd and a love of the tortured pun.... For die-hard fans of the game of American politics, the witty and astute commentary of *One-Car Caravan* is a must read."—*Rocky Mountain News*

"The book's fly-on-the-wall anecdotes will delight the politically obsessed."—*BusinessWeek*

"Armed only with a deep passion for the process, and a bracing dose of skepticism and good humor, Shapiro has returned from his journeys [with the candidates] with a treasure trove of solid insights into who these people are, and how they think."
—Jeff Greenfield, CNN Senior Analyst

"Shapiro offers some funny anecdotes and insight into how presidential candidates go from a single car to the bus motorcade and the rambling remarks to the stump speech."—**Nashua (NH)** *Telegraph*

"Real, raw, behind-the-scenes stories ... [Shapiro] remains true to his craft and gives readers the full picture of the candidates—the good, the bad and the ugly."—*National Journal*

"[A] comprehensive, witty, and altogether compelling look at contemporary politics and politicians.
—Wendy Wasserstein, playwright

Contents

Introduction to the Paperback Edition

Political reporters are supposed to be hard-bitten cynics free from partisan loyalties and detached from any human emotion beyond a natural crankiness. Yet at the risk of jeopardizing my press card tucked into the hatband of my fedora, I will confess to feeling a sense of authorial pride on the misty morning of July 7. In a few minutes, John Kerry and John Edwards would be stepping before the cameras in their first joined-at-the-hip appearance as the 2004 Democratic ticket. Never in my quarter century covering presidential campaigns have I known two candidates so intimately. Delving beneath their public personas, I had gained the hard-won access required to understand their off-stage personalities, their private motivations, their strengths and limitations, their dreams and drive. My journalistic secret was to play the early bird and get a worms-eye view of these two senators before they were surrounded by camera crews and smothered by handlers. For I had been out there on the road, often alone, with John Kerry and John Edwards back during those long-vanished, hope-and-heartbreak days when their campaigns were indeed one-car caravans.

The setting for Wednesday morning's meticulously choreographed ticket-mate two-step, which will be broadcast live on the network morning shows, is a newly mown field atop a Pennsylvania hillside, just outside of Pittsburgh. The imagery suggests the simple life—or as close as Teresa Heinz ever gets to a milkmaid existence on her baronial 88-acre hideaway quaintly billed as a farm. Finally, the candidates and their wives—accompanied by their children—glide hand-in-hand across the meadow as if they were the von Trapp family in a road-company version of *The Sound of Music.* One hundred reporters and photographers, who have been idling for an hour on scenic hay bales trucked in for the occasion, leap to their feet in anticipation of news. Okay, not "news" rigorously defined as being unexpected, but at least "news" in terms of being a new photo-op.

Kerry, sensitive to the vaudeville adage about the risks of competing with animal acts and small children, playfully decides to turn the spotlight on tow-headed Jack Edwards, a four-year-old who had blithely assumed that his political role at his father's big moment would be limited to thumb-sucking. "We want to announce today that we have a new campaign manager," Kerry says as a smile undermines the mock-gravity of his tone. "Jack Edwards has taken over everything." Elizabeth Edwards, the mother of the newly-installed campaign manager, attempts to gently dislodge Jack's thumb, while six-year-old daughter Emma Claire silently signals that she needs to be fortified with a hug. This is a cute-children scene perhaps unmatched since Shirley Temple dined alone. Kerry cannot disguise his pleasure in the way his vice-presidential rollout has turned into "Take Your Running Mate's Children To Work Day." The Democratic nominee gleefully recounts Jack's first unimpressed words on learning of his father's selection: "I can swim with my head above water."

All but forgotten on this morning of good-ship-lollipop merriment is the uncertainty that accompanied Kerry's second-banana deliberations. Just thirty-six hours earlier, Edwards had been a politician with no fixed address and no firm future, not knowing whether he would be heading home to North Carolina when his Senate term expired at the end of the year. The courtroom-charmer-turned-senator, who had chosen the pursuit of the presidency over a re-election race, was in Boston that Monday gamely headlining a series of Democratic fund-raisers. Ardent backer Fred Baron—widely hailed and sometimes reviled as the nation's most successful tort lawyer—arranged for Edwards to informally chat with Cam Kerry, the candidate's younger brother and closest adviser. This unofficial hour-long meeting turned into a bonding session, but on the late-night flight back to Washington, Edwards and Baron still had nothing tangible to go on but their hopes. Baron, a veteran of countless waits for jury verdicts, was struck by how unflappable Edwards seemed at a moment when his political future hung in the balance. As the two men separated at Dulles Airport, Edwards's final words to Baron were, "Whatever is, is." That fatalistic sentiment appears to have been the family mantra, since Elizabeth Edwards wrote in an e-mail to a friend Monday afternoon, "Que sera sera."

Almost at the precise moment when Edwards's plane was touching down at Dulles, Kerry was unveiling his veep pick to Jim Johnson, who handled the vice-presidential vetting, and campaign manager Mary Beth Cahill. To continue the dramatic cross-cutting, this was also about the time when the *New York Post* was going to press in its tabloid bid for Dewey-defeats-Truman immortality with the front-page screamer, "KERRY's CHOICE—Dem picks Gephardt as VP candidate." Not until Tuesday morning did Edwards get his formal invitation to spend part of a putative Kerry administration in what the current White House likes to describe as an "undisclosed secure location." As Edwards recalls at Wednesday's ticket-punching ceremony, "When I got the call from John, my assumption was it was another reporter calling to say, 'Do you know anything?'"

I spent the rest of Wednesday inside the bubble, following the Democratic duo as the campaign bounced from Pittsburgh to rallies in Cleveland and Dayton. (Dear Lord: Would it disturb some vast eternal plan if someday you made Hawaii a battleground state?) Without reviewing my notes or replaying my tapes, I have no memory of a single word that Kerry or Edwards uttered at these outdoor events, although I do recall this off-kilter boast by Teresa Heinz in Cleveland: "I'm not a lawyer. I only talk people talk." What stayed with me instead was a sense of distance from Kerry and Edwards, both physical and emotional. Campaign travel at this point in the political calendar means that a reporter gets the privilege of being permitted by the Secret Service to be in the same ZIP code as the candidates, but the vantage point is usually the press bleachers at a rally. This is what it generally means when a talking-head journalist boasts on TV, "I was just out with Kerry in Ohio."

As a veteran of seven presidential campaign cycles, I have become inured to the weirdness of this face-in-the-crowd style of coverage. But a few days after Edwards joined the ticket, I went to a baseball game at Yankee Stadium. Seated in prime real estate behind home plate, I had one of those breakthrough realizations—the sort that normally take place in a room with a couch and a bearded psychiatrist—as Derek Jeter came up to bat. My God, I thought, I am closer to the Yankee shortstop than I ever was to Kerry and Edwards in Ohio. The big difference is that baseball fans don't rush home to brag, "I was just out with Derek Jeter at Yankee Stadium."

This anecdote helps explain the theory behind the book that you are about to read. Even though I never before put it in Jeter-esque terms, I sensed that the under-chronicled early days of the 2004 campaign were my last chance to take the measure of would-be presidents and vice presidents as people instead of theorizing about them from afar as they recite speeches off TelePrompTers. That was the original guiding star that inspired me to write *One-Car Caravan*. In adding new chapters to this tale of the most unpredictable race for the Democratic nomination since Jimmy Carter learned to smile, I have decided to keep the original version intact so that you can relive the anything-can-happen immediacy of the drama. Hindsight and the aura of omniscience that comes with it are laudable virtues in writing history. But nothing—absolutely nothing—can compare to having been there as a reporter witnessing first-hand and close-up both John Kerry and John Edwards embark on their rendezvous with destiny.

Author's Note

When I was a boy back in the 1950s, movie theaters were tolerant places that allowed patrons to come and go as they pleased without this multiplex fandango about having to buy a ticket specifically for the 5:30 show. My grandmother was comically lax about bureaucratic details like starting times, so on my visits to New York we would invariably slip into a darkened upper Broadway movie house halfway into the performance. This, of course, meant that we would also leave in the middle of the next showing, stumbling down the aisle, blocking views, tripping over sprawled feet and upending popcorn containers with my grandmother apologetically murmuring, "This is where we came in."

As I write these introductory words during the summer of 2003, I feel peculiar elbowing my way toward the exit at a time when most Democratic voters are just beginning to follow the plot lines and the character arcs of the 2004 Democratic race. The difference is that this time—unlike my early movie-going adventures—I depart with only the haziest suspicions about how the story is going to end. It is tempting to stick around to chronicle what promises to be a spine-tingling drama about the lust for fame and power against the backdrop of the Great Game of democracy. Not since the 1970s can I recall a year in which the nomination fight was bathed in so much uncertainty as five, maybe six, candidates headed into the fall before the primaries with plausible scenarios for victory.

So why then have I chosen to conclude this presidential campaign saga before the end of the first reel?

Campaign chronicles, which traditionally appear after the election is over, have sadly become a dying genre. No matter how beautifully crafted and meticulously researched, these now-it-can-be-told political narratives suffer from a built-in flaw—readers know the inevitable conclusion before they get to the first page. Even as a card-carrying political junkie, I would find it hard to curl up right now with a backward-looking recap of, say, the 2000 race filled with passages that begin, "Bill Bradley was nervous ... "

That's why I thought that it would be glorious fun to publish at the precise moment when Americans are becoming transfixed with the battle for the 2004 Democratic nomination. At the risk of sounding as earnest and self-congratulatory as a public-television station during a pledge drive, I also preferred to deliver my insights about the candidates and the process to Democratic voters before, rather than after, they cast their primary ballots. Moreover, as someone whose normal idea of adventure travel is crossing my Manhattan block against the light, I uncharacteristically succumbed to the daredevil factor. There was an irresistible challenge to clambering out on the high wire to describe the early phases of a presidential contest while the political ground kept shifting beneath my feet.

There were advantages to starting early. The most telling glimpses of the candidates came when they were just beginning to step into the cauldron of ambition. This was the time when their lines were still unscripted and their public veneers hung loosely like a suit that they had not yet grown into. Yet most of the stories from this period were buried in the back pages of the newspapers. With a war in Iraq and other breaking news stories, who can blame editors for decreeing that full-tilt coverage of the presidential campaign could wait until the hurly-burly leading up to the Iowa caucuses and the New Hampshire primary? But what this means, in practice, is that most Americans tune in to the campaign at the point when the Democratic contenders have thrown off the last vestiges of spontaneity—and virtually every syllable they utter is an echo of an earlier speech, question-and-answer session or interview. Journalistic convention, with its emphasis on what happened yesterday, does not often allow reporters to backtrack in order to explain the roots of a candidacy. So in the normal course of political coverage, the meaningful material from the initial stages of the campaign ends up consigned to the memory hole.

It was also liberating to cover a presidential campaign before the living-room wars of dueling television commercials. I find it frightening to contemplate how much time I have squandered over the years sitting passively in hotel rooms with the TV set turned on so that I could monitor campaign spots. It is a strange calling that requires hours of viewing soporific programming in order to see the ads as voters do. (My vision of hell involves being damned to eternally watch the last half hour of celebrity fodder and happy-talk cooking tips on the network morning shows.) Campaigning is far more revealing when the candidates are still making all their pitches to Iowa and New Hampshire voters in person rather than merely using public appearances to reinforce the imagery of their thirty-second commercials.

There is a famous *Twilight Zone* episode about a man who is given a pocket watch with the miraculous ability to stop time dead in its tracks. Everything is frozen except the person who controls the watch. This being Rod Serling's universe, our hero decides to rob a bank and, of course, drops the watch as he is wheeling out the cash—and is thereby doomed to spend eternity in a lifeless place where the clocks never move. Even though I am a law-abiding sort, I confess that I craved that freeze-frame power in my headlong rush to write this book. How I longed for the candidates to go into the Witness Protection Program for a few months—or at least refrain from committing news—so I could catch up with everything I had missed. Here I was just adjusting to John Edwards's prowess as a fund-raiser in the first three months of 2003 when suddenly Howard Dean blew by him with his Internet-powered rocket pack. A presidential campaign waits for no man—not even, alas, a frenzied reporter with a looming book deadline.

As a result, I decided not to attempt to be comprehensive. I lavished my attention on those aspects of the pre-primary caval- cade that I found to be revealing, riveting or risible. Rather than filling in gaps in the chronology by calling on the work of my peers in the press pack, I have almost completely limited this narrative to events that I witnessed personally or reconstructed through my own interviews. (A major exception is the reporting by my research assistant, Yael Kohen, which provides much of the non–East Coast detail on political fund-raising.) Aside from public speeches, virtually all quotes from the candidates, their aides and other political players have been drawn from my own interviews.

My approach is also premised on an abiding belief in the pres- ent tense. As much as I admire books such as Richard Ben Cramer's magisterial *What It Takes* about the 1988 presidential race, I consciously chose to leave the task of delving into the life histories of the candidates to others. So there are no cameo appearances by college roommates, no tales from bygone political campaigns and no gotcha efforts to sift through birth certificates, arrest records or marital histories. What I have mined instead is the rich vein of political life from mid–2002 until mid–2003, that under-appreciated period when the candidates decided to run, first organized their campaigns, raised the early money and made their initial forays into Iowa and New Hampshire.

Alert readers may notice that a character named George W. Bush hovers in the background of this narrative without ever striding onto center stage. This neglect is intentional, since I didn't think that the world needs more bromides about the White House's message discipline, the president's fund-raising prowess or Karl Rove's purported genius. For all the claims by the Democratic contenders about their electability, the validity of these premises will only be tested after the primaries. Some things in politics are unknowable—and I saw no reason to camouflage my deficiencies as a seer with evanescent survey data, theoretical discussions of swing states and self-serving quotes from Republican operatives.

Contemporary political coverage revolves around the Poll-ish Corridor, that seemingly empirical outlet into the seas of public opinion. But too often polls foster a false sense of certainty and mask the volatility of the popular mood. This was especially true during the early days of the Democratic race and, as a consequence, there is minimal discussion of survey data in this book. Part of the reason is aesthetic—it is nearly impossible to compose interesting sentences built around percentage points and margins of error. Also, national polling about Democratic candidate preferences is virtually worthless months before the primaries, since it measures little more than name recognition and dimly felt and easily changeable impressions of the candidates. Iowa is a pollster's nightmare; it is nearly impossible to predict with precision which Democrats will make the major commitment to leave their warm homes on a blustery winter's night to attend the caucuses. New Hampshire polls are notoriously fickle, and placing too much weight on them in the early going minimized the potential for the late-breaking surges of Gary Hart in 1984 and John McCain in 2000.

Now for the true confession that undergirds my skepticism about polls. In 1984, covering my first campaign for *Newsweek,* I became bored with writing if-clauses and employing flaccid conditional verbs to describe the contest for the Democratic nomination. So in the issue of the magazine that hit the newsstands the day before the New Hampshire primary and arrived in many mailboxes after the votes were counted, I embraced the seemingly unequivocal polls and flatly declared that Walter Mondale's "lead in New Hampshire appeared unassailable." Flying to New Hampshire on primary day—and thereby missing the exit poll numbers—I arrived at the Sheraton Wayfarer Hotel, the press corps' favorite watering hole, blithely unaware of Mondale's stunning defeat. But I got no further than the hotel lobby before Michael Kramer, then the political columnist for *New York* magazine, stopped me to say, with words that echo in my ears even today, "You blew it!"

Enough reminiscences of bygone campaigns, since I have one final task to complete. I must explain why, following the model of *What It Takes,* I am presenting this book without an index. All of us on the fringes of the political game have stood in book stores riffling through the alphabetized final pages of a new book to see if we are mentioned. This egoistic ritual inspires either the transient joys of relevance or the lasting agonies of rejection. To spare everyone further emotional turmoil, I have dispensed with the editorial feature that has caused more heartbreak than the senior prom.

But there is also a serious reason for this willful omission. I did not write this book as a scholarly reference work or a dense study of the political process. Rather, it is the tale of one reporter's adventures with this season's political dreamers, who each fantasize that he will become the forty-fourth member of an illustrious historical chain dating back to George Washington. The joy of this book, I hope, is in the narrative, not in the roster of names mentioned on specific pages. So, please, put aside the yellow highlighter and the serious expression. Instead, if I am lucky, you will read it in bed late at night with a smile on your face.

CHAPTER 1

Rubes on the Road

In the beginning, there is only one declared Democratic presidential candidate, one car and one reporter.

As the lone car with a Vermont state trooper behind the wheel heads south toward a Democratic dinner in New Hampshire, the slate-gray late afternoon sky and the premature reddish tint to the foliage serve as mournful reminders that this is the last Saturday of summer 2002. But Vermont Governor Howard Dean is too wound up with coiled energy to be disheartened by the change of season. As outlandish as it seems for a candidate without money, campaign staff or national following, Dean is consumed by a seductive fantasy: the self-confident conviction that come July 2004 he is destined to be standing alone on the stage of the Democratic Convention, bathed in a sea of light, his hands held high in exuberant triumph, as he accepts the presidential nomination of the party of Roosevelt, Kennedy and Clinton.

That may be the dream, but the momentary reality for Dean, the doctor turned five-term governor, is defined by a black-and-white photostat of the first brochure of the 2004 campaign season. From her perch in the front seat, Kate O'Connor, the governor's lone traveling aide, hands the folded, envelope-size

"Dean for America" flier to the candidate for inspection. With pursed lips, Dean scrutinizes it with the intensity of a president reading a memorandum from his national security adviser. After noting several typos, the trim, buttoned-down Dean points to a photograph of himself on the inside flap and complains, "This picture makes me look like Dick Cheney. Like I have Bell's palsy." But the candidate's middle-aged vanity is assuaged by the cover photo montage, which shows him smiling in white shirt sleeves and tie against the over-orchestrated backdrop of an American flag and, yes, the White House. "This is really excellent," he says, before asking nervously, "Did we get a price on this?" There is something weirdly incongruous about the question. Here is a man who might, just might, someday be deciding the Pentagon's budget—and he's worrying about minor printing costs.

In a one-car caravan, it is hard for a reporter to maintain journalistic detachment. Soon Dean and O'Connor are debating a rarified question of political packaging: the merits of a phrase describing him as "an avid downhill skier." The candidate broods, "People think that skiing is a rich man's sport, that it costs as much as golf. So make it 'an avid outdoorsman.'" Dean turns to me, his backseat focus group, to validate his linguistic sleight of hand. I offer a political hack's judgment that I have never seen a single ski pole during a quarter century of reporting trips to Iowa—and, perhaps, the sport does have elitist overtones. As a populist alternative, I suggest, "an avid outdoor bowler." (In the end, the brochure merely describes Dean as "an outdoorsman . . . [who] hiked all 270 miles of Vermont's spectacular Long Trail.")

Nothing in politics compares to the enforced intimacy of sitting with a candidate in the backseat on a long car ride. There are no distractions, just two guys talking, as the one with the tape recorder tries to take the measure of the other who wants to be president while the topics range from Jean-Paul Sartre (Dean has an encyclopedic memory of his political philosophy courses at Yale) to the lineup of the 1961 Yankees. Up until now, Dean, the governor of a rustic bed-and-breakfast state, has been something of a stealth candidate—and this is only his third lengthy interview with a national reporter. During the early days on the campaign calendar, you can still pose an obvious question and receive a candid rather than canned response. So, I ask, how did you decide to run for president? "It's a hard question to answer," Dean begins. "The answer should be that I deeply care about it, and I thought it all out. But the way it happens is that I'm very intuitive, so I was driven toward running before I knew why I was doing it. I know that doesn't make any sense. It sounds like I'm just a very ambitious person who wants to be president."

I resist the temptation to mention that naked ambition has spawned countless other candidacies. But Dean does it for me: "There's a big difference between me and some of the other Democrats. There are two Democrats running because they want to be president, that's all they can tell you." (An obvious, if slightly petulant, reference to probable rivals John Kerry and John Edwards.) "I want to be president because I want health insurance, I want to balance the budget, I want a decent foreign policy. I want to lead people, not follow. I don't want to just do what it takes to be elected." (Whoops, here comes the stump speech.)

Surprisingly, Dean opts for something suspiciously close to honesty: "I decided in August [2001] that I wasn't going to run again [for governor]. It then quickly came to me that I had a choice of joining boards and swearing at the *New York Times* every morning and saying how outrageous it was. Basically, I was in a position where I thought I could run for president, so I decided that I was going to."

That answer is about as unvarnished as an experienced politician ever gets. For all his sincere, if still vague, sentiments about health care, the economy and foreign policy, Dean is not running as an embodiment of a political movement. There were no "Draft Dean" websites or trial balloons floated by his fellow governors. Rather, faced with a life change in his early fifties, Dean recoiled at the vision of the road ahead—a few corporate boards, a blue-

ribbon commission or two, the semi-retired, didn't-you-used-to-
be-somebody, bland life of a respected former governor. Having
stared into the abyss of irrelevance, Dean preferred to roll the dice
at a craps table soon to be filled with other candidates who would
arrive with huge piles of chips and chits earned in Washington.

Sure, Dean's impetuous decision to be the first declared candidate means arduous weeks on the long trail in Iowa and New
Hampshire, endless car rides to small towns along two-lane
blacktop, never knowing if at the next stop there will be a half
dozen apologetic party officials or an eager crowd of two hundred Democrats, and evenings ending in the spare bedrooms of
local supporters. This quest also brings with it a repetitive diet of
breakfasts and lunches with New York investment bankers and
other party fund-raisers (the Regency Hotel one day, the University Club the next), always wondering if practiced patter, a smile
and a shoeshine are enough to close the deal. For the frugal and
underfunded Dean, the closest thing to relaxation is solitary time
in the backseat of his state car, a motorized luxury that he will
lose when his final term as governor ends come January. Amid
the blur of cities, handshakes and speeches, there will be days
when Dean's air of crisp determination collides with rebuffs and
disappointments, when his self-created candidacy seems to be
held together with duct tape and stubbornness.

But there will be other days of bright sunshine and clamorous
applause. Maybe he could capture the mood and the moment.
Maybe he would be transformed by the revelation: By God, there
is nothing more exhilarating than an audience enraptured with
me, Howard Dean, its new hero, rising to its feet with every line,
the cheers and the chants—and, most of all, the hopeful faces of
Democrats who have come to share my ego-driven dream. This is
life, this is history, this is Mickey Mantle playing center field in
the 1961 World Series. Who wouldn't take this madcap odyssey
over a comfortable existence in Burlington, Vermont, punctuated
by visits to New York for a meeting of the Council on Foreign
Relations or lunch at the Ford Foundation?

Running for president requires, among other essential ingredients, a quart of Vermont maple syrup. As we cross the New Hampshire line en route to the annual dinner of the Cheshire County Democrats in Keene, Kate O'Connor suddenly remembers that she has forgotten to bring Dean's contribution for the silent auction. Her emergency solution: a cell phone call to her sister in nearby Rutland instructing her to pick up the emblematic Vermont product on her way to the dinner. An hour later, the jug of syrup, autographed by Dean, sits awaiting bids on a white paper–covered table in Keene, along with a North Carolina T-shirt signed by Edwards, a Kerry-donated Senate paperweight, a Dick Gephardt souvenir plate and a remainder-table copy of Joe Lieberman's 2000 book, *In Praise of Public Life*.

It is a tribute to the democratic vibrancy of the first primary state (or a reflection of the limited social possibilities in Keene) that 250 Democrats are willing to spend Saturday night at long tables in a non-air-conditioned former Masonic hall, dining on limp spaghetti and overcooked meatballs, all for the sake of their party. Despite the steamy temperature, these stalwarts are in no hurry to hear their featured speaker. This is New Hampshire, where presidential contenders come and go but local politics endures forever, so there are individual stand-and-wave introductions of dozens of candidates for county commissioner and state representative, hokey rituals such as the raffle for the chrysanthemums that decorate the stage, plus full-length speeches by the candidates for senator and governor. Slipping outside for a breath of fresh air during the endless preliminaries, I am introduced to Andi Johnson, the organizer of the dinner and a member of the Keene city council. She confesses that the local party had a desperate time searching for the main speaker before settling for Dean. As she puts it, "Dean's okay, I guess. But he's been here a lot—and, well, we had hoped to do better."

* * *

Jimmy Walker, New York City's Jazz Age mayor, claimed, "No girl was ever ruined by a book." But this middle-aged boy, as I have grown to be, certainly had his life upended by one. After reading Theodore White's *The Making of the President 1960* as an adolescent, I began dreaming about enlisting in the privileged brotherhood of campaign reporters. To witness history being forged, to share the confidences of candidates on the cusp of the White House, to take part in the hype and hoopla of our quadrennial rite of democratic decision—that all seemed a splendid adventure. How noble, how naive. I was like a boy who grew up thrilling to stories about powerful locomotives and Casey Jones only to sign on with the railroads in the era of Amtrak. The job description may read the same, but it's not like it was in the age of coal-fired boilers.

I have covered every presidential race since 1980, each time feeling more disheartened by the poll-propelled, focus-group-fixated mechanics of modern politics. My journalistic credentials, dangling from a chain around my neck, are in good order. But there is nothing ennobling about being in the middle of a hundred-person press pack, surrounded by technicians wielding boom mikes as lances and camera tripods as battering rams, elbowing and shoving, as I hold my tape recorder aloft in the hopes of catching the front-runner robotically utter a banality like, "I'm running because I want a better life for all Americans." The rat-a-tat of attack ads, the charges and counter-charges, the petulant press conferences, the opposition research e-mails and snarling spin doctors all reduce politics to a Hobbesian jungle.

Name an American airport, and I have probably trudged across its tarmac, lugging a laptop computer, bedraggled and sleep deprived, stumbling past eager advancemen on my way to another press bus. From the bygone days of three TV networks when chain-smoking correspondents carried portable Olivetti typewriters and complained about their hangovers, I have seen the campaign entourages swell into electronic armies as TV cameras overwhelm the story they are purporting to cover and print reporters, deprived of access, are reduced to regurgitating self-serving quotes from manipulative press secretaries.

But for all my cynicism about presidential politics in election years I still thrill to the innocent simplicity of the off years when it all begins. The speeches in New Hampshire living rooms, the pancake breakfasts in Iowa diners, the question-and-answer sessions on South Carolina lawns—and even the silent auctions and the chrysanthemum raffles. For all the blather about how candidates are transformed by climbing Heartbreak Hill during the presidential marathon, they are the same confident, complex and committed contenders at the start of the race as they will be in 2004 when they near the finish line. The only difference is that in these early days all the Democratic strivers are open and accessible to reporters instead of bubble-wrapped by image-sensitive handlers and cordoned off by the Secret Service. For all the deadline-driven journalistic obsession with what the candidates said yesterday at syncopated airport rallies and during flag-draped photo ops, the best way to gauge their personalities, their intellects, their motivations and their aspirations is to be there at the beginning when everything seems possible, even the presidency itself.

This opening-gun phase of the presidential contest—the time when the candidates are honing their stump speeches, concocting their messages, assembling their staffs, courting party activists and wooing fund-raisers—has become known as the Invisible Primary. The phrase was invented by journalist Arthur T. Hadley in his 1976 book called (surprise) *The Invisible Primary*. Hadley formally defined it as "that period of political time between the election of one President and the start of the first state primary to determine the next political candidates." Of course, the presidential campaign unfolded at the leisurely pace of a Trollope novel during Hadley's era, when nomination fights were rarely decided until the California primary in June and underdog contenders still dreamed of dramatic upsets on the floor of the convention. These days, thanks to the fast-forward

frenzy of modern politics, the Invisible Primary is best understood as that period of preliminary presidential positioning that
occurs before the first TV spots are aired and typical primary voters tune in. But make no mistake, this isn't Grapefruit League
baseball when the regulars are preoccupied with their condition-
ing and timing rather than the outcome. In presidential politics,
every pitch matters, even if the only people watching are the
managers, the scouts and the eager denizens of the press box.

Built into the American ethos is a steadfast belief that there
are objective statistical measurements for everything, from the
life potential of a gawky seventeen-year-old (SAT scores) to the
chance that you will impulsively buy a refrigerator on the way
home from work (Index of Consumer Confidence). But what
makes the Invisible Primary so intriguing is that it takes place in
an alternative universe where no one has learned to count. "This
is a period when no one can keep score," says Harrison Hickman,
the pollster for Edwards. "The political process is a spectator
sport, but there is no scoreboard. Yes, there are two empirical
measures: the polls and fund-raising. But you have two great
Texas examples—John Connally in 1980 and Phil Gramm in
1996—where money didn't matter. And the third empirical measure, which is hard to tally, is the opinion of those at the center of
the process."

Political reporters, along with the candidates and the consultants they chronicle, are dedicated students of recent history
with a brightest-kid-in-the-class eagerness to find parallels to
prior campaigns. But this time around, these tribal memories of
the 1976 Iowa caucuses or 1988 Super Tuesday primaries serve to
obscure the Big Story. The rarely acknowledged truth is that the
2004 Democratic race is radically different from any earlier contest—and that presidential politics has entered a post-modern
phase as dissimilar from the 1992 Clinton crusade or even the
2000 Al Gore campaign as John Kennedy's TV camera charisma
was from Adlai Stevenson's cerebral eloquence.

What makes 2004 so distinctive? It isn't just the sheer number of candidates, even though the field is as cluttered as the list of potential co-respondents in Tony Soprano's divorce. After all, back in 1976 (the year of Fred Harris, Milton Shapp and Frank Church), there were enough Democrats running to restage *Cheaper by the Dozen*. Nor is it war with Iraq or the lingering sorrows and fears from September 11. Rather, the twenty-first-century difference arises from the interplay of four factors: (1) a ludicrously front-loaded and truncated primary calendar, (2) inflationary political costs that belie the flatline Consumer Price Index, (3) the universally accepted belief that politics is a four-season sport and the only way to win is to wage the permanent campaign and (4) the rise of influential Internet political tip sheets (most notably, ABC's "The Note" and the CBS "Washington Wrap") that spread hyperactive judgments of the campaigns and the candidates. Nobody planned it this way, but the inadvertent result is the creation of a warp-speed political culture that undermines deliberation by the candidates, the press and, ultimately, the primary voters. To update Woody Allen, a presidential candidate is like a shark. Either he relentlessly moves forward, earlier than ever before, or his dreams of the White House die.

It wasn't long ago that would-be presidents dedicated the odd-numbered year before an election to wrestling with their ambitions and mapping out the route to the nomination. As chronicled by Teddy White, the initial planning session for JFK's 1960 campaign took place at Hyannisport in late October 1959. Bill Clinton, according to David Maraniss in *First in His Class,* spent June and July 1991 quizzing "scores of friends about whether he should run for president." That same year, New York Governor Mario Cuomo, the fabled Hamlet of the Hudson, dithered until the December 20 filing date for the first primary before deciding, with a plane waiting to whisk him from Albany to Concord, New Hampshire, that this was one campaign that would never get off the ground.

Cuomo's protracted inner agonies now seem as quaint as Dear

Abby columns on the dangers of teenage petting. Today's candidates no longer have the luxury of leisurely indecision, despite retired General Wesley Clark's year-long dithering on the sidelines. Where once presidential politics was a hand-tooled industry, now, due to changes in the calendar, it's a frenzied assembly line. Beginning with the 1996 Republican race, the major caucuses and primaries were compressed into an adrenaline-pumping six-week period in February and March. (This irrational new system ended up nominating septuagenarian Bob Dole. Go figure.) Leave it to the Democrats to take a bad system and make it worse. This time around, the Democrats decided to quicken the pace in 2004 by advancing the Iowa caucuses and the New Hampshire primary to January, knowing that many other states would jump their nomination contests to early February. The result is a slam-bang schedule with all the subtlety of a Saturday night during Fleet Week. No longer can underdog candidates like Gary Hart in 1984 follow the strategy of winning the New Hampshire primary and then using the newsmagazine cover burst of publicity to replenish their finances. Presidential politics these days is a merciless all-cash business with no pity for a candidate who does not have money in reserve to blanket California with thirty-second spots. As a result, any serious White House aspirant has to begin early in order to meet his daunting sales quota of raising at least $15–$20 million by the end of 2003. With a maximum contribution limit of $2,000, it requires wooing tens of thousands of individual donors, one checkbook at a time.

That's why, with the eager Dean in the forefront, the real Democratic race began earlier than ever before—right in the middle of the 2002 congressional elections. By fall 2002, five Democrats (six, if you count the flamboyantly self-promoting Al Sharpton) were actively preparing their campaigns. Even late entrants like the doggedly determined Bob Graham and left-wing gadfly Congressman Dennis Kucinich had fluttered past the starting gate by spring 2003. The candidates, at least the more self-aware among them, understood the personal consequences of their fast-off-the-mark decisions to run. As Joe Lieberman confided to a private luncheon of New York fund-raisers in March 2003, "I've made this decision not casually. This is a decision to live a life that is not a normal life for at least a year, hopefully two years. And as somebody said, 'If you get really lucky and get elected, you'll live an abnormal life for the rest of your life.'"

The Democratic contenders undoubtedly felt at times discouraged by George W. Bush's poll ratings and daunted by the Republican fund-raising machine, but rarely in modern history have opposition-party candidates been less awed by the intellect or the erudition of the incumbent president. Where a humbled Harry Truman declared on ascending to the presidency, "I felt like the moon, the stars and all the planets had fallen on me," the 2004 Democrats worried far more about surviving the campaign than actually governing from the White House.

An emblematic example of this hell-I-can-do-that mentality came from Buddy Menn, Graham's chief of staff, who described a spring 2001 conversation with the Florida senator. The two men were in the bedroom of Graham's Capitol Hill townhouse as the senator was packing for a trip home. Menn casually mentioned that at this moment they might have been chatting in Dick Cheney's guarded compound at the Naval Observatory if Al Gore had selected Graham as his 2000 running mate and thereby carried Florida. That prompted Graham, who had never breathed a word of his presidential ambitions, to muse aloud, "You know, Buddy, at this point in my career, you learn that the person at the other end of Pennsylvania Avenue puts his pants on the same as you and I." Graham's one-leg-at-a-time imagery may have been hackneyed, but the sentiment was real. Despite the terrorist threat and the chilling international climate, every serious Democratic hopeful—from Edwards, the first-term senator, to veteran legislators like Dick Gephardt and Kerry—was animated by the certainty that he was far better prepared to wield globe-girdling power than that shallow and callow man in the White House.

* * *

How quickly it all changes from a quiet waltz in the corner with the gramophone playing to the blaring bedlam of a Rolling Stones concert. On a Wednesday morning in late February 2003—just five months after my visit to New Hampshire with Lonely Guy Howard Dean—I was standing in a full-fledged campaign press room set up in an elementary school in St. Louis. As several dozen reporters banged out their stories heralding Gephardt's just completed formal launch of his candidacy, I realized that I was getting my first glimpse of what the campaign will eventually become. Once the Gephardt announcement tour was over, the oversized press entourage vanished like Brigadoon—and the former House Democratic leader, like his rivals, went back to traveling light. But, for the moment, the temporary scene in St. Louis seemed so familiar, so reminiscent of other years and candidates. The occasional bursts of chatter were comforting in their predictability. A TV producer, worried about phone connections, announced triumphantly, "Josh has got a land line." A nervous local reporter confided to a colleague from the Missouri press corps, "I hope I'm on the list for a Gephardt interview." A national correspondent, tapping out the lengthy list of the other candidates, called out for help, "Is Howard Dean still the governor of Vermont?" (No.) Gephardt pollster Ed Reilly asked, in words so commonplace for those of us in the bubble, "What time does the filing end?" (Soon.)

Then, in a reenactment of that enduring campaign cliché, it was time for the traveling press to cram into press vans for the drive to the airport in the middle of, yes, a ten-vehicle motorcade led by a police car with lights flashing. Free for the moment from deadline pressures, the mood was jaunty as we acclimated ourselves to a rambling life stripped of such pesky annoyances as red lights and airport security. This was the first leg of a campaign (or "Camp Pain" as it is sometimes called) reunion tour. Once aboard the American Airlines jet to Des Moines—the first press charter of the 2004 political season—I found myself sharing a row with Susan Milligan from the *Boston Globe,* a fellow wayfarer during the last months of the 1992 Clinton campaign. A few rows back, Alexandra Pelosi (the former NBC producer who transformed her handheld camera footage from the 2000 Bush campaign into the charming HBO movie *Journeys with George*) whooped with glee when the flight attendant offered her the same unvarying campaign lunch that she mocked in her film: a cellophane-wrapped ham sandwich.

Down the aisle came Dick Gephardt, his coat off and his smile on, to share a few minutes of easy banter with the reporters in each row. Even though it had been twenty-six years since he entered Congress and fifteen since his last bid for the Democratic nomination, the sixty-two-year-old Gephardt still had the look of a freckle-faced kid perched on a stool at the neighborhood soda fountain. He was warbling about the wonders of a St. Louis specialty, the frozen concoctions of Ted Drewes. "Heavy cream, honey and eggs," said this milkman's son now running for president. "It's the best frozen custard in the world. On a hot summer's night, there might be a hundred people lined up outside the store." This summer night's reverie was interrupted by the voice of the pilot over the intercom: "We're delighted to have aboard with us today the future president of the United States, Congressman Dick Gephardt." After a moment's hesitation, the candidate broke into an aw-shucks grin and, for one shining moment in the skies above Iowa, he was indeed the emperor of ice cream.

Etched in my memory are images of so many other campaign flights. A gallant John Glenn—accompanied by a new country music mother-and-daughter duo called the Judds—playing out the string during the sad-eyed days of the 1984 primaries. A nearly comatose Bob Dole sitting motionless in an aisle seat the morning after he blew his lead in the 1988 New Hampshire primary. Most of all, I recall the sleep-deprived and adrenaline-fueled ecstasy of the Clinton plane in the final hours of the 1992 campaign—the blur of takeoffs, landings and exuberant airport rallies—as candidate, spouse, staff and scribblers all sensed the impending victory.

A campaign plane is like a Japanese office: everyone knows his or her place. There is a beguiling comfort in the routine from the assigned seats and detailed itineraries to the unvarying rhythms of speeches and filing times. But it is also a self-contained universe in which real voters, penned up behind Secret Service rope lines, become little more than the faceless Hollywood hordes in Nathanael West's *The Day of the Locust.* When you are aloft in a campaign plane, most of America is viewed as part of the great flyover. From 30,000 feet, the presidential race is reduced to an abstraction of states, media markets and demographic groups. Inevitably the campaign takes on the cynical trappings of an us-versus-them contest—and they are not the opposition candidate and party, but rather the poor rubes stuck on the ground.

How different it is at the beginning of the journey, when everyone from the fledgling candidates to the ever hopeful reporters are rubes on the road to the White House.

CHAPTER 2

Testing the Waters

John Kerry looks more like a president than any other Democrat poised to run in 2004—tall and lean, with a thick no-Rogaine-needed shock of gray hair and a chiseled face that seems to belong on a Roman coin. But sometimes a public image can mask private disarray.

So it is with Kerry on this Boston Sunday morning in mid-August 2002. An aide has ushered me into the dimly lit downstairs study of the senator's townhouse on Louisberg Square, one of the grand properties that he owns with his second wife, the heiress Teresa Heinz. Feeling a bit like the intrusive tabloid reporter portrayed by Jimmy Stewart in *The Philadelphia Story*, I take an inventory of the furnishings: several large-scale models of whaling ships in the foyer; a macabre oil painting featuring a skull over the fireplace; and a wall of books ranging from Winston Churchill's *World Crisis 1915* to Jules Witcover's account of the 1976 presidential race, *Marathon*.

My *Architectural Digest* ruminations keep being interrupted by sounds akin to a wildebeest on a feeding frenzy. It is an overwrought Kerry rooting around in the adjoining conservatory, frantically searching for a missing cell phone. The distressed senator, dressed in a light green polo shirt and white Dockers, eventually wanders into view long enough to nod at me before resuming his search. Kerry even borrows the aide's phone to call the van waiting on the street in front of the house to see if the missing object is on the front seat. Finally, World Crisis 2002 is averted when the absent-minded senator discovers the phone in his briefcase. "Rock and roll," Kerry announces, a Vietnam-era phrase he frequently employs to signal movement.

Kerry is something of a stranger to me. After intermittently watching him for more than a decade in the Senate, my impression is that he is a haughty, overly ambitious patrician who is a bit too slick in his eagerness to exploit his heroism in Vietnam. In short, I'm not imagining a buddy movie in which I play Ben Bradlee to his Jack Kennedy. But I'm also open to the possibility that I may have misjudged Kerry from afar. The point of these initial journeys with the leading presidential contenders is to get beyond the shallow Washington clichés and the snarky back-of-the-press-conference put-downs. Lurking behind every cardboard campaign poster is a real person—sometimes as complex as Bill Clinton, sometimes as one-dimensional as George W. Bush—and the challenge of political reporting is to find him.

On the thirty-minute drive to Hanscom Field, a private airport outside Boston where we take off for Keene, New Hampshire, Kerry keeps up a running travelogue for my benefit. He points out the Mormon tabernacle, where Republican gubernatorial candidate Mitt Romney worships, before wistfully musing, "I wish I knew more about comparative religion." As we pass through Lexington, Kerry offers his practiced Gray Line tour guide spiel, pointing out the road along which the Minutemen marched on their way to "the rude bridge that arched the flood." A stand of oak trees prompts Kerry to recall dragging his daughters (now adults) on fall foliage tours of New Hampshire, adding the mournful note that he told them, "When I'm dead, think of me when you see a tree." Just as I begin to dismiss the cell phone interlude as a strange aberration, I get a brief glimpse of Kerry's control freak side. As we approach the barred gate of the airport, Kerry pointedly instructs the woman staffer driving the van to back up and try again so that she won't have to open the door to announce his arrival on the speaker phone.

Maybe, in originally arranging my day with Kerry, I should have noted something suspicious when press secretary David Wade asked, "You don't mind small planes, do you?" That question did not invite an honest answer—unless I yearned to be left on the ground as the candidate flew to New Hampshire. Perhaps, on the drive to the airport, I should have listened more carefully when an aide told the senator that there would be an airshow in Keene. Kerry immediately joked, "Maybe I'll try some barrel rolls on the way in."

That should have been my first whiff of danger. But I can be pretty oblivious. Only after I am strapped into the back of the twin-engine Cessna 340 do I notice that the pilot, the trained professional who owns the rented plane, is sitting in the wrong seat. For unless Massachusetts is a fly-on-the-left state, Kerry (yikes!) is my pilot in more than a metaphorical sense.

The short flight, on this sparkling August Sunday, is uneventful (and free of barrel rolls) until Kerry begins the long turn to line himself up for landing in Keene. At that moment, the lost-and-found cell phone in Kerry's back pocket begins to ring. "Don't answer it," I pray. The man who wants to pilot the nation's destiny reaches for the phone in an overconfident display of multitasking. I am thinking, "It's illegal in New York, where I come from, to talk on a cell phone while driving a car. And we're landing a plane. Is this what New Hampshire means with its license plate slogan, 'Live Free or Die'?"

Luckily, the real pilot takes the ringing instrument from Kerry. But this trained professional can't figure out how to work the flip-top phone. So Kerry grabs it, opens it, hands it back—and then proceeds to make a perfect landing in the center of runway 2.

Kerry's cell-phoniness can easily fit the caricature of him as a heedlessly arrogant and self-important politician. But that would be grotesquely unfair. That morning, the senator's eighty-nine-year-old mother, Rosemary Forbes Kerry, made an unexpected return visit to the hospital with life-threatening bronchial problems. Kerry's cell phone has become a symbolic lifeline to his mother's bedside—the number that his sister, Diana, would repeatedly use to call from the hospital.

It is a reflection of Kerry's fortitude, and his ambition, that he gamely stuck to his heavy, prearranged New Hampshire schedule. The senator at times radiates eagerness about the coming Democratic contest, saying, "I feel that people are ready to get things going with the presidential race. It can't happen soon enough." But during long periods in the van driving between events, Kerry would sit silently in the front seat seemingly absorbed with his briefing book, which contained nothing more than the day's itinerary and brief bios of local political figures. He would at times feign animation, for example, telling media consultant Jim Margolis and myself about his tour of Google headquarters on a recent trip to the West Coast. Midsentence the cell phone would ring, and there would be a hushed conversation with Diana about the latest medical reports. Then Kerry would again turn toward the backseat and, picking up where he left off, start asking, "Do you know how many searches Google has on an average day? Three hundred million."

On that afternoon filled with private turmoil, Kerry is still months away from commissioning the stump speech and the scripted sound bites that would someday define his campaign for the White House. Instead, like all the other Democratic hopefuls at this premature stage, his speeches are a personal "Greatest Hits" album—applause lines from his Senate campaigns, tropes that he has been using for years, flights of rhetoric salvaged from his mental attic—fascinating in their own right as a Baedeker to his political persona.

There is a time warp quality to Kerry's words as the calendar keeps drifting back to the 1960s, the decade that carried him from Yale to the Mekong Delta as a navy officer (where he received a

Silver Star, a Bronze Star and three Purple Hearts during two tours of combat) and eventually transformed him into a disillusioned crusader against the Vietnam War. Part of this '60s nostalgia is linked to the lost Kennedy legacy, which Kerry invokes both painfully and passionately. Standing on a chair in the old Masonic lodge in Keene, now the local Democratic headquarters and already a familiar spot for me, Kerry begins his speech to about one hundred party activists with the tired jibe that Massachusetts is an Indian word "for land of many Kennedys." In a passage that is a staple of his campaign oratory, Kerry also recalls returning to California on a troop ship, after his first tour of duty in Vietnam, on that searing 1968 evening when Robert Kennedy was assassinated. Kerry solemnly repeats the slightly mangled George Bernard Shaw quote that served as the epitaph of that foreshortened Kennedy campaign: "Some men see things as they are and ask why. I dream things that never were and ask why not." Then, because he has yet to find the words to top Kennedy quoting Shaw, Kerry concludes awkwardly, "Our politics needs to get back to asking why not and dreaming a little bit."

Late that afternoon at a party fund-raiser in Londonderry, standing this time on a rock in a sprawling backyard, Kerry speaks with fervor about another 1968 campaign—the anti-war insurgency of Gene McCarthy. Fatigued after three lengthy speeches and brooding over his mother's health, Kerry offers raw emotion rather than polished diction as he conjures up the turbulent decade that molded him: "One thing that was authentic, honest, that came from the gut and the passion of people was the notion that as individuals we could make a difference in the life around us. And when people saw that the war was wrong, Gene McCarthy and a bunch of kids came up here, the peanut-butter-and-jelly brigade, and they went out there, living off those sandwiches and knocking on the doors. And he sent the president of the United States a message that he couldn't continue to be president of the United States and wage that war."

Despite the White House's orchestrated aria of operatic challenges to Saddam Hussein, Kerry is not alluding to the contemporary anti-war movement. Rather he is riffing on Democratic idealism, but his vague conclusion fails to support his dramatic peroration. "They gave birth to a still unfinished agenda in this country," he declares. "They gave birth to the environment. We didn't have an EPA, we didn't have a clean water act, a clean air act, a safe drinking water act ... "

Huh? How did we go from the Gene McCarthy crusade to a history of Nixon-era environmental legislation? I get the sense that Kerry is still trying to work through the '60s, still trying to capture something elusive from his youth, and yet the answer remains just beyond his mental grasp like an emotion-laden dream that vanishes with the first rays of daylight.

Throughout the long day, I have been clutching my tape recorder waiting for the proper moment to pose the standard reporter's questions about Kerry's presidential plans. But in deference to his mother's health, I continually hold back, not wanting to intrude. Still, I recognize that I have gotten an unexpected glimpse of Kerry Unplugged, alternately emotional and wistful, solitary and gregarious. Now, after the last event of the day, a low-key meeting with his fellow veterans, I am waiting awkwardly in the darkness on a lawn in Manchester for a good-bye handshake with Kerry. When he finally wanders over, I mention that I didn't press him with questions in light of the burden he is bearing. Kerry looks directly at me, taps my right shoulder with his fist and says, "Thanks, man. We'll do it again."

Short of designing the compensation packages for Enron executives, it is difficult to conceive of a more selfish endeavor than campaigning for president. Sure, the Democratic candidates all harbor sincere dreams about the programs they would sign into law in the White House Rose Garden and stud their speeches with uplifting visions of the future. But the sheer act of running turns each personal encounter into a functional transaction.

Every handshake and hurried conversation brings with it the hope of a vote, a check, or a favorable press clip. At their most human and vulnerable, presidential candidates crave reassurance: "How did I do?" But mostly, every moment of their day, every decision about what to do and whom to see is predicated on a single question: "What's in it for me?"

For these ego-driven presidential contenders, no torture was more exquisitely calibrated than the off-year 2002 congressional elections. Rather than blatantly trumpet their own cause, the candidates were compelled to pretend to subordinate their egos as they stumped for other Democrats and raised money for the party—a charade that reduced them to the political equivalent of warm-up acts on a Jerry Lewis telethon. By chance, both Iowa and New Hampshire were battleground states with hard-fought statewide races and five Republican-held House seats theoretically in play. So the presidential contenders dutifully warbled the praises of such House candidates as Katrina Swett in New Hampshire and John Norris in Iowa, only to watch from the sidelines as all the non-incumbent Democratic congressional candidates in both states—including New Hampshire Governor Jeanne Shaheen running for the Senate—were upended in November. Only Senator Tom Harkin and Governor Tom Vilsack at the top of the ticket in Iowa emerged unscathed from the Democratic debacle.

Yet the value of these initial forays into Iowa and New Hampshire cannot be measured by the dismal Election Day 2002 scorecard. The self-abnegating presidential hopefuls snagged some key endorsements. After the election, Norris signed on as Kerry's Iowa state director and Swett, the daughter of California Congressman Tom Lantos, ended up backing Joe Lieberman. But more than anything, the 2002 campaign offered a low-risk environment in which the Democratic contenders could begin the arduous process of self-definition, which is the centerpiece of a successful presidential candidacy. Sometimes a spontaneous throwaway comment at a house party in Portsmouth will produce a refrain that becomes transformed into a guaranteed applause line in a stump speech. Sometimes a story that was successful in prior political travels consistently falls flat and is stricken from the candidate's repertoire. (Memo to Kerry: Ax the "land of many Kennedys" joke.) No presidential candidate (not even Bill Clinton in 1992) is born with perfect pitch. The melody that comes to define a candidate is assembled note by note, speech by speech, in the continuous feedback loop that is grassroots politics.

With the exception of Bob Graham, who kept his presidential yearnings in a private lockbox until after the congressional elections, the five other leading presidential contenders logged more air miles and stumped for more candidates in 2002 than virtually anyone in the Democratic Party. (Their only challengers for this all-good-men-must-come-to-the-aid-of-their-party crown were Democratic chairman Terry McAuliffe and Senate leader Tom Daschle, who was poised to enter the presidential fray in early January 2003 until he was stricken with a last-minute change of heart.)

Each of these five early birds strode onto the stage with his own musical accompaniment. You could almost imagine Howard Dean with a top hat and a cane tap-dancing his way from the back row of the chorus line to center stage, clicking his heels at the sheer I-was-nobody-and-now-I'm-Fred-Astaire improbability of it all. Every time John Kerry evokes the failed idealism of the 1960s, you cannot but hear the sadder-but-wiser voice of Richard Burton recalling the faded glories of Camelot. Joe Lieberman's have-tallis-will-travel-except-on-Saturday good humor and his upbeat only-in-America message definitely require the lilting refrain of "Hava Negila." (No one with a wife named Hadassah can complain about ethnic stereotyping.) How about an old-fashioned barbershop quartet crooning "Sweet Adeline" for fair-haired Midwesterner Dick Gephardt? Assuming, of course, that all the harmony makers are paid-up members of the musician's union. And John Edwards—the handsome, always smiling, preternaturally youthful North Carolina senator—should be introduced to the sound of the smooth jazz you might find on an easy-listening station, with just a hint of a Clinton saxophone solo in the background.

At this early phase, as the orchestra is still playing the overture for the presidential procession, there is an incestuous no-secrets quality to the maneuvering in which the slightest stage whisper is immediately amplified on the Internet. This political echo chamber effect was demonstrated for my benefit in Manchester on a Monday morning in mid-October 2002.

I was chatting with Peter Sullivan, a New Hampshire state representative, as we waited to hear Joe Lieberman speak to a small party rally. Sullivan mentioned that Wesley Clark, the former NATO commander, had just been in town meeting with Democrats to discuss a putative presidential bid. This odd but intriguing rumor made me feel as if I'd already panned a small nugget from the stream after just ten minutes of on-scene reporting. Moments later, I ran into James Pindell, an energetic young reporter for politicsNH.com, an on-line newsletter. Pindell proudly announced that his exclusive story about Clark's expedition was ballyhooed in the ABC political digest "The Note," which I had not read because I had to get up at 5:00 in the morning to fly to New Hampshire. Such is the speed at which buzz travels in contemporary politics. I was sadly behind the curve because I was reporting in New Hampshire rather than sitting at home in New York reading the on-line gossip sheets.

I will confess a residual affection for Lieberman, an affinity that is primarily based on our shared Connecticut heritage. I grew up in Norwalk, just ten miles from Lieberman's hometown of Stamford, a city where my father, Salem, was urban renewal director in the 1960s. This is an admittedly fragile bond, but reporters are not immune to the blandishments of Tip O'Neill's dictum that "all politics is local." Lieberman, whom I had interviewed maybe a dozen times on topics ranging from the Clinton scandals to his hard-line foreign-policy views, has the knack of remembering to ask about my ninety-four-year-old father. But this connection only carries me so far. For all his engaging manner, I have always found the 2000 vice-presidential nominee to be strangely impenetrable. There are questions, there are answers, but the transaction only takes you so far. As I discovered anew on this pre-election visit to New Hampshire, it is impossible to get too close to Joe Lieberman.

Behind a lectern, Lieberman is adept at feigning a pseudo-intimacy with his soft-spoken tone that seems free of bombast even when he is making naked political claims. In Manchester, he introduced a critique of Republican attack ads by confiding, "I was on the treadmill literally, not figuratively, at the fitness center here this morning watching television. And I got to see some of the ads, the negative stuff, the slashing back and forth." As he would throughout the day, Lieberman went on to portentously announce, "How the Senate and House go will be determined here in New Hampshire." Lieberman then took this obvious boilerplate line and gave it a twist. "I don't want to put too much pressure on you," he added amid growing laughter. "But the fate of Western civilization hangs in the balance." The humor was conspiratorial, signaling to his audience a rye-with-corned-beef detachment from aggressive partisanship, even as Lieberman was claiming that if the Republicans control Congress "nothing will protect us from the far-right agenda."

On occasion Lieberman gently mocks his own religiosity. Emerging from his car in Keene outside—yes, you can do it from memory—the former Masonic temple that is now the Democratic headquarters, Lieberman suddenly bent over to touch the ground. Then turning to me, he announced, "This is not some weird Jewish ritual. I'm just stretching." Lieberman's speech in Keene was mostly notable for the exuberant and decidedly non-ironic praise that he lavished on Katrina Swett (the congressional candidate who will endorse him in early 2003), gushing about "the extraordinary experience that she possesses and the great experience that she has." Had Lieberman slathered on fewer superlatives, Swett might well have ended up backing Dick Gephardt.

There was a good-humored quality, as well, to the way Lieberman handled what he called his "unique situation," his promise not to run if Al Gore, his political benefactor, sought the 2004 nomination. That pledge was so ironclad that Lieberman had earlier waved off a reporter (Nick Lemann from the *New Yorker*) who provided a series of passages from the Talmud explaining religiously acceptable reasons for breaking an inconvenient promise. But during our interview between New Hampshire stops, the only time I am allowed to ride with the if-Al-doesn't-I-will candidate, Lieberman explained what turned out to be his prescient strategy. "I decided that I had to do a lot of things that a potential candidate would do just to keep my options open," he said. "What it means is raising money, helping Democrats around the country, giving them money and campaigning for them."

No matter what the topic, there is a rehearsed quality to Lieberman, a sense that every syllable has been lifted from a prior conversation with someone else. Some of it may be learned behavior, stay-on-message techniques Lieberman picked up from the press-averse 2000 Gore campaign. During our interview, Lieberman recalled being instructed by his vice-presidential handlers not to wander to the back of the campaign plane to talk to reporters because "you'll step on your own story." (That is, Lieberman's impromptu comments would have overshadowed the scripted sound bites of the day's speech.) The almost–vice president also admitted, with some embarrassment, that a "devilish reporter" in 2000 lured him into a politically ill-advised discussion of interfaith marriage in which he expressed "a more benign view than some Orthodox Jews." Oy vey, we must talk to the rebbe about this.

So sure, I could call Joe Lieberman "my homey" in a strictly Connecticut sense. Sure, I could laugh at his jokes and enjoy the act that has been called "Shecky Lieberman." But I couldn't delve beneath his avuncular veneer. And I couldn't shake the feeling that Lieberman brandishes his surface affability as a weapon to keep other people, especially reporters, at a distance.

Every time I see Dick Gephardt, I remember with embarrassment our initial encounter in late 1987, at the beginning of the St. Louis congressman's first race for president. I had been invited to speak at a conference on "Campaign '88" at Dartmouth, and my wife Meryl and I were flying to Hanover that Saturday morning on a puddle-jumper from LaGuardia Airport. As the lead political writer for *Time*, I had pulled a news magazine all-nighter getting home from the office just in time to shower and dress for the trip to Dartmouth. In the midst of this sleep-deprivation experiment, social graces, such as modulating my tone aboard the plane, fell by the wayside. Rehearsing my talk on the candidates for Meryl in an inadvertently stentorian voice, I worked myself into a scornful fury about Gephardt: "What a joke, the guy has no eyebrows. And that fake populism and all that posturing about how we're losing jobs because of trade. Who does he think he is? The second coming of William Jennings Bryan?" At that moment, the red-haired man seated a row in front of me, whom I had not noticed, abruptly moved to a vacant seat in the front of the plane. It was only later—when the moderator of the Dartmouth panel announced, "And we have with us today presidential candidate Dick Gephardt" and I glimpsed a familiar shade of red hair—that I shamefacedly figured out who my traveling companion had been.

It wasn't as if I had spent the ensuing fifteen years making amends. Over the years on Capitol Hill, I had seen Gephardt work himself into an apocalyptic frenzy about "Republican greed" at countless press conferences and heard him mouth focus-group platitudes about "kitchen-table economics" during interviews. Even being invited, along with two friends who are political reporters, to an off-the-record dinner with the then House minority leader in early July 2002 did not inspire me to overhaul my all-too-glib assessments. During a post-interview drink with my journalistic colleagues at the bar at Washington's Tenpenh restaurant, I mockingly announced, "The dinner made me feel better about Gephardt. But not that much better."

Cynicism is to political reporters what combat fatigue is to soldiers, an occupational hazard that comes from living too long in the trenches. As an antidote to this temptation toward overly facile mockery, I was in St. Louis on a Saturday morning just before the 2002 elections to visit Dick Gephardt's political roots. This journey of rediscovery began at a community center with a get-out-the-vote rally for St. Louis County Democrats. Here the dress code was simple: Wear a windbreaker, preferably inscribed with a union logo like "Sprinklefitter Local 268." Gephardt had opted for a simple blue jacket over his khaki slacks, while his wife Jane went with a tan leather coat. As Gephardt began to speak to this hometown crowd, he announced, "This is like family." But familiarity did not deter Gephardt from reminding his political kinfolk of the biographical detail that is his touchstone: "My dad was a Teamster, a milk-truck driver." He went on to talk about "the values that we all grew up with," as he pointedly added, "That's what my mother told me every day." Hearing those words about her ninety-four-year-old mother-in-law, Jane Gephardt murmured, "Still does."

The local-color selling point for this trip was getting to watch Dick and Jane Gephardt reprise the good old days when they were both precinct captains in the mid-1960s and when he was running for Congress for the first time in 1976, tirelessly knocking on virtually every door in the district. But a congressional leader who will soon be running for president can't go home again ... without an entourage. In addition to Dick and Jane, the Saturday morning door-knocking party consisted of several aides with registered voter lists and brochures, a press secretary, Gephardt's post-9/11 security guard, a reporter from the St. Louis *Post-Dispatch,* a two-man C-Span team filming for later broadcast, longtime press-bus colleague Roger Simon from *U.S. News*, accompanied by a photographer, and me. Lambeth Street, a cul-de-sac in blue-collar Lemay Township, didn't know what hit it. As the posse approached the first doorway, Gephardt made the obvious joke: "They probably think we're from Publishers Clearing House."

There was a jaunty mood to the Lambeth walk past brick bungalows with tidy lawns and festive pre-Halloween displays of skeletons, witches and goblins. At one of the first houses we reached, the yawning middle-aged woman who answered the door matter-of-factly explained that she had worked until 2:00 in the morning in the back office of a local brokerage house, while her husband was on the day shift. And they have four children. In short, husband and wife barely saw each other five days a week. As we departed, Gephardt said to me with fierce intensity, "That's why it's so hard to educate our children. The parents are working so hard. My mom was there for me after school until I was in the sixth grade." A few houses later, we encountered eighty-one-year-old Dorothy Pauley, who told Gephardt, "You made it possible for me to go to computer school at the senior center. You got a grant for the program." She added for good measure, and you could just see Gephardt beam, "You care for the little people, that's why I like you." Then like a Democratic pollster's fantasy, she urged, "Do something about the cost of medicine. That's my problem."

Every presidential candidate extrapolates his image of America from that which is most familiar. Michael Dukakis, to give an extreme example, always believed that his affluent, ethnically diverse hometown of Brookline, Massachusetts, represented a microcosm of the nation. Dick Gephardt entered the twenty-first century as one of the last Old Economy Democrats—and voters like Dorothy Pauley constantly vindicate his belief that elections are won, and lives are uplifted, by government programs. This truth was underscored at a house up the street where Gephardt found a set of house keys lying in the driveway. The desire to return the keys, rather than the need to add to the ersatz meet-the-voters drama, prompted him to knock loudly and repeatedly on the front door. Finally, a portly, shirtless middle-aged man answered, blinking at the bright autumn sunlight. "They're my mother's keys," he explained. "I must have dropped them when I came in from the night shift." As we walked down the driveway, Gephardt said, "What you learn doing this, what you see everywhere, is how hard people work." That comment would seem tinny and phoney at a Capitol Hill press conference. But here on Lambeth Street, it reflected the striver reality of Dick Gephardt's America.

Just as tourists form premature mental images of their vacation itineraries by devouring guidebooks, political reporters prepare for a maiden voyage with a presidential candidate by wading through electronic clip files. Often the clichés embedded in these prior news stories take on the power of self-fulfilling prophesies much as a first-time visitor to Japan is pre-disposed to constantly search for women in kimonos and salarymen practicing phantom golf swings on Tokyo train platforms. My armchair impression of Howard Dean, before my initial 2002 trip with him to New Hampshire, was that of an accidental politician—a doctor who was dabbling at being Vermont's part-time lieutenant governor before he was elevated into the governor's office by the sudden death of the Republican incumbent in 1991.

But during our lengthy backseat conversation, I discovered that Dean was, in fact, a "pol" in the best sense of the word, with a shrewd grasp of the tactics and strategies that accompany his second career. My first glimpse of the calculating side of the stethoscope-wielding governor came when I asked him to explain an odd detail that I had gleaned from the news clips: his 1988 endorsement of Gephardt for president, a peculiar choice given that Dukakis was the governor of an adjacent state. "Part of it had to do with the fact that I would have been the seven-hundred-and-fiftieth person in New England who was in on the Dukakis bandwagon—and the first for Gephardt," Dean said with the frankness of an old-time ward boss explaining the rules for awarding sewer contracts. "Also, I just liked the guy. He was an up-and-coming congressman who was smart and doing all this stuff with tax policy. He's a very decent person, I think." Against the backdrop of the 2004 race, it was intriguing that Dean's initial visit to Iowa came in the role of a little-known lieutenant governor stumping for Gephardt before the 1988 caucuses.

Darting from topic to topic in a conversation designed as much to pass the time as to probe Dean's fitness for the White House (which at that moment seemed an outlandish proposition), I began to understand the advantages of running for president with the non-Washington perspective of a governor. Unlike his congressional rivals for the nomination, Dean presciently grasped the political implications of George W. Bush's so-called No Child Left Behind education bill, which he ridiculed in his speeches as the "No School Board Left Standing" bill. As Dean explained to me, "School boards around the country are getting what this bill does and they don't like it. And that means that the taxpayers won't be far behind. The bill is a disaster from an educational standpoint. It's going to lower standards and raise property taxes. The folks in Washington had no idea what they were doing." (A year later, virtually all the Democrats running for president were emulating Dean by studding their speeches with vitriolic attacks on Bush's failure to properly fund his education plan).

It is a time-honored journalistic technique to enliven sit-down interviews (even one conducted in a moving vehicle driven by a Vermont state trooper) with detailed descriptions of the subject's body language. But Dean, who removed his suit jacket for the journey but was otherwise crisply attired in a button-down white shirt and striped tie, presented a challenge to colorful writing.

From his salt-and-pepper hair to his shined lace-up black shoes, Dean is a compact man who seemed to be constructed with absolutely no wasted bodily attributes and who disdained flamboyant gestures. At the Democratic dinner in Keene, I kept losing sight of him in the crowd. Dean struck me as less a presidential candidate than as prime spy material, since he is blessed with the uncanny ability to blend into the background. During our car talk, whether in daylight or in rain-drenched darkness, the only thing distinctive about Dean was the unabashed self-confidence in his voice.

At this early stage of the race, Dean was his own campaign manager and strategist. But even sixteen months before the Iowa caucuses, Dean the Pol displayed a deft understanding of how to position himself for the long haul. A prime example was his skepticism about far-reaching national gun-control legislation, a staple of liberal Democratic orthodoxy. "My position on guns for the presidential race is that states can do whatever they want," Dean explained. "And if California wants to have gun control, let them have as much gun control as they want—just don't pass it nationally. We should close the gun-show loophole. We should have that and the Brady bill, and then just let the states do what they want and get it off the Democratic agenda."

Now I am about as likely to keep a pet camel in my Upper West Side Manhattan apartment as I am to own a gun, but I also recognized the electoral logic behind his argument. Dean—a political realist who understands rural America as well as the limitations of feel-good liberal legislation—argued, "There is no point in pushing gun control in states like Vermont and Wyoming, all it does is get Democrats defeated." The shoot-from-the-hip governor went on to say, "You'll lose 6 to 10 percent of union members on this issue alone. It's ridiculous."

Ever since Illinois-born Hillary Clinton shamelessly announced in the midst of her 2000 New York Senate race that she had always been a closet Yankee fan, I have become a tad cynical about the shifting baseball allegiances of political figures. So when Dean mentioned that he had recently undergone a religious conversion and had begun rooting for the Boston Red Sox, I immediately thought, "How convenient for the New Hampshire primary."

Normally, the governor of Vermont would be assumed to be a life-long member of the Red Sox Nation, but Dean grew up as a passionate Yankee fan in Manhattan and still cheers for New York basketball and hockey teams. Yet the thing about Dean is that, even when you suspect ulterior political motives, he offers a superficially convincing explanation. His Yankee-go-home transformation was prompted by the conduct of Bronx Bomber pitching ace Roger Clemens who beaned Mike Piazza, the star catcher for the Mets, during the 2000 regular season and then threw part of a broken bat at him during the World Series. "So I became a Red Sox fan," Dean explained. "And I understand for the first time, the futility and the pain involved with that." But then, who better than a long-shot presidential candidate to appreciate the allure of rooting for the underdog.

I love New Hampshire living rooms. No setting better conveys the wondrous intimacy of the Invisible Primary. It seems outlandish that in the twenty-first century a candidate theoretically can go in little more than two years from standing in front of a fireplace addressing seventy-five voters to governing a nation of 280 million. That is why, whatever happens in the coming election, I will long remember my first living rooms of the 2004 campaign season.

This being New Hampshire, politics was, of course, the attraction on this Saturday night in the early summer of 2002. The event in this sprawling post-modern farmhouse near Portsmouth was nominally a fund-raiser for the state party, but none of the seventy-five Democrats working their way along a lavish buffet table overflowing with smoked salmon or milling around in small groups as they sipped pricey chardonnay believed that cover story for a moment. They were here, as the sun set on a plowed field visible through the floor-to-ceiling windows, to watch John Edwards try out for the biggest role of his life.

Edwards, who had the gumption or the temerity to get ready to seek the Democratic presidential nomination just three years after he arrived in the Senate, had been auditioning all day. He began with a brunch with party activists in an unadorned living room in Mount Vernon, located in the back of a vintage farm-house whose wide-beam floors probably were already sagging when Daniel Webster first entered politics. This late-morning crowd throbbed with cause-oriented earnestness, epitomized by a woman with a shaved head who hectored the senator on the evils of suburban sprawl and the woeful expansion of the tourist industry. Then it was on through the pouring rain to a Democratic Party pig roast in Wye, where Edwards shared the celebrity limelight with Senate candidate Jeanne Shaheen. There the senator's wife, Elizabeth, on only her second out-of-state trip of this exploratory season, already had a glazed look in her eyes as she confessed, "I have no idea where we are. I just go where they take me."

Now Edwards was standing before a massive fireplace, dressed in an open-necked blue Oxford shirt and cream-colored slacks, his boyish face framed by a shock of light brown hair, his whole being a study in inchoate charisma. Like Jimmy Carter and Bill Clinton before him, Edwards represents the beguiling Democratic myth that a handsome champion can emerge from the South, head north toward his true political home and smile and glad-hand his way into the Oval Office. Though I had studied Edwards in Senate committee rooms and in his home state, today marked the first time that I had seen him flash his plumage outside his native habitat. As Edwards began his speech, laying out his populist pedigree, I mentally footnoted his oratory:

- "I grew up in a little town in North Carolina; my dad worked in the cotton mills all his life." (Left unmentioned was that his father worked himself up to mill supervisor.)
- "When I became a lawyer, I decided that those people who I wanted to represent were those who worked in the mill with my dad." (Awkward truth: Edwards was so successful as a personal injury lawyer that he is worth about $25 million and funded most of his own 1998 Senate campaign.)
- "What people think about what's going on in Washington is exactly right. We get off the elevator to vote and you can barely get to the floor for all the people who want to talk to you. Most of them have very fancy suits, representing powerful interest groups. And they're going to make sure that the people they're representing are heard." (This one may be a keeper.)
- "We ought to use a little North Carolina and New Hampshire common sense." (Ouch.)

The speech was interrupted by applause only once (when Edwards repeated the Democratic mantra that prescription drugs should be covered by Medicare) and there were no on-the-spot conversions. The reaction was that of a friendly audience which realizes that this play still has first-act problems, but knows that they are fixable. The allure of living-room politics in New Hampshire is not the stump speeches, but the obligatory questions from voters with a craftsman's pride in quizzing would-be presidents. Edwards cleanly fielded the first two queries on taxes for small business and funding for special education. Then came the first sense that we might be witnessing a candidate with the potential to become more than the sum of his position papers. The questioner was a middle-aged woman wearing expensive gold jewelry, a peach blouse and white slacks. Palpably uneasy at speaking in public, she pointedly referred to September 11 as she said, "It sort of feels like the Marx Brothers are running security in this country. Truly, it's scary. How can Americans feel safe? Tell me something that will make me feel safe."

Edwards knew that she wanted him to look her in the eye and promise with his hand over his heart that the New Hampshire seacoast is far from any known terrorist target. But the senator had spent too many days behind the guarded doors of the Senate Intelligence Committee to offer this kind of balm. Edwards simply could not do it. Nor did he direct his attention to his questioner. Instead his gaze was fixed on a young woman in the front row holding on to her eight-year-old son. (Afterward Edwards told me that he was thinking, "How can I answer that question honestly without scaring the kid?")

Finally, in a soft voice, Edwards responded, "Well, we can't get that assurance. That's what I would say." But the would-be candidate understood that he could not leave it there, that he had to give his audience some basis for optimism. So without missing a beat, he immediately launched into a knowing critique of the FBI's efforts to combat terrorism, studding his remarks with an agenda for reform. It was less what Edwards said and more the calm confidence that he projected in saying it. Years of addressing juries in small North Carolina towns as a trial lawyer enhanced Edwards's natural ability to radiate sincerity. Watching the faces in the room, I noticed the fear dissipating by the time Edwards reached his conclusion: "The best way to stop these potential attacks is not to catch every single person who might be getting on an airplane, but the way to stop it is to get inside it, and stop it before the plot even gets started."

Late that night as I sat with the senator at a table in the bar of a Portsmouth restaurant (Elizabeth Edwards, press secretary Mike Briggs and Meryl rounded out the party), I was seized by a revelation. After twelve hours of campaigning, Edwards had been elevated to a secret planet that only he (and maybe Elizabeth) occupied. He was on a pure adrenaline high, glassy-eyed with the crack of politics, too pumped up for ordinary conversation, still reveling in the memory of every handshake and every encouraging smile, replaying every line of his stump speech in his mind. This is why they all do it—this is why otherwise prudent men condemn themselves to harrowing days on the road, hamburgers on the run and Holiday Inns for rest, this is why they risk derision, dejection and defeat, all for the fleeting chance of becoming president.

CHAPTER 3

I Nominate Me

During late 2002, every Washington lunch with a top Democratic political operative followed an identical ritual. A handshake, a few murmured words of greeting, a cursory glance at the menu— and then ten minutes of rumor repeating, scuttlebutt sharing and tea-leaf testing. All this intense gossipmongering revolved around the same overarching topic: Was Al Gore running? There was no hint of ambiguity about the intentions of John Kerry, Dick Gephardt, Howard Dean and John Edwards. But the pivotal slot, belonged to either Gore or his self-appointed stand-in, Joe Lieberman.

Today's lunch at Bistro Bis, one of the better eateries on Capitol Hill, adheres to the predictable flight path. My companion, a senior adviser to one of the Democratic Definites, doesn't have much news to offer on the Gore front, saving both of us from endlessly chewing over an indigestible morsel on the order of "I just talked to someone who spoke to Carter Eskew who said that Peter Knight was claiming that Gore..." Instead, midway through the meal, my lunch mate casually drops the bombshell that he's heard that Edwards is having serious second thoughts about getting into the race.

I'm stunned. There hasn't been a word about Edwards's indecision in either the papers or the on-line political newsletters. I realize that Edwards is up for re-election in 2004 and that a premature
presidential bid could transform the golden-haired freshman senator into a modern-day Icarus, tumbling to earth without a Senate
seat or a political future. But I know Edwards—or at least I think I
do. My wife profiled Edwards for *Elle* magazine in early 2001 and
Meryl and I subsequently had two off-the-record dinners with the
would-be candidate and his wife Elizabeth during which every
vibe, every joke, every conversational gambit was premised on the
shared assumption that he was going for the White House. Could
my inner divining rod, which twitches at the slightest hint of presidential ambition, have been that out of kilter? Edwards certainly
radiated I'm-ready-so-let's-get-on-with-it certainty when he shared
top billing with Kerry and Dean at the annual Jefferson-Jackson
fund-raising dinner of the Iowa Democratic Party in mid-October.
Was the whole Edwards presidential edifice (the senior consultants, the young aides with their eyes on the main chance, the preliminary funding from trial lawyers and the lavish purchases of
desktop computers for the Iowa Democratic Party) all a Potemkin
village?

The Edwards enigma prompted me to schedule a lunch with
the vacillating candidate's most trusted adviser, the one person
sure to be privy to his inner deliberations: Elizabeth Edwards. So
on a snowy Thursday in early December, with the capital's icy
streets treacherous enough to warrant the assistance of the ski
patrol, Meryl and I take a cab out to Chez Edwards sprawling
rented house in the suburban-looking Spring Valley neighborhood of Washington, easily recognizable from the eight-foot-tall
plastic snowman from Costco perched on the front lawn. Elizabeth, dressed in jeans and a sweater, greets us in an entry foyer
filled with a jumble of children's coats, mittens and boots, a testament to the presence of the mid-life additions to the household—four-year-old Emma Claire and two-year-old Jack.

Our initial efforts at conversation are tinged with awkwardness, as if the three of us were onstage in a drawing room comedy without ever having seen the script. Elizabeth—a bankruptcy attorney until their sixteen-year-old son, Wade, was killed in a freak automobile accident in 1996—normally projects an air of bemused confidence. But here she is in the kitchen, fluttering nervously over the simple act of toasting the white bread for our lunch of egg-salad sandwiches. Some of the anxiety, on my part as well as hers, is rooted in confusion over appropriate roles. Up to now, we've primarily seen each other in social settings. Despite Meryl's presence, this is an interview; I've arrived with a notebook and tape recorder, the tools of a reporter's trade. As the sandwich preparation proceeds at the pace of Freudian analysis, it becomes obvious that Elizabeth is also tense for reasons that have little to do with my journalistic persona. With her husband arriving home this very afternoon from a four-day, burnish-the-foreign-policy-credentials visit to NATO headquarters in Brussels, the uncertainty and the waiting are taking their toll on the home front.

Finally we are seated at a table in the sprawling, comfortable library that serves as the casual center of family life. Nearby is the computer that Elizabeth uses to thread her way through strand after strand of the latest campaign stories, typing her husband's name and those of his putative rivals into the Google News search engine. The awkwardness dissipates as soon as I switch on my tape recorder, since now we have our assigned parts. I'm the sympathetic questioner, puzzled by Edwards's late-developing doubts. And Elizabeth is a hybrid, not the standard-issue willfully bland political spouse (she laughingly calls herself the "un-Barbie"), but also far too candid and emotionally engaging to play Hillary Clinton redux.

Elizabeth immediately confirms the rumors. Yes, they had intense discussions about the pros and cons of the race when their eldest daughter, Cate, was home from Princeton over Thanksgiving. They've met with many people here at the house and Edwards has been talking with his fellow senators. "John

could probably make his decision by the end of the week," Elizabeth announces. "He has Cate's and my permission to do whatever he wants to do. It's his decision to make. We're on board if
he wants to do it. And we're not disappointed in him if he
doesn't choose to do it."

In my quarter century of covering presidential politics, I have
always hungered for fly-on-the-wall moments like this when you
get a sense of the internal debate before a decision is made. At
my request, Elizabeth outlines the case for not running this time
around: "That John's doing it too soon. Should he wait and do it,
if he's going to do it, in 2008?" She pauses and then adds, "The
first question that he has to ask doesn't have to do with the field,
it has to do with himself. Am I up to this? Not only am I up to the
job of the campaign, but am I up to the job of presidency."

This is the deep, dark-night-of-the-soul quandary, the question
that should leave any self-aware politician in fear and trembling
about the implications of his own ambitions. John Edwards has
not had a moment's pause in his headlong rush to the top; he was
in the Senate for little more than a year when—in a tribute to
both his southern base and his courtroom–honed skills as an
advocate—he popped up on Gore's short list of potential 2000
running mates. Politics as a second career has come easily to
Edwards, perhaps too easily. But no would-be president is ever
prepared for what awaits him the moment he steps into the Oval
Office. I recall, for Elizabeth's benefit, that in 1994, while war
raged in Bosnia and Croatia, Bill Clinton expressed regret that he
had come to power without knowing anything about the Balkans.
And then there's Bush.

She waves off the Bush comparison: "John said that you can't
use Bush. The bar is too low if you use Bush." The real question,
although Elizabeth doesn't use these precise words, is whether
Edwards is ready to play at the top of his potential game. His
years as a trial lawyer have given him a quick-study ability to
master complex material, skills that might translate well to the
White House. But is that enough? Has he come far enough along

his personal learning curve to grapple with a fast-changing and threatening world?

For Elizabeth, a woman who listens to C-Span radio in her car, the other side of the equation is the risk of four more years of a Bush presidency. Her voice brimming with partisan zeal, she runs through the standard litany of issues from the red-ink tax cuts to the president's ill-advised judicial appointments. "We have to win," declares La Pasionara of Spring Valley. "We have to win. The nation can't afford for us to lose. And I think they [Bush and company] are exercising some restraint right now. There are things that won't happen until after 2004 because they're holding back to wait for the re-election. And it's going to be our worst nightmare."

This fear of a permanent right-wing ascendancy drives the debate in the Edwards household. Electability is normally a strategic consideration in nominating a candidate, but to Elizabeth it also possesses a moral component: Edwards is simply the Democrat most likely to defoliate Bush. Sounding like she's read more than her share of polls, Elizabeth argues that her husband is the candidate most likely to attract white males, the reverse gender gap core of the Republican Party. In her view, it all comes down to the contrast in backgrounds between Edwards (a high-school football player in the North Carolina hamlet of Robbins) and Bush (a prep-school cheerleader). Sure, it helps that Edwards is a southerner. But it's a mistake to view his appeal solely through a regional prism. As Elizabeth puts it, "I just think that he's more likable, warmer and more engaging than any of the other Democrats. And I also think he beats Bush on that score."

This isn't spin, since Elizabeth immediately qualifies her beat-Bush prediction with a rueful "Maybe I'm wrong." Her comments reflect a mixture of honesty, wifely pride and a can-do optimism that is a hallmark of both her and her husband. Any obstacle (excluding the loss of Wade) can be overcome with hard work, a broad smile and innate intelligence. But now she finds herself on the outside looking in as this practiced attorney argues the case for and against running for president in his own mind. She thinks he's going to do it, she hopes he's going to do it, but she isn't confident that's what he'll decide. Finally, gesturing toward the front door, she says, "Maybe he'll come back from this trip and know the answer." Meryl and I swivel our heads in the expectation of witnessing this dramatic homecoming scene complete with the long-awaited announcement. Elizabeth laughs as she says, "I'll have to get him not to walk in the front door and yell it out to me."

Not to worry about loose lips. John Edwards was in no position to blurt out his secret, since his trip to Europe never granted him time for quiet reflection. So it went in the Edwards camp, another day, another implicit deadline missed, and the senior staffers working on this campaign-in-waiting were beginning to fret. There were problems on other fronts as well. Ted Kennedy, who served as a Senate mentor to Edwards, bowed to Bay State political realities and came out for Kerry, while the rumors were spreading in Washington that media consultant Bob Shrum would defect as well. Although Edwards's advisers claimed that methodically thinking through the rigors and rationale of a presidential campaign is a useful and even high-minded exercise, they had assumed that this was a slam-dunk leading to only one possible conclusion. After all, they were certain enough to dedicate the next eighteen months of their lives to nominating John Edwards for president. Why then was the candidate of their dreams having these doubts? The Edwards loyalists were, for the most part, younger and hungrier than the campaigners for his likely opponents. Having never experienced the birth pangs of a presidential candidacy, these staffers were palpably eager to be present at the creation.

None was more determined than David Ginsberg, the campaign's wunderkind communications director, whose scraggly beard and distracted manner make him seem like a graduate student brooding that he's chosen the wrong dissertation topic. Early on the Sunday night of Thanksgiving weekend, Ginsberg was driving back to Washington from New Jersey with his wife, Ellen, when Edwards called on the cell phone to say, "I'm going to make this decision tonight. We're gathering some people at the house." But there was a hitch: Ginsberg was snarled in the kind of post-holiday traffic jam for which the New Jersey Turnpike is rightfully notorious. While Ellen frantically changed lanes, Ginsberg was thinking, "I'm not going to miss the meeting where the decision is made." The breathless Ginsberg, the first staffer hired in early 1998 by the nascent Edwards-for-Senate campaign, made it to Spring Valley in time to participate in the historic discussion. Serious questions were raised and options were seriously considered before producing the conclusion that (gulp!) they should all talk again.

Instead of clarity, the Edwards dialogues generated more false climaxes than a Beethoven symphony. Once again opting for hope over experience, the campaign staff decided that since the week before Christmas is a traditionally slow news period, it would be an ideal time for Edwards to unveil his candidacy. A few days after Edwards returned from Europe, Jonathan Prince, a former Clinton speechwriter now a senior strategist with the campaign, and Ginsberg made the trek to the senator's home to argue for the virtues of this tentative rollout date. A little skittish, Prince and Ginsberg organized their mission under the guise of showing the candidate the new campaign logo (surprise: a star-spangled flag motif). When they casually inquired whether the senator had any firm plans for the week of December 16, Edwards snapped, "I'm not going to rush this decision just to get a little more press."

Throughout this period, the questions that Edwards kept raising were similar to those previewed by Elizabeth: "What does it mean to be ready to be president? Is the time right? Can I improve my skills without undermining my long-term potential?" Veteran pollster Harrison Hickman, who had advised Edwards since the 1998 Senate campaign, tried to rebut the I'm-not-sure-I'm-ready concerns: "What, you want to be a better talk show host? What skills and knowledge will you pick up being in the Senate for six more years? Part of the problem of staying in Washington is you end up trying to fill the expectations of the people who live here." Miles Lackey, the chief of staff in the Senate office, argued that by waiting until 2008 Edwards would end up staking his future on the one factor that he can't control: the political environment four years from now.

Edwards knew, ever so wrenchingly, that there are many things in life beyond his control. It is impossible for an outsider to gauge what role the memory of his son Wade (whose Outward Bound pin Edwards wears in the lapel of his suit jacket) played in his inner struggle over seeking the presidency. Neither Edwards nor Elizabeth ever mentioned Wade in any of the meetings at the house, but his presence, even six years after his death, hovered softly around both of them. An Edwards adviser who understandably did not want to be quoted by name explained, "Someone like John Edwards is painfully aware that life moves quickly and things are precarious. We never talked about it, but it has to be part of his thinking." Others in the inner circle suggested that Wade's death made Edwards impervious to the fears that govern the lives of other politicians, fears like losing an election. As Hickman put it, "After you have to get up on a table in a medical-examiner's office and hug your son good-bye, there's nothing they can ever do to you."

Right after Christmas, Edwards indulged in the most sybaritic luxury ever granted a would-be president: unstructured time absolutely alone. To escape both the flurry of phone calls probing his intentions and the clamor and chaos of a household revolving around two small children, Edwards retreated (as he often did before major trials) to the family's North Carolina beach house on Figure Eight Island near Wilmington. There, over three days, he finally made his decision. There was never a Eureka moment, just the gradual arc of inevitability. Discussing that period in retrospect, Edwards automatically lapsed into the practiced cadences of political message. "I went away for the purpose of deciding a couple of things," he said. "Whether I felt strongly enough about the direction that the country was going and the extent to which it needed to be changed. And, second, whether I brought a perspective to the presidency that was important for the American people who were largely being left out in my view ... It was about that simple."

Really? C'mon, wasn't there a moment of who-me humility? Edwards had spent too much of his life before skeptical juries not to concede the obvious. "Of course, many times," he replied. "If I was looking for the single most powerful push-back against doing it, that would be it. Thinking why in the world me? Why should I be the person who could best represent the American people and lead them?" So, what convinced you that you were indeed that person? Rather than hinting at the depths of his soul-searching, Edwards returned to his campaign theme of soft-edged southern populism: "People like my own family and people whom I have seen my whole life not get the opportunities that I thought they were entitled to. That was really what did it."

Even though Edwards the Reluctant became Edwards the Candidate, he somehow could not bring himself to make an explicit announcement to his staff. (Such an admission would, of course, have made him Edwards the Confessor.) The senator's phone conversations with the campaign high command after he returned from the beach were suggestive, but curiously elliptical. Staffers were reduced to joking among themselves: "He'll never tell us directly that he's running because he's afraid that we'll leak it to the press." Even during a New Year's Eve meeting in Raleigh to plan the round-robin TV interviews on January 2 that would trumpet his candidacy, Edwards continued these odd circumlocutions. Driving back to Washington with Ginsberg and Robert Gordon, the legislative director on the Senate staff, Hickman said, "I hate to bring this up. But in all the conversations that he's had with me, both privately and publicly, he's never said, 'I'm going to run for president.' I've read a lot of the books with campaign tick-tock—Teddy White and the others—and candidates don't wait until they appear on national TV to say for the first time, 'I'm running.'"

Political reporters might well take as their muse the duchess in *Alice in Wonderland* who told a certain small girl with long hair, "Everything's got a moral if you can only find it." If I and my colleagues in the press pack can construct elaborate theories about a candidate based on a mere slip of the tongue during a campaign debate, then surely there are larger lessons to be derived from the month that this fresh-faced senator spent pondering the outer limits of his own ambition.

On the credit side of the ledger for Edwards are both his recognition of the need for solitude and his refusal to be stampeded into seeking the presidency by the restlessness of his staff. Setting up a campaign structure to make it possible to run inevitably creates the expectation that you must run. "John and I had several conversations about having to fight against that," recalled Elizabeth Edwards in a follow-up conversation. "It was necessary for him to say, 'You have to do it on its own merits.' And not because people expected you to or even that they turned down another job to take this prospective job with you."

But all that has to be balanced against the sophistry of his professed rationale for running. As Edwards told Matt Lauer in the *Today Show* interview that launched his campaign, "I want to be a champion for regular people, the same people I fought for my whole life, people like my family . . ." Who are the people that the other Democrats are fighting for? The Baker Street Irregulars? The issue is not Edwards's sincerity, but his outsize pride in his trademark phrase "regular people." Those two words, which Edwards somehow regards as the Rosetta Stone for deciphering his political essence, were the culmination of his lonely days at the beach. "The message came from me, nobody else," he said with the aggrieved tone that Lincoln might have used to defend his authorship of the Gettysburg Address. "Nobody else played a role in this message. This was me."

No other Washington-based Democratic presidential candidate put himself through anything comparable to Edwards's ordeal of indecision. The presidency beckoned, this was their moment, so there was no need to strut across the stage doing their rendition of "To be or not to be?"

This fits the modern pattern in which presidential candidates are self-nominated. Gone is the era when a trainload of cigar-smoking party leaders wearing derby hats would descend on the hometown of a respected governor or senator begging him to run. Just a half century ago in 1952, the nominees of both parties (Dwight Eisenhower and Adlai Stevenson) had to be formally drafted with petition drives and write-in campaigns in the primaries. But the age of coyness vanished about the time Henry Cabot Lodge won the 1964 New Hampshire GOP primary without ever leaving his post as ambassador to South Vietnam.

All the men (and also, in a technical sense, scandal-scarred former Illinois Senator Carol Moseley Braun) lusting after the wide-open 2004 Democratic nomination are the spiritual descendants of Jimmy Carter, the ultimate self-made president. In his 1976 campaign autobiography, humbly entitled *Why Not the Best?*, Carter writes about meeting, as Georgia governor, all the 1972 candidates from Richard Nixon to George McGovern, Hubert Humphrey and Ed Muskie. The lesson Carter derived from his initial exposure to the leading political figures of his day: "I lost my feeling of awe about presidents. This is not meant as a criticism of them, but it is merely a simple statement of fact."

Aside from Edwards, the most wrenching decision made by any of the 2004 hopefuls had nothing directly to do with the presidency. The day after the dispiriting 2002 elections, Dick Gephardt, who resembled Sisyphus in his efforts to win back the House, stepped down as minority leader.

Two days later, on the Friday of election week, Gephardt was perched on a couch in his palatial, soon-to-be-relinquished leadership office in the Capitol. Over his head was a dramatic rendering of the romance of the Industrial Age—an oversize 1873 painting of the Eads Bridge, the first railroad crossing of the Mississippi River, which was slated to be returned to the Saint Louis Art Museum. Gephardt had been conducting continuous interviews since the election. Although his words were practiced, the anguish over falling on his sword was still audible in his voice. The renunciation of his leadership post was not exactly a surprise, since many had assumed that it would be the logical response to the expected Democratic defeat. But Gephardt insisted that he made the decision with his wife, Jane: "We came back here after the election and we sat most of the day at home. And we decided that I didn't want to do this any more. I wanted out." So what comes next, heh-heh? Gephardt, at this point, kept up the pretense of being elusive: "I want to do something different. What it is, I don't know at this point; I haven't figured it all out."

Fast-forward to my next conversation with Gephardt—a fast figure-it-outer who was now an active presidential candidate—in late January 2003, the day of the State of the Union Address. This time, because of a bomb scare, we took refuge in Gephardt's former hideaway office off the House floor, to which his staff still held the key. The walls, once filled with cartoons and other memorabilia from his 1988 presidential race, had been stripped bare. When I asked about the decision to run, Gephardt made a surprising admission: "It's always a hard decision. I guess the decision to step down as leader was harder."

Those words made me think of Bob Dole wandering forlornly across America in mid–1996, ruing the day that he let his handlers convince him that resigning the Senate seat he loved was the only way to demonstrate his determination to oust Clinton from the White House. But Dole was Senate majority leader, while Gephardt, if he had stayed on, would have been stuck with heading the toothless House Democratic opposition at a time when the Republicans had no interest in bipartisanship. Gephardt, in his early sixties, had come to a point in life when the House was not a home. His reasoning was understandable— having hungered after the White House for nearly two decades, he felt entitled to one final turn of the wheel. It was place your bets, up or out, and hopefully no lasting regrets if you lose.

If you believe the venomous critics of John Forbes Kerry, he's been running for president since his prep-school days when he first realized the implications of the initials "JFK." Yet for all the sneering put-downs of his overweening ambition, here he was— as Kerry himself took pains to point out—only getting around to his first race for the White House after nearly two decades on Capitol Hill. Sitting in his Senate office on an early spring day in 2003, Kerry gestured toward a burnished leather sofa and said, "I didn't think about it for ten seconds in '92 when Paul Tsongas sat on that red couch and asked if I was thinking about running for president. He told me that he was, and I said no I wasn't." (Tsongas, a former Massachusetts senator who died in 1997, proved to be Clinton's most serious competitor for the 1992 nomination.) Kerry, like Gephardt, made preliminary noises about challenging Gore in 2000. Yet for a range of factors (impeachment, Gore's prowess, Bill Bradley's candidacy and, he insists, concerns about divisiveness in the party), Kerry never entered the fray.

This time there was no hesitancy, at least on his part. As Kerry explained, "I felt so frustrated and angry about the [2002] election, angry about what happened to Max Cleland, angry about the voicelessness of my party and determined to make a difference. That resolved it for me, fairly quickly and easily." Cleland, a Vietnam veteran confined to a wheelchair because of his war wounds, was defeated in his Senate re-election bid in Georgia by a vicious GOP campaign that assailed his patriotism.

Well, it wasn't quite that simple. There was also the Teresa factor. As a traditionally adoring political spouse, Kerry's second wife is to Nancy Reagan as a woodpecker is to a cooing dove. The most talked-about article during the Invisible Primary was a devastating June 2002 *Washington Post* portrait of the senator and his mega-wealthy wife by Mark Leibovich that began, "Teresa Heinz is getting up a full head of rage, while her husband John Kerry fidgets"—and went downhill from there, painting Heinz as a harridan and Kerry as her hen-pecked enabler. Teresa Heinz is the kind of figure who would be intriguing to a novelist but endlessly exasperating to a campaign staff. The Mozambique-born, European-educated widow of Pennsylvania Republican Senator John Heinz and heiress to a half-billion-dollar-plus condiment fortune, she is smart, often charming and frequently self-absorbed.

During a February interview in her Washington office at the Heinz Foundation, she demonstrated a detailed knowledge of health-care policy, offered shrewd insights about her husband and displayed her penchant for lengthy digressions that invariably guided the conversation back to her own life. As a longtime student of senators on both sides of the political and marital aisle, she understands the presidential bug. A young-looking sixty-four (call me naive, but I thought her secret was great genes and not, as she later revealed to *Elle* magazine, Botox injections), she appreciates the time-is-fleeting pressures on her husband as he nears that day of reckoning with a sixty-candle-power birthday cake. "This is his fourth term," she said, "and he like a lot of us, maybe it's age-related, maybe it's the state of the world, feels a certain urgency to talk about certain things." As she explained, "I think he viewed this as an opportunity to finally get things off his chest and go for broke. Just go for broke."

Teresa, who adopted the last name Kerry for the campaign, admitted that she was initially troubled by the notion of a presidential race because she was keenly aware of the strains that the campaign would put on her and the marriage. "We talked about it a lot over the last year or so, off and on," she said. "Mostly, it was how do we cope with this? How do we live our lives? Is it really the right thing for us at this time?" Dressed in a black jacket and skirt highlighted by a white crocheted blouse and a large bejeweled cross encrusted with diamonds, she explained her initial reluctance: "I cherish privacy. I like to go to the supermarket. I like to talk to the shopkeeper. That's a big sacrifice for me, because I love doing those things." (That quote has been shortened out of necessity, since she veered off on a tangent halfway through before returning to the topic of Kerry's presidential ambitions.)

Here was how she framed what to her was the Big Question: "Do I, caring as much as I do about so many issues, have the right for selfish reasons, personal reasons, not to be part of his trip? And the more I thought about it—hiking by myself and just thinking, just out there with nature and God—the more I thought that I have to help him because of what he had to say, the questions that he had to raise."

And what a strange, strange trip it is sure to be, both for Kerry and the most uncontained political spouse in recent memory.

When is a dream born? It is a Washington cliché that every senator peers into his shaving mirror and sees the next president. But Joe Lieberman—no stranger to ego, although he masks it well— was different. His curious lack of the presidential gland didn't primarily stem from any concern over being too Jewish or too hawkish. Rather, before 2000, he always regarded himself as a man of the Senate. Even with his family, he never allowed himself to muse aloud, "Well, maybe, someday, if everything goes right..." Even when a conservative newspaper columnist would occasionally, very occasionally, suggest that the Democrats should abandon their foolhardy leftist ways and look to someone like Lieberman, the Connecticut senator would wave it off with a bemused air. As Rebecca Lieberman, his thirty-three-year-old daughter from his first marriage, recalled, "He never talked about running for president. He never talked about it with us."

Of course, everything changed as soon as Lieberman ended up a hanging chad away from the heartbeat-away job of vice president. Small wonder. Every vice-presidential nominee in the past thirty years, with the conspicuous exception of Geraldine Ferraro, has at one time run for president. Now that he was kosher-certified presidential timber, Lieberman was poised to be a candidate, except for his old-fashioned loyalty to Al Gore, the man who single-handedly raised the Connecticut senator's sights beyond someday being chairman of the Armed Services Committee.

Throughout most of 2002, Lieberman was animated by the intuition—more a hunch than any solid nugget of information—that Gore wouldn't do it. But by late fall, as Gore roared back in the headlines with his book tour and a foreign-policy speech assailing Bush's Iraq policy, Lieberman began to develop a frisson of doubt. After all these careful if-I-run preparations, was his career again destined to be defined by a near miss? Lieberman, though, was absolutely certain about one thing: Gore had said he would announce his decision in early January. The senator expected to learn more when the two of them got together at Gore's Washington-area home on Monday morning, December 16, for a long-scheduled chat.

But Lieberman didn't have to wait. Instead, the news broke mid-afternoon Sunday. Lieberman had just returned from Connecticut to his Georgetown home in one of Washington's rare gated communities. His wife, Hadassah, was in New York City, and the senator was sharing the house with their fourteen-year-old daughter, Hani. Suddenly he got a message from a Senate staffer on his BlackBerry wireless console: There's a rumor that Al isn't running. Lieberman and his daughter immediately switched on CNN to learn that Gore would indeed announce on *60 Minutes* that he had chosen not to be a candidate. A surge of adrenaline shot through Lieberman as he thought, This is what I hoped for, this is what I dreamed about and, uh-oh, this is just the beginning of a long and grueling ordeal that can end who knows where. Hani, a deeply religious teenager, let loose with what even Orthodox rabbis would agree was the only appropriate response: "Holy shit!"

About an hour later on this BlackBerry Sunday, Lieberman received a text message from Gore formally confirming everything and asking to postpone their meeting so that the former vice president could work through his must-call list. When Matt Lieberman, a teacher in New Haven, got through on a low-tech device called the telephone, he found his father's mood to be well-modulated enthusiasm (more "How about that?" than "Yippee!") mixed with an undertone of seriousness about the gravity of the undertaking. At the moment, the mostly vacationing Lieberman loyalists were a far-flung lot, since they had been operating under the assumption that the first hints of a Gore decision would not come until after Christmas. So the residents of Lieberworld—the loyalists and staffers plus the senator and his family—got together on a conference call that evening and merely decided that Lieberman would hold a Monday press conference to announce that he "probably is a candidate." But that was a mere fig leaf of plausible denial. For during the call, Rebecca Lieberman concluded, "It's definite all right. We're doing this."

The yarmulke was in the ring.

As the outgoing chairman of the Senate Intelligence Committee, Bob Graham was rather good at keeping secrets, especially big ones about himself. Graham didn't lurk in the shadows like a CIA agent operating a safe house in Damascus. The sixty-six-year-old Florida senator logged more appearances on the Sunday morning talk shows in 2002 than any other public figure. Rather in the spirit of Poe's "The Purloined Letter," Graham was adept at hiding the truth in plain sight. Though he intimated this to no one outside his immediate family, Graham had spent most of 2002 contemplating a bid for the White House.

This reticence was largely based on Graham's conviction that any hint of partisan ambition would undermine the joint Senate-House inquiry into the intelligence failures leading up to September 11, which he had been co-chairing with his House counterpart, Porter Goss. Ever disciplined, Graham didn't even explicitly raise the topic of a presidential race with his wife, Adele. But as she recalled, "When he was discussing the problems with the intelligence investigation, I could tell he was thinking about it. You don't have to say it to feel it."

At a family Thanksgiving, Graham jettisoned this don't-ask-don't-tell policy. He felt liberated because the congressional 9/11 investigation was finally completed (although the eight-hundred-plus-page text of the report was not released until July 2003). The senator and his wife were spending the holiday at one of the places he loves best: the farm in Albany, Georgia, where Grahams have been raising Black Angus cattle since the 1920s. With them was the eldest of their four daughters, Gwen Logan, and her family, who had driven up from Tallahassee. Unlike anyone else, Gwen had actually been talking with her father about the presidency, off and on, throughout the year. Now she put it to him directly, "Dad, do you have the desire to do this?" Graham admitted that he had the yen. He recalled the words of his late sister-in-law, Katharine Graham, that every president she ever knew had "the depth of passion to do all the difficult and sometimes unpleasant things necessary to be elected and serve." Suddenly the White House, rather than the Black Angus, became the dominant weekend topic. When Gwen and her father wearied of their own suppositions and speculations, they went on-line to sift through the political news and then plotted some more.

After thirty-six years of elective office, including two terms as governor and three in the Senate, Bob Graham is the most successful politician in modern Florida history. Yet rather than immediately assembling a team of veteran advisers to map out a late-starting presidential race, Graham did nothing for two weeks. Absolutely nothing. Finally, without giving a reason, he asked his Senate chief of staff, Buddy Menn, to arrange a private meeting with the most famous political strategist in America not named Karl Rove.

James Carville was the first outsider to whom Graham confided his deep-cover aspirations. The thirty-minute chat at the senator's Capitol Hill townhouse was conducted in the friendly but formal fashion that is Graham's natural metier. No stranger to such conversations with would-be presidents seeking their learner's permit, Carville offered his standard advice about the rules of the road: "You've got to know why you're running ... It's not a position, it's a job ... The one thing you know in every instance without fail is that the person with the most money in the bank on January 1 of the election year gets the nomination." Graham, famous for his color-coded notebooks in which he records the hour-by-hour details of his day, jotted down the highlights of Carville's lecture. Although Graham never said anything definitive, Carville left the townhouse thinking, "Hey, this guy's going to run for president."

Four days later, on December 13, ABC's "The Note" ran this intriguing one-sentence item: "For those who think the Democratic field is pretty set, what would you say if you heard that Senator Bob Graham of Florida has initiated some 'serious discussions' with people about whether he might put together a strong 2004 presidential campaign?" But the senator, afflicted with what seemed to be a case of the slows, still did nothing overt beyond getting ready for a six-day, pre-Christmas cruise to Mexico with Adele. Graham was literally at sea when Al Gore made the announcement that turned the presidential race into "Anything Can Happen Day" for the Democratic Party.

For all his senatorial solemnity in Washington, Graham's hallmark in Florida is his "work days," media stunts in which he tries to replicate the on-the-job experiences of his constituents, doing everything from mixing mortar to grooming circus animals. Work day no. 385 on December 23 involved no heavy lifting; the gray-haired senator was slated to spend the day at Radio Carnivale in Miami's Little Haiti section. It began with an appearance behind the microphone on a morning call-in show. There, in response to a series of questions about his future plans, as some callers even mentioned the White House, Graham blurted out, "I'm seriously thinking about options, including the option of running for president." Never before in the nation's proud melting-pot history had anyone ever unveiled a presidential candidacy on a Haitian-American radio show. (As Graham later explained to me, his logic for opting for Radio Carnivale over, say, *Meet the Press* was simply that "I didn't want to be disingenuous.")

The meticulous Graham, of course, had brought along to the radio station his tiny green notebook to chronicle the day's events, large and small. Arriving at 7:45, he wrote, "Difficulty opening door—what if they had a radio show and nobody could [get in]." Entering the studio at 7:55, he dutifully noted "round table—2 mikes," detailed his pre-interview preparations ("clear throat"), and mentioned that the announcer boasted that he was "the only talk show host with a USS," which is Graham's acronym for "United States Senator." Later in the broadcast, he described drinking "coffee—heavy sweet & sugar." Most of Graham's thirteen pages of jottings for the day referred to the concerns of the senator's Haitian-American constituents.

Hey, haven't we buried the lead? What about Graham's bombshell revelation that he was running for president? History should note that Graham devoted exactly two entries, totaling fifteen words, to the entire topic. During the call-in portion, sometime after 8:00, he scrawled, "repeated urging to run for President." Around 8:45, Graham also jotted down the words of the host who mentioned that his senatorial guest may be "moving to a new job [on] Pennsylvania Avenue." In short, running for president got equal billing with Graham's summary of a news break: "9:45—traffic—many accidents."

Others close to the senator, though, were more literarily exuberant. Adele Graham, who started keeping her own set of notes on the presidential race just the day before, wrote, "'Oui,' is the sound of enthusiasm coming from Haitian Carnivale Radio. Over and over, Bob was asked if he would run for president—and finally a child brought forth a positive response. I was listening and heard a confirmation of what I had expected. The press filled in the details throughout the day announcing the possibility of a presidential run. Our youngest daughter was very surprised. Our oldest daughter [Gwen] was his greatest advocate. All four [daughters] expressing comments of excitement and concern. The phone began to ring—longtime friends who had suggested it for years."

Two weeks later, the Grahams were back in Washington, returning home after a dinner across the Potomac in Great Falls, Virginia, with their daughter Suzanne and her husband, Tom Gibson. As Adele described it in her journal, "Bob is on the right path. A private breakfast with Warren Buffett. A ride by the White House on the way home from dinner with the Gibsons with [Bob's] statement: 'Maybe we'll be in that house over there in a couple of years.'"

CHAPTER 4

The Money Primary

As John Kerry peers down the long conference table at his two dozen breakfast companions on this mid-December 2002 morning, it is easy to imagine that he sees dollar signs along with such familiar faces as investment banker Felix Rohatyn. Assembled in the Park Avenue office of equity-fund manager Alan Patricof are some of Manhattan's leading Democratic fund-raisers, a group shell-shocked and adrift following Al Gore's precipitous withdrawal from the presidential race just two days ago. This long-planned meet-the-candidate session involves nothing so crass as the exchange of campaign cash. Rather, it is akin to a backer's audition for a Broadway musical. If the would-be theatrical angels leave humming the title tune, they will undoubtedly ante up later.

Suffice it to say that I am probably the only person at the table who worries about paying his monthly American Express bill. I had originally gone to see Patricof, whom I knew socially, after word had leaked out that he had gathered a small group to hear a preliminary pitch from General Wesley Clark, that intriguing figure always hovering on the fringes of presidential possibility. Patricof mentioned that I also had just missed a closed-door breakfast with the little-known Howard Dean. Then he invited me to the Kerry tryout and upcoming sessions with the other candidates. It was a surprising offer, since reporters are rarely permitted to witness the most clandestine courting ritual of the Invisible Primary—the wooing of checkbook Democrats. So here I am, feeling like I just landed a walk-on role in the political version of *Upstairs, Downstairs.*

After two trips with Kerry during the run-up to the 2002 elections, I am familiar with his standard pitch to Democratic activists in New Hampshire and Iowa. What intrigue me are the ways that he adapts his spiel to appeal to this politically sophisticated Manhattan audience. Running through his résumé, for example, Kerry emphasizes the anti-war aspects of his Vietnam persona rather than the medals he earned as a navy officer. Liberated from worrying about how his comments might come across in tomorrow's newspapers, Kerry is scathing about the Democrats' failure to offer a coherent message during the off-year campaign and the refusal of his Senate colleagues to approve legislation establishing the Department of Homeland Security before the election. Kerry does not, however, go so far as to point out that the politically ill-advised battle over the lack of union protections in the Bush administration's homeland-security legislation was orchestrated by Joe Lieberman.

Even though Kerry is the only man in the room who removes his suit jacket in an effort to appear informal and relaxed, he comes across as tense, defensive and curiously tone deaf. Keenly aware of the recently orphaned Gore contingent in the room, Kerry makes a maladroit effort to empathize with the former vice president. In a bizarre biographical riff, Kerry likens Gore's bowing out to his own long-ago decision not to mount a second attempt to win a Massachusetts congressional seat in 1974 after losing an initial effort in 1972. Kerry portentously explains that he chose instead to give his support to Paul Tsongas because he didn't want to contribute to the Democratic divisions in "our country . . . er, my state, my congressional district."

By this point, Kerry is beginning to lose his audience; the man sitting across from me is visibly reading the *New York Times.* Before he answers questions, Kerry first poses a rhetorical one of his own: Can a Democrat from Massachusetts win the White House? His response, an almost word-for-word repetition of an argument he made to me in October, is that Massachusetts is not the liberal bastion that people imagine. Four of the state's last five governors have been Republicans (Kerry leaves unmentioned that he served as lieutenant governor under the exception, a fellow named Michael Dukakis), Massachusetts voted for Ronald Reagan both times and in the 1976 presidential primary, the state backed Scoop Jackson, the most conservative Democrat in the field. As Kerry revs up the way-back machine, I half expect him to mention that a Massachusetts Republican senator blocked the League of Nations in 1919.

Kerry's presentation provides the first intimations of a flaw in his candidacy—he tries so hard to be reassuring and is so conscious of the "Massachusetts liberal" label that he fails to make clear his rationale for running. Stressing his own moderate credentials and pandering a bit to presumed Wall Street sentiment, Kerry points out that he backed the 1996 welfare reform legislation and has supported a wide variety of business-oriented tax cuts. He speaks so effusively about his tax-cutting zeal, in fact, that several Democrats in the room mistakenly assume that Kerry voted for the deficits-be-damned 2001 Bush tax bill.

During the forty-five-minute question period, Kerry candidly outlines his fund-raising plans. Brimming with confidence, he declares that he can raise at least $30 million before the primaries, which, with federal matching funds, translates into a hefty nearly $50 million campaign budget. My ears perk up as Kerry casually mentions his intention to participate in the matching-funds program, under which the government doubles individual campaign contributions up to $250. Although he never spells out the significance of this declaration, I grasp it immediately. It means no ketchup money from the funds he jointly shares with his Heinz heiress wife, Teresa. Under the law, a candidate who donates more than $50,000 to his own campaign is automatically barred from receiving federal matching funds.

Kerry also serves up a lengthy and factually accurate exegesis of how George W. Bush corralled the 2000 GOP nomination. The secret was that the leading Republican fund-raisers collectively decided in early 1999 to unite around Bush, thereby depriving such potential rivals as Lamar Alexander, Elizabeth Dole and, yes, Dan Quayle of the cash to survive the 1999 preliminary skirmishing. That's why the iconoclastic John McCain ended up as Bush's only serious challenger. Embedded in Kerry's narrative is an obvious lesson for Democrats who want to avoid a fratricidal nomination struggle in 2004. When Patricof asks about the potential for a divisive primary fight, Kerry makes this message explicit: "Alan, it's up to you and the rest of the people in this room. You can coalesce around a candidate and squeeze out everyone else. Or we'll have to depend on everyone being on good behavior [in the primaries]."

Kerry's unite-around-me appeal prompted memories of a boast that Gore adviser Ron Klain made to me back in mid–1998 when the vice president was trying to clear the field for an unchallenged romp to the 2000 nomination. "There are only 30,000 proven big givers in the Democratic Party," Klain said with unequivocal certainty. "And we've already signed up 27,000 of them. There's no way that anyone can raise the money to oppose Gore." Whoops! What the Gore high command failed to consider was that "Dollar Bill" Bradley had carefully nurtured his own fund-raising base outside those 30,000 big-ticket donors. While Bradley had liabilities as a candidate, the former basketball star was able to match Gore dollar for dollar until he was upended in the New Hampshire primary.

These cash-and-Kerry fantasies similarly misjudged the dynamics of the 2004 money primary. In a contest without an

obvious favorite, there is small incentive and large risk for fund-
raisers to prematurely anoint any candidate as the Daddy Warbucks of the Democratic Party. If they bet on the wrong horse,
they could end up following the next Democratic administration
on CNN rather than from, say, the embassy in Stockholm. The
GOP's 2000 rally-around-the-president's-son movement to Bush
reflected the ingrained royalist tenor of Republican presidential
politics; the disorganized Democrats, in contrast, have consistently failed to clear the path to the nomination for anyone, even
for an incumbent president like Jimmy Carter in 1980. A handful
of glowing news clips, some promising New Hampshire polls
and a consultant-heavy campaign staff were not nearly enough to
cloak Kerry in an aura of inevitability.

Kerry, to be sure, ended up collecting more than $12 million
during the first six months of 2003, the most of any Democrat and
close to matching the pace that he had forecast at the Patricof
breakfast. But measured by the quarterly reports to the Federal
Election Commission (FEC), Kerry's position in the fund-raising
derby was analogous to that of Mo Udall, the liberal Arizona congressman who kept finishing second in the 1976 primaries. Each
time around, the Kerry number prompted oh-yeah yawns from
the political cognoscenti, who were galvanized by the dramatic
narrative line coming from another campaign. At the end of the
first quarter, John Edwards won the headlines with his ability to
belly up to the bar with the trial lawyers. And on June 30,
Howard Dean became the big story. The once impecunious Dean
had for the first time in political history miraculously found a
way to harness the small-contribution power of the Internet. The
tectonic plates had shifted, the continents had moved, and never
again would campaign finance be viewed solely through the old-
fashioned prism of who had the largest group of proven Democratic fund-raisers in his corner.

But for all the justified fascination with Dean's web-slinging
exploits on the Internet, the relative financial competitiveness of
the Democratic presidential race was also due to another far less

ballyhooed factor. Yes, it is time to talk about the landmark 2002 McCain-Feingold campaign reform bill. I will concede that those who are obsessed with the details of campaign reform are like nineteenth-century devotees of Esperanto as a universal language. There may not be many of them, but their passions about the topic are so intense that they are best avoided at cocktail parties. But in all the abstruse debates that surrounded the legislation and its subsequent Supreme Court review, little attention was devoted to a minor provision that made all the difference for the Democratic hopefuls.

A drum roll if you please, maestro. McCain-Feingold increased the maximum legally permissible individual campaign contribution in a primary campaign from $1,000 to $2,000. That seemingly innocuous double-your-pleasure-double-your-fun numerical change probably kept Dick Gephardt, Lieberman and even Edwards in the race. Do the arithmetic—a candidate can now harvest twice the campaign cash from the same two hours spent in a Fifth Avenue living room or at a beach house in Malibu. For a presidential contender who must put all his begs in one ask-it, the implications are enormous. Most of the 2004 Democrats, especially in the early stages of the campaign, depended on contributors who could "max out" with a single check. During the first three months of 2003, both Gephardt and Lieberman received more than 85 percent of their funding in increments of $1,000 or more. The new $2,000 limit illustrates the truism that a rising tide lifts all candidates. Taken as a group, the Democratic hopefuls in the first quarter garnered roughly an additional $10 million in $1,000-plus contributions that would have been impermissible under the old law.

The rule of thumb is that a White House hopeful needs to raise at least $15 million (not counting federal matching funds) in 2003, though mileage may vary based on driving conditions. This change in the contribution limit makes it likely that most, if not all, of the serious Democratic contenders will make it. (Bob Graham—who was supposed to rake in more money in his home state of Florida than Disney World—is likely to prove to be the conspicuous exception.) Never before in modern political history have this many presidential candidates entered the fall before the primaries with the financial resources in place to seriously joust for the nomination. The financial terrain of a presidential campaign will never be level, but this $2,000 wrinkle has dramatically lifted the barriers to entry that have blocked generations of underfunded White House dreamers.

Jesse Unruh, the rotund leader of California Democrats during the 1960s, famously declared that "money is the mother's milk of politics." Applying Unruh's colorful metaphor to the 2004 Democratic hopefuls might make John Edwards the most ardent proponent of breast-feeding. All the presidential candidates needed money, but Edwards craved it with single-minded intensity. Invisible in the polls, inexperienced in Washington and innocent of long-standing ties to traditional national fund-raising networks, Edwards banked on a dramatic breakthrough in the early money primary. Nick Baldick, Edwards's campaign manager, confided in mid-December 2002 that the strategy for the first quarter was to risk neglecting the early caucus and primary states to concentrate exclusively on fund-raising. "Trips to New Hampshire are helpful for Kerry because he already has a support base there from Boston television," Baldick said. "But people there don't know who we are."

What the North Carolina senator had going for him was the willingness of his fellow attorneys to take him on appeal. The dirty little secret of the Democrats, explained to me by a leading fund-raiser, is the narrowness of the party's financial base. Without the mainstream business support of the Republican Party, the Democrats disproportionately depend on just three groups: Jews, unions and trial lawyers. But wealthy litigators have traditionally bought their way into the Democratic Party through "soft money," the fat-cat five- and six-digit donations that were banned by McCain-Feingold. When it comes to rounding up campaign checks the old-fashioned way, in bunches of $1,000 and $2,000, trial lawyers were as inexperienced as a fledgling law-school graduate arguing an appeal before the Supreme Court. "At our first law-firm event, we got every type of check," said Eileen Kotecki, who oversees Edwards's fund-raising, in mid-January. "I had to explain that a law-firm check or a numbered account is not going to work. It has to be a check from your personal account." (This may partially explain why an Arkansas law firm is under federal investigation for allegedly illegally reimbursing its employees for their donations to the Edwards campaign, which returned $10,000 in questionable funds.)

Nothing—not even following the house-beautification doctrines of Martha Stewart—is more labor-intensive than early political fund-raising in a presidential campaign. Every free hour of every day carries a price tag of, say, $5,000. Big-ticket donors are not satisfied to merely see the candidate in a living-room setting; they also demand five minutes of his time to privately press their views on Iraq or, in Edwards's case, the iniquities of tort-reform legislation.

Scorning sleep and hitting the road the moment the Senate ended pressing business, Edwards spent more time with lawyers than a CEO facing criminal indictment for insider trading. Part of what carried him forward was an unflagging optimism. "I'm going to do everything in my power to get your support," he explained to me, "but you're not going to get every vote and you're not going to get every fund-raiser. If that man or woman doesn't work out, you go on to the next one with equal energy." Every night, whether traveling or home in Washington, Edwards would call Kotecki and ask, "Eileen, how much money do we have? We've got to be number one."

That quest led to Jeffrey Anderson, a fifty-six-year-old trial lawyer with his own firm in San Antonio, who contributed $2,000 in March to the Edwards campaign. Anderson, who admits that he could end up voting for Bush in the general election, met the candidate at a Sunday afternoon reception organized by his friend and fellow lawyer Frank Herrera. Anderson and Edwards chatted for about five minutes about foreign policy and their shared concerns about the drive to cap medical-liability settlements. There was no hard sell; money was never mentioned. But afterward, Anderson sent his check to the campaign via Herrera. "Mr. Edwards is an interesting individual," Anderson explained. "I find if you meet with individuals personally, you get a better feel for their charisma or their knowledge and sincerity than if you see them in sound bites or orchestrated ads."

Let's follow the daisy chain of mutual obligation back to Herrera, the host of the fifty-person San Antonio event that netted $45,000 for Edwards. Herrera, sixty, was recruited by high-powered Dallas trial lawyer Fred Baron, the financial chairman of the Edwards campaign, with whom he had worked on several lucrative asbestos cases. Although he had never met the candidate, Herrera was already committed to Edwards: "It was an easy choice for me because obviously he is in the same profession I'm in." The son of an auto mechanic from Edna, Texas, Herrera was also attracted to Edwards's hard-scrabble heritage. So when Baron called to urge him to host an Edwards fund-raiser, Herrera recalls, "I leaped at the chance because I had not had the chance to visit with him personally."

No stranger to the political money circuit (he held a six-hundred-person Democratic event featuring Bill Clinton before the 1998 congressional elections), Herrera possessed the three essential qualifications of a successful fund-raiser: a large Rolodex, a willingness to work the phones to call in favors and a jaw-dropping home. With just two weeks to prepare, Herrera sent out two hundred faxed invitations (mostly to lawyer friends) and made about one hundred follow-up phone calls. "They know that if I'm calling two or three times a day," said Herrera, "I'm calling for a political reason."

Part of the allure was the house: 10,000 square feet, with a living room the size of a basketball court, set on ten acres in Hill Country Village, just outside San Antonio. The Edwards campaign prefers events in private homes, since the host can legally spend up to $4,000 on food and decorations without any of it counting as a campaign contribution. So the Herrera home was filled with fresh flowers and the caterers set up a Mexican lunch of beans, rice, fajitas and tortillas. After meeting privately with Herrera and former San Antonio mayor and Clinton cabinet member Henry Cisneros (who later endorsed Kerry), Edwards spoke for fifteen minutes and then worked the crowd, with his host standing next to him making the introductions. For Herrera, the success of the event was defined by a number: He exceeded his target of $40,000.

At the end of a fund-raising quarter, when contributions must be reported to the Federal Elections Commission, it is traditional for campaigns to announce their totals well in advance of the official release of the information by the FEC. All day Tuesday, April 1, political junkies waited for the Kerry camp to release its pace-setting number. Tiring of this Alphonse-and-Gaston routine a little after 4:00 P.M., the Edwards campaign sprung its surprise: $7.4 million. Not until the following afternoon did the crestfallen Kerry team issue a press release headlined, "John Kerry Tops $7 Million for First Fundraising Quarter."

John Edwards got his wish; he was number one. But never did a presidential candidate owe so much to a single occupational group. According to a *Washington Post* analysis of the Edwards filings to the FEC, the senator received a whopping 55 percent of his money from individuals who identified themselves on disclosure forms as lawyers. (That figure does not count spouses and adult children of attorneys nor does it include real-estate developers, owners of plant-watering services and other vendors with business ties to law firms.) If the Edwards campaign had an unofficial slogan, it might well be "Torts 'R' Us."

For all his medical training, Howard Dean rightly describes himself as a "technophobe." As Vermont governor, he did not begin using e-mail until late 2001, and through the early months of 2003 he traveled without a computer. While rivals such as Lieberman were wedded to their BlackBerry wireless handheld consoles, Dean made do with a cell phone, though he sometimes had trouble playing back recorded messages. In short, Dean began his presidential bid with about as much chance of being the darling of the Internet as Chance, the simpleton gardener, played by Peter Sellers in *Being There,* did advising presidents. But then virtually everything about the Dean crusade seemed to be based on serendipity. The candidate, who is also not a TV fan, happily adopted the suggestion of an early supporter to call his campaign "Dean for America" without having the foggiest notion that the slogan was borrowed from *The West Wing.*

Dean's original approach to raising money resembled that of every other Democrat, except that the sums he was questing after were far more modest. In late January 2003, I attended one of Dean's initial fund-raisers, a low-key reception held at the Washington home of former Clinton cabinet secretary Christine Varney, where the stated but timorously enforced price of admission was a $500 contribution. Speaking to this room filled with curious but mostly uncommitted veterans of the Clinton administration, the candidate artfully delineated the Dean difference. "Now I'm going to tell this group of insiders, who know a lot about politics, why I can win," he declared. His reasoning can be boiled down to a single argument: I'm from outside the Beltway. "If you're from Washington," he said, with a slight sneer audible in his tone, "you get trained to nuance all your positions so that they appeal to as many people as you possibly can ... Your biggest claim to fame is that you can say that you introduced a bill."

But governors, Dean declared without having to directly invoke Clinton's pedigree, march to the beat of a different drummer. "If you're a governor, you get paid to offend people," he said, getting a small laugh. "You get paid to make very tough decisions. I don't think we can possibly beat George Bush unless we have as an alternative somebody who's direct, somebody who knows who they are and who is comfortable with their message." Drumming the point home, Dean declared, "I don't think you can win with Bush Lite. As Harry Truman said, 'If you have a choice between a Republican and a Republican, the Republican is going to win every time.'" (Bigger laugh.) Afterward I chatted with former Clinton strategist Harold Ickes, who expressed the conventional view that while Dean was impressive, he probably could not raise enough money to be competitive.

Really? Four months later, I was listening to Dean fund-raising director Stephanie Schriock giggle at the memory of her job interview with the candidate. We were sitting in her office in the Burlington headquarters, which was filled with odd bits of political memorabilia like a 1984 Walter Mondale for President poster (a token of her Minnesota roots) and dominated by a wall chart detailing every fund-raising event planned for the second quarter. Like many of her fund-raising counterparts in other campaigns, the blond, enthusiastic thirty-year-old Schriock is a recent alumna of the Democratic Senate Campaign Committee. Recruited by Dean media consultant Steve McMahon, with whom she worked on an abortive Senate race in Oklahoma, Schriock finally sat down with the Vermont governor during the Democratic Governors Association convention in Austin, Texas, right after the 2002 elections.

What was, in hindsight, the comic moment came when she asked Dean, whose most expensive re-election race had cost $1 million, how much money he hoped to raise. "We're looking at $10 million," he said, probably exaggerating for her benefit. Schriock bluntly responded, "If we only do $10 million, we lose." That confident answer clinched the job. As Schriock recalled, "I really think he was expecting me to frown and say, 'Uh-oh, that'll be tough.'"

Schriock could laugh about that conversation now that it was the end of May, since the campaign was then on pace to raise more than $7 million during the first half of 2003. (The final total turned out to be more than $10 million—Dean surpassed his most optimistic projections for the entire campaign seven months before the Iowa caucuses. And the money kept rolling in throughout the summer.) But in late 2002, Dean was in financial terms akin to the Duchy of Grand Fenwick declaring war on the United States. Kerry and Edwards chartered jets for their travels, while Dean traveled coach. Even in the spring of 2003, after a late-night fund-raiser in Manhattan, Dean thought nothing of cramming into a rented sedan with his aides for the five-hour drive back to Burlington. Getting ready to leave New York around 10:00 P.M. on an April evening, Dean was shocked to discover that his staff had rented a Cadillac, albeit at a bargain rate. "How much did we raise today?" he asked grumpily. Only after hearing the five-digit total did he grudgingly say, "Well, okay."

Dean was outpacing his mainstream rivals because he had tapped into that half-forgotten vein of Democratic campaign cash: cause money. Even with Dean's passionate dissent from war with Iraq, it took a while for his own campaign to fully grasp the financial implications of his maverick candidacy. "On March 1," Schriock recalled, "I thought we were going to do $1 million in March. That said, neither Governor Dean nor the campaign manager [Joe Trippi] thought we'd do $1 million." While other campaigns desperately raced to impress the press with their first-quarter figures, Schriock confessed that "we had no expectations for March 31." Reflecting this otherworldly approach, the Dean campaign actually scheduled its first $1,000-a-person fundraiser for April 1 in New York, the day that the books opened for the second quarter.

It is funny how a new means of communication is often used to replicate the emotions that accompanied the technology that it replaced. The Dean campaign's first Internet breakthrough—the moment that in political terms equaled Alexander Graham Bell shouting into a primitive telephone mouthpiece, "Mr. Watson, come here, I want you!"—was built around something as ordinary as a postcard. On March 27, the campaign sent out to the

30,000 supporters on its e-mail list a retro-style facsimile of a
having-a-wonderful-time-wish-you-were-here Vermont vacation
greeting complete with a mock twenty-three-cent stamp. The
postcard featured an old-fashioned, almost-full mercury ther-
mometer that looked like it was borrowed from a 1950s local Red
Cross fund-raising campaign. "Dear friend," the printed text read.
"We're close to our goal, but we need your help. We're only
$83,000 short of our target for the first quarter FEC deadline."
Small public radio stations beg for $83,000, not serious presiden-
tial campaigns. But the results from this modest mass e-mailed
appeal were dramatic enough to justify an IPO. Dean collected
$400,000 over the Internet in just five days.

Even in late May, when I spoke with Schriock about Internet
fund-raising, she projected the slightly nervous tone of a 1920s
aviatrix about to attempt a cross-country flight. "Someday just
like direct mail, it's going to be a science," she said. But right
now, she admitted, there was just too little of an on-line track
record to hazard a realistic second-quarter projection. Working in
tandem with Internet sites such as meetup.com (which orchestrated heavily publicized monthly gatherings of Dean supporters)
and MoveOn.org (a Democratic activist network), the campaign
had seen its e-mail list swell to more than 100,000 addresses. Yet
no one in the Dean domain—not even Trippi, the Internet-
obsessed campaign manager who had worked in Silicon Valley—
fully grasped the stunning fund-raising potential of the list. They
were all like high-school science students who had thrown a
bunch of volatile chemicals into a beaker and had no idea if they
were going to spark a chain reaction. As the evocatively named
Zephyr Teachout, a former death-penalty lawyer who now oversees Internet organizing for Dean, put it, "The learning curve for
all of this is extraordinary."

Not nearly as extraordinary as the results. On June 29, two
days before the second-quarter deadline, the campaign issued a
breathless press release heralding the news that Dean had raised
more than $6 million since April 1, with $2 million coming in

over the Internet in the prior eight days. During the final count-down to midnight June 30, the Dean web page featured a baseball bat–shaped graphic that updated the fund-raising total each half hour. More than just a simulation of the final frenzied minutes of an ebay auction, this Dean telethon conveyed the participatory message that all who pointed and clicked their way to even a $50 contribution were an integral part of something larger than them-selves. The final number was a pace-setting, jaw-dropping, $7.6 million for the quarter, with more than half of the money coming over the Internet. Howard Dean was the church mouse who roared.

The Democrats may be the self-professed party of the people, but, aside from Dean, their fund-raising habits over the last decade have transformed them into the party of the (rich) people. The flagrant abuse of the campaign laws governing large unregulated soft-money contributions began with a desperate Bill Clinton—reeling from the loss of the House in the 1994 elections—who would meet with anyone, even Chinese-speaking rogues running hustles out on the Pacific Rim, to raise the big bucks to pay for his Dick Morris–dictated re-election advertising blitz. During the subsequent 1997 Senate hearings on the Clinton fund-raising scandals, I came to admire Lieberman's bravely independent stance as the only Democrat pressing for a fair-minded investiga-tion instead of a whitewash of the ethically challenged president.

Even though congressional Democrats voted overwhelmingly in 2002 to approve campaign reform legislation, many party lead-ers, from Chairman Terry McAuliffe on down, mourn the passing of soft money. The transition to hard money (individual contribu-tions of up to $2,000 that pay for presidential primary cam-paigns) has been particularly wrenching for the party's fund-raisers who were used to a more latitudinarian system. "Bill Clinton was a double-edged sword for the Democrats," explained fund-raiser Eileen Kotecki. "He trained a generation of Democratic fund-raisers who know how to sell a photograph with the president for $25,000. But they don't know how to work data bases and do prospecting and field work to get donors. We've lined up a generation of political fund-raisers who don't know how to do hard money."

The same can be said of Democratic donors. Many investment bankers, accustomed to writing $50,000 checks to the party and receiving deference from the likes of Tom Daschle in return, have neither the time nor the inclination to assemble the same amount for a presidential candidate by putting the arm on twenty-five separate donors for $2,000 each. In the new fund-raising universe, it is less a question of your personal net worth than how much you are worth in casting the net. "Guys with a lot of money are now irrelevant," says Gregg Hymowitz, a Wall Street money manager who is national co-chairman of the Gephardt campaign. "What you want are guys with a lot of friends." The best hard-money fund-raisers are those with a large social network built around a latticework of mutual obligation based on business, friendship or charitable giving. A member of Kerry's fourteen-person New York (fund-raising) steering committee boasts that his personal "A-list" consists of people who only ask about the candidate when they want to know what name to put on the check.

Wealthy New York Democrats, especially those who had been keening for Al Gore to run, were slow to commit to a presidential candidate. This post-Gore indecisiveness explained the prevalence of occasions like the Patricof breakfasts—events where a candidate makes an hour-long appearance just as he does at a fund-raiser, but collects nothing in return other than the names of possible prospects to add to future call lists. Small wonder that campaigns bristled at these frequent only-in-New- York tryouts. As one campaign fund-raiser sniffed, "Now that soft money is gone, showing up late means getting a seat at the back of the bus." In the end, Patricof backed Wesley Clark.

As a reporter, I found these prospecting sessions to be far more revealing than the half dozen private closed-room New York fund-raisers that I also wangled my way into. It was the differ-ence between watching an eager-to-please candidate try to win over an audience of doubters and seeing that same presidential contender confidently translate the well-practiced cadences of his New Hampshire stump speech to the social setting of a sprawling loft in Soho.

For example, when Lieberman appeared before the Patricof group, he was confronted with the question that has consistently cast a pall over his fund-raising efforts: Can a Jew really be elected president?

Lieberman first responded with the answer that I have often seen him give in public settings, an only-in-America trope that begins, "The 2000 experience was really inspiring, we didn't face any anti-Semitism at all." But the audience sitting around the table in a Park Avenue conference room wanted more than just another gooey remembrance of the Gore-Lieberman campaign. Prepared for this skepticism, Lieberman came equipped with polling numbers or, as he preferred to call them, "data points." In 1960, the year of the Kennedy-Nixon election, only 71 percent of Americans said that they would vote for a Catholic for president. "Today," Lieberman declared, "asked about voting for somebody Jewish, it's 92 percent."

But there were more goodies in the grab bag of data points pro-vided by pollster Mark Penn. "You'll get a kick out of hearing about one of the polls I did nationally before I decided to run," Lieberman said. "All the candidates were described in a positive way [without their names]. And in my description to half the sam-ple, we didn't say what my religion was. And in the other half of the sample, we said I was Jewish." Lieberman paused as if he were the announcer in the old which-hand-has-the-M&Ms TV commercial. Then with an open-palms gesture, he revealed, "I ran better in the half in which they said I was Jewish. So go figure."

Even though he had a hard time winning converts, Lieberman, who is after all the senator from an adjoining state, can easily project a New York state of mind. But I never figured that Dick

Gephardt—whom I always picture in a union windbreaker pledging to "fight for working families"—would ever play well here. Seeing Gephardt in Manhattan seems akin to meeting Ed Koch on a safari. Sure travel is broadening, but this is ridiculous.

But on a mid-January morning, a year before the Iowa caucuses, Gephardt had been speaking for ten minutes to two dozen influential Democrats who were raptly following every word in his rap. There was a sense of drama in the room (this Patricof prospecting breakfast was held at an East Side restaurant) as Gephardt told a story that I have heard before about his White House meeting with Bush the day after the World Trade Center towers crumbled. "I told the president," he recounted, "'You've got to trust us and we've got to trust you.'" But with his voice rising in anger, he then detailed all the ways in which Bush has betrayed that trust. "This president," Gephardt declared, rapping the table for emphasis, "is not talking to the American people about the nature of the challenge we face." This was not a crowd used to presidential candidates using tables as punctuation marks, but somehow, strangely enough, it worked.

Unlike Kerry in his appearance before the group, Gephardt came across as confident rather than defensive. After Patricof challenged him by saying, "A lot of people in New York are concerned about your class-war rhetoric, beat the rich," Gephardt offered a lengthy tour of his economic views that ended with a self-deprecating anecdote about a friend who told him, "Dick, you're such a nice man, why are you always screaming on television?" Gephardt was also repeatedly pressed on everything from his opposition to the 1993 NAFTA treaty to the perception that he is in the pocket of the unions. Other politicians might have pandered ("I'm as concerned with business as I am with labor") or groveled ("NAFTA was then, this is now") or even grown testy ("It's easy for you to criticize working families"). Instead, Gephardt just doggedly plowed ahead with an opaque refusal to recognize the semi-hostile nature of the questions.

Afterward, I found myself chatting with Ellen Chesler, the

biographer of Margaret Sanger and friend of Hillary who heads reproductive-rights programs at George Soros's Open Society Institute—in short, the quintessential upmarket Manhattan Democrat. "If I had time to get involved, I really might support him," she said to my surprise. Another friend at the breakfast, whom I consider the Mikey of presidential politics ("He hates everybody"), confided, "I thought Gephardt was pretty good. I walked away more impressed than I thought I would."

Much like Scarlett O'Hara vowing that she will never be hungry again, presidential candidates swear they will never be down to their last thirty-second commercial. Gephardt, unlike his rivals for the nomination, knows from bitter experience what it feels like to become the Invisible Man on TV screens at just the wrong moment. As Gephardt frequently tells it (he used this anecdote at the Patricof breakfast), he came south for the 1988 Super Tuesday primaries with just $1 million compared to $3 million each for Dukakis and Gore. (Against the free-spending backdrop of contemporary politics, it seems ludicrous that a presidential nomination could ever be decided based on who had $3 million.) The Missouri congressman recalled checking into a Texas hotel room late one night, switching on the TV set and enduring three Dukakis ads and three Gore commercials in half an hour with nary a Gephardt spot in sight. With the pain from that poignant memory audible in his voice, he said, "That's when I knew it was over."

Yet Gephardt seems doomed to always be singing the "St. Louis Blues" when it comes to money. It probably stems from that same glitz-and-glamour gap that makes him the least likely Democratic hopeful to be profiled in *Vanity Fair*. During the first half of 2003, he finished fifth in the fund-raising derby with $7.4 million, though he augmented that figure with $2.4 million that he had squirreled away in his House re-election account. An inherent danger in political reporting is over-emphasizing the predictive importance of early green-eyeshade fund-raising numbers. Yes, history does show that the candidate with the most cash going into the primaries generally wins the nomination. But since presidential campaigns are only waged every four years, truisms that cover the last quarter century are actually based on a limited number of occurrences. Nothing this time around dictates that money will be the determining factor in a wide-open race. So for all of Gephardt's fund-raising woes, let us violate the norms of journalism for a brief moment to accentuate the positive.

Picture an early June evening at the River House, the legendary Manhattan apartment building on Sutton Place. The windows of a long, cream-colored living room, decorated with modern art that might make the MOMA envious, were open wide to admit the late spring air and to display the classic view of the East River and the sparkling lights of ... well ... Queens. The four dozen Democrats assembled here—an eclectic mixture that includes former United Nations ambassador and every Democrat's putative secretary of state Dick Holbrooke, Bette Midler and my friend Ellen Chesler—had all responded to an invitation that read, "Lady de Rothschild and Ambassador Felix Rohatyn Invite You to the Gephardt Fund-Raiser Reception."

After a brief introduction from Rohatyn (who had played a similar role at a Kerry event the prior week) and a few welcoming words by Lynn Forester (married to Lord Evelyn Rothschild), the candidate, the Robespierre of the union halls, took the place of honor in front of a marble fireplace. "Let me first thank Felix and Lynn for doing this; they are dear friends," he said. "It's always a little difficult to get involved in a primary election. But they have been willing, along with all of you, to give me some help at an important time in the campaign."

The words that followed were far less important than the occasion at which they were spoken. For on this glittering evening, the long financial struggles of Dick Gephardt were momentarily forgotten as he nurtured the hope that maybe this time he would not be left bereft in a strange hotel room watching the TV commercials of his well-heeled rivals as his dreams of the White House vanished before his eyes.

Presidential fund-raising would be a lot more convenient for Capitol Hill Democrats if George Washington had not been seized by the wacky notion of moving the nation's capital from New York to a dreary swampland between Maryland and Virginia. While California, Florida and all those flyover states play major roles in the money primary, the greed-locked streets of Manhattan remain the spot for one-stop shopping. In the spring of 2003 you literally couldn't cross a block in midtown without encountering a presidential hopeful. One day, John Edwards was leaving lunch at *Rolling Stone* magazine when he spotted a familiar driver standing by an empty Lincoln town car on the other side of the street. Calling out to the chauffeur, whom he had employed on prior trips to New York, the ever-friendly Edwards asked, "Who are you driving for today?" Back came the answer: "Senator Bob Graham."

That same evening, Graham was at a cocktail party in the Fifth Avenue apartment of Richard Gardner, a former ambassador to Spain and Italy, now a law professor at Columbia University. Designed to introduce Graham to Manhattan's Democratic elite, this no-contribution-required reception was the kind of prospecting event that the other presidential contenders held earlier in the campaign cycle. But Graham was starting late, in part because he had lost six weeks in February and March to heart surgery. As tuxedo-clad waiters circulated among the three dozen guests with trays of melon wrapped in smoked salmon and potatoes topped with sour cream and a dollop of caviar, it was apparent that Graham had attracted the right bold-faced names—former Governor Mario Cuomo, George Soros, cosmetics heir Leonard Lauder and Kennedy administration legends Ted Sorensen and Arthur Schlesinger. Danielle Gardner, the hostess, had pointedly set out a plate of bakery-fresh Graham crackers in honor of the candidate.

As the silver-haired senator got ready to speak, positioning himself in front of a window with a stunning, normally only-seen-in-the-real-estate ads view of the Central Park reservoir, Adele Graham noticed that the setting sun would be shining right into the eyes of his audience. Taking her husband by the sleeve, she led him to the other end of the living room. In his new venue, Graham began in his trademark orotund style, "My wife, who is an extremely wise as well as beautiful person, has urged me at considerable risk to my personal well-being to be brief." Then Graham announced with a bizarre slip of the tongue, "I'm going to answer two questions: Why am I running for president and why do I think I can beat Clinton?" (No one in the well-mannered crowd broke in to inquire whether Graham was inadvertently referring to the former president or the current junior senator from New York.)

There was a gracious formality to Graham as he predicted to this roomful of friendly strangers, "As you come to know me, you will have a comfort level that will allow you to support our mission." But the candidate was not above the language of the counting house. In response to a question, he candidly explained, "I think the overall primary campaign which will get us to January, when we get federal matching funds, will have to be in the range of $15–$20 million. We think we can raise 40–50 percent of that in Florida. We have already raised $6–$7 million or have what I consider to be reliable commitments."

These commitments, alas, turned out to be as reliable as the promises of Florida real-estate hustlers during the 1920s land boom. Graham ended up collecting a paltry $2 million in the second quarter for a half-year total of $3.1 million. Asked about this embarrassing shortfall, Graham campaign manager Paul Johnson ruefully responded, "I think what Senator Graham is learning, and what most of us already knew, is that you have to discount what people promise. One gentleman pledged that he would raise half a million dollars. He didn't have that ability, but he tried really hard."

That might well serve as the epitaph for the Graham campaign, announced on a Haitian-American radio station just before Christmas 2002 and abandoned during a CNN interview with Larry King the following October. He tried really hard, but never had the ability to convince his longtime supporters back home in Florida that he was a credible candidate. So these Graham grandees glumly wrote $250 checks to the campaign rather than ponying up the anticipated $2,000. But even in early October, after the resignation of Johnson and most of the hired-gun campaign staff, the Florida senator resisted the inevitable. At a poised-to-surrender campaign summit at his daughter Suzanne Gibson's home, Graham clung to the quaint notion that he could still find a forum to talk about terrorism, Iraq, and the other ideas that had fueled his ill-fated presidential campaign. As Senate chief of staff Buddy Menn explained, "These guys run for office because they believe that they're going to be the next president of the United States. That's why the senator was the last one to agree."

But ultimately Graham had to bow to the gimlet-eyed financial realities of politics—TV stations in Iowa do not take promissory notes. In a perfect world, presidential candidates would be judged on the weight of their ideas, not on the heft of their campaign bank accounts. But for all the noble ideals of democracy, for all the old-fashioned courting of individual voters in New Hampshire and Iowa, for all the romance of the campaign trail, the quest for the most powerful office on this whirling orb of a planet invariably comes down to, as Wordsworth put it, "Getting and spending, we lay waste our powers."

CHAPTER 5

The Staff of Life

Jano Cabrera's life is in disarray, even by the permissive single-beer-in-an-otherwise-empty-refrigerator standards of young political operatives. The diminutive and puckish Cabrera—a veritable Hispanic elf—has just returned to Washington in mid-January from a vacation in London, which had been repeatedly rescheduled because of Al Gore. Cabrera is moving to a new apartment, which means that the suits and ties of his adult wardrobe are all in storage. And, oh yes, Joe Lieberman wants to meet with him immediately to discuss the job as his campaign spokesman.

After earning his wings in the rapid-response "war room" during the 2000 campaign, Cabrera had been Gore's public voice during the will-he-or-won't-he phase of the Invisible Primary. Jano (as he is universally known in politics without any more need for a last name than Madonna) earned a footnote in modern aviation history on that fateful December Sunday when Gore suddenly decided to go on *60 Minutes* to announce his presidential plans. Unaware of his boss's intentions, Cabrera was aboard an early afternoon US Airways shuttle, heading back to Washington following Gore's appearance on *Saturday Night Live.* Moments after the plane pulled away from the gate, Cabrera illicitly answered a cell phone call from a Gore staffer instructing him to rush back to Manhattan for an emergency meeting. With artful persuasiveness, Cabrera convinced the US Airways crew to return the airplane to the terminal so that he could hop off.

Now, a month later, Cabrera is the former Gore staffer most coveted by other presidential campaigns. But he lacks the clothes to close the deal. He sheepishly alerts Lieberman recruiter Jim Kennedy—the senator's longtime press secretary now working for the post-presidential Bill Clinton—that his sartorial options are closer to PU than *GQ*. Retrieving what passes as his best sweater from the dry cleaner and still looking like a high-school student on his first field trip to Washington, Cabrera nervously arrives at the candidate's Senate office for the interview.

"I thought you'd be wearing sweatpants," Lieberman says by way of greeting. For the next fifteen minutes, Lieberman banters with Cabrera, whom he knows slightly from the Gore campaign, mostly asking questions about his hometown (Pomona, California) and his family. This is not the kind of probing interrogation that Cabrera had come to expect from a presidential candidate who would be picking the person to serve as the public face of his campaign. As Lieberman continues to crack jokes instead of breaking out the bright lights and rubber hoses, Cabrera realizes that this campaign could actually be fun. Finally, as the interview draws to a close, Lieberman asks if he needs more time to make a decision. "Yes," Cabrera says, "I'd like to talk things over with Vice President Gore." As for Lieberman, he's convinced. "We want you," he announces as if the matter were never in dispute. "I know what your concerns and issues are [a reference to matters like salary and title] and as far as we're concerned, they're settled."

(As Cabrera tells me this story, I find myself drifting back to 1976 when I was an impoverished writer for the *Washington Monthly* desperately angling for a job with Jimmy Carter's campaign. My wardrobe in that era was limited by both finances and, embarrassing in hindsight, taste. On the summer day that was to seal my political fate, I was wearing an exuberantly rainbow-hued Madras jacket, electric-blue pants and a drip-dry shirt. Suddenly the phone rang with the encouraging news that senior Carter aide Stu Eizenstat wanted to interview me in just twenty minutes before he caught a plane. Even though my outfit was not touted by dress-for-success manuals, I was filled with the youthful certainty that my coat of many colors could not possibly blind the Carter campaign to my inner merit. Boy, did I learn a life lesson! The look of horror on the face of Eizenstat, an uptight Atlanta lawyer, eloquently instructed me that the interview was effectively over before we had a chance to shake hands.)

For Cabrera, who was also courted by Howard Dean and John Edwards, it was the combination of Lieberman's avuncular tone and his decisiveness that made the difference. Every campaign takes on the personality of the candidate and, as Cabrera put it, "I now know why Senator Lieberman has people on his staff who have been with him for decades."

Cabrera had talked with Dean by phone, but the former Vermont governor, nervous about being able to afford extra staff, had said that he planned to wait a few months before hiring a press secretary. There was also a thirty-minute face-to-face interview with Edwards and his wife, Elizabeth, that was closer to the law boards than Lieberman's laid-back approach. The senator, as he did during most first-time meetings, began the session by bluntly stating, "This is how I can win." In lawyerly fashion, Edwards then peppered Cabrera with questions: "What are my positives as a candidate? What are my negatives?" This friendly but arduous conversation ended without a formal job offer being made. (Edwards soon hired Jennifer Palmieri from the Democratic National Committee as his press secretary.)

A few days after his meeting with Lieberman, Cabrera tapped out an e-mail message to Jim Kennedy. Entitled "The Decision," it followed the familiar contours of a MasterCard commercial:

> Cost of a new BlackBerry: $300.
> A new campaign cell phone: $100.
> Hearing Jano speak Yiddish: Priceless.

* * *

Just as the run-up to a wedding replicates all the stresses (money, in-laws, choice of china patterns) of a long marriage, so the endless presidential campaign mirrors the challenges of serving in the White House. That anyway is the best excuse around to justify our cockamamie presidential-selection system. The long and winding road toward November 2004, punctuated by the bumper-car bedlam of the primaries, tests the mettle and maturity of would-be presidents. If a candidate goes ballistic at a press-conference in Iowa or melts under the bright lights of a pre-primary debate, it is a safe bet that he will have problems with recalcitrant congressional committee chairmen, let alone French diplomats.

But nothing better approximates the challenges of the White House than the seemingly straight-forward task of selecting a campaign staff. For the presidency is, at its core, a management challenge. The choice of a pollster may not have the same global implications as picking the Pentagon boss, but the approach to decision-making is probably similar in both cases. Nothing better reveals a candidate's management style and philosophy than the personnel decisions inherent in constructing out of nowhere a $30-million national enterprise to win the nomination. And nothing more closely replicates the fateful choices that a soon-to-be-inaugurated president would have to make as he selects his cabinet and the roughly 400-person White House staff in the frenzied ten weeks following the election.

Yet many of the Democrats seeking the presidency in 2004 have never managed anything larger than a congressional staff. Dean, to be sure, was the governor of a Lilliputian state and Lieberman back in the 1980s served as Connecticut's attorney general. But only Bob Graham, whose tenure as Florida governor ended while Ronald Reagan was still in the White House, boasts anything resembling major-league administrative experience. There is a theory that suggests that voters instinctively sense that slipping an amendment into a congressional conference report and giving passionate speeches from the floor of the Senate does not add up to the best prep course for the presidency. After all, devotees of historical precedents point out that since the nine-teenth century only two presidents (John Kennedy and Warren Harding) have moved directly from Capitol Hill to the White House. But while I worry about managerial expertise, I am also leery of such rigid historical determinism, since it requires premising an overarching theory on the hapless presidential races of Senators Bob Dole, George McGovern and Barry Goldwater.

What is puzzling, though, is how little press attention is devoted to how presidential hopefuls cobble together their campaign teams. A candidate can't simply go to the bookshelf and take down management manuals with titles like *Who Moved My Primary?* and *The Leadership Secrets of Alf Landon.* All campaigns are different, though the unhappy ones always provide the best stories. Every Democratic presidential contender is determined not to replicate the revolving-door 2000 Gore campaign in which the indecisive candidate changed strategies and discarded consultants like a hypochondriac with a permissive health plan. Even Lieberman, Gore's ever-faithful running mate, told me, "I didn't want to end up where Al was in terms that there weren't people around him with longtime histories with him." But there is more to constructing a campaign than simply putting on a bracelet inscribed with the acronym WWAD—What Would Al Do?—and then doing the exact opposite.

Each candidate must make a series of decisions as he assembles his staff. Does he place a premium on personal chemistry and decades of loyalty or entrust his fate to political hired guns with impressive pedigrees? Should he opt for youthful potential or jaded experience? Is he a micro-manager or a passive delegator of authority? Will he tolerate rival power centers or emphasize staff harmony? And, most of all, how will the candidate react when he hits those inevitable potholes on the road to the White House? Does he angrily purge his staff as Bob Dole did in 1988, literally leaving two ousted aides on the tarmac in Jacksonville, Florida? Then there is the model of Bill Clinton, who regrouped during the dark days before the 1992 New Hampshire primary

and ended the indecisiveness of unwieldy, multi-operative conference calls by effectively placing James Carville in command of
the campaign. Even more inspirational in some ways was the
way that George W. Bush loyally stuck with Karl Rove and Karen
Hughes after his humiliating defeat in New Hampshire.

As the only Democratic contender to have run for president
before, Dick Gephardt boasts the most clearly articulated theory
of staffing a campaign. "I always wanted to use mostly people
who I had worked with before," he said. "This [running for presi-
dent] is hard to do. And for me, it was so much better and easier
and more reasonable to do it with people who you worked with
before. Especially some from '88. They know you and know what
you want to do, and you don't have to explain it." The irony here
is that the 1988 Gephardt campaign, as chronicled by Richard
Ben Cramer in *What It Takes*, was notoriously fractious, with the
cabals and purges traditionally associated with losing efforts.

But like a dysfunctional family that has been together so long
that they have learned to adjust to each other's personal idiosyn-
crasies, the Gephardt team, at least in the early going, has been
harmonious. As pollster Ed Reilly, who performed the same role
in 1988, put it, "If you go through a fight like that, there's a
bond." The campaign had an initial misstep when Washington
lobbyist Tom O'Donnell signed on as campaign manager in
December 2002 and then resigned within the month. His replacement, Steve Murphy, ran Iowa for Gephardt in 1988. Before he
took the job, Murphy asked the candidate, "Dick, are you sure
that Bill Carrick doesn't want to do it?" Instead, the California-
based Carrick, the 1988 campaign manager, is the media consultant. Murphy, Carrick and Reilly, all in their fifties, laughingly
refer to themselves as the "Cryogenic Corps." Other top staffers
such as consultant Steve Elmendorf and press secretary Erik
Smith are veterans of Gephardt's congressional leadership office.

Trying to characterize the staffs of the other candidates is a
trickier enterprise, since they don't fit into a cubbyhole as neatly
as the Gephardt operation. By reputation—though not by the

actual early spending totals for salaries and consulting fees—
John Kerry's campaign is seen as a behemoth on a par with General Motors. In early July, twenty-one senior staffers and advisers
(eighteen of them male) attended a Kerry strategic-planning session on Nantucket. And after the opening-bell South Carolina
debate in early May, Kerry dispatched two media consultants,
two pollsters and a passel of press aides to spin webs for
reporters. Gesturing at the oversize Kerry team, Dean media consultant Steve McMahon cracked, "It's the Noah's Ark campaign.
They have two of everything."

Kerry's Washington-based campaign manager, Jim Jordan, a
veteran of the Democratic Senate Campaign Committee, embark-
ing on his first presidential race, faced the most daunting diplomatic challenge since Colin Powell tried to sell the Iraqi war to
the Security Council. He had to cope with a phalanx of Boston
consultants with long-standing ties to Kerry and battle scars from
the 1988 Dukakis campaign. Throw into this volatile mix late-
arriving media consultant Bob Shrum, who is a charming addition
to any campaign as long he gets his own way. Then there is Kerry
himself, the Democratic contender who most keenly relishes the
feints and maneuvers of politics. This love of the sport can be an
asset, but it also fosters a well-justified reputation for micro-
managing his own campaigns. Before signing on as campaign
manager, Jordan extracted from Kerry a promise that he would
concentrate on being a candidate instead of moonlighting as his
own consultant. But as the campaign turned into a reenactment of
the Battling Bickersons, Kerry fired Jordan in early November.

The Edwards operation is, well, curious. At times during the
early months of 2003, it seemed less a campaign than a fund-
raising machine and a candidate. This was a period when
Edwards was shedding consultants while his rivals were aug-
menting their teams. Shrum, along with his partner Mike Donilon,
defected to Kerry; Steve Jarding, who had fallen into disfavor
while running Edwards's political action committee, enlisted with
the Graham campaign. That left an inner core of the campaign that

was both close-knit and a trifle jejune. As a well-respected young political operative who interviewed with Edwards back in January asked, "Where are the adults in the campaign?"

Like the acerbic Dean, whom he does not otherwise resemble, Edwards is blessed with preternatural self-confidence and conveys the impression that the master plan for the campaign resides primarily in his head. No matter what the organization chart says, the Edwards campaign is really a series of concentric circles revolving around the candidate and his wife. "He's very clear about his priorities," said campaign manager Nick Baldick, who ran New Hampshire for Gore in the 2000 primary. "He'll say, 'I want you to do X, Y and Z.' But then he lets you do it. He doesn't expect to be involved in figuring out the budget for Ohio."

Lacking the longtime national political connections of a Gephardt or a Kerry, Edwards initially assembled his team from alumni of his 1998 Senate race (veteran pollster Harrison Hickman and twenty-eight-year-old communications director David Ginsberg) and upwardly mobile political warriors attracted by his potential (Baldick and speechwriter-strategist Jonathan Prince from the Clinton White House). The balding thirty-five-year-old Baldick, who joked, "I wish I had a candidate who looked older than I do," first met Edwards in mid–2001. At the time, Baldick was searching for a mount for the 2004 presidential race much like a jockey checking out thoroughbreds in anticipation of the Kentucky Derby. He had three criteria: a candidate he liked, a candidate who could win the general election and a candidate who believes what he says. (This last factor was a telling reflection of the political culture.) Baldick explained his emphasis on viability in the general election: "If I'm I going to do all this, and be away from children and my wife, I just couldn't spend my time working for a guy who can get his butt handed to him."

A presidential candidate with just one aide is akin to an impoverished nineteenth-century Russian aristocrat trying to keep up appearances in three squalid rooms with only his samovar and long-suffering manservant for company. Throughout most of 2002, Kate O'Connor was the Howard Dean campaign. She was the person most likely to pick up the phone if you called the fledgling campaign's Burlington office, and she and a Vermont state trooper were the governor's only companions on the road. Small wonder that the thirty-nine-year-old, brown-haired O'Connor laughingly calls herself "long-suffering," although others who know her well from Vermont politics prefer such descriptions as "territorial" and "overprotective." Having worked for Dean since he was a part-time lieutenant governor, O'Connor exudes small-town Vermont—neither flashy nor sophisticated, but quietly competent and blessed with a sense of the comic absurdity of the original rickety venture. Each time she's asked if she has a family, O'Connor gives the same answer, "If I had been married when this campaign started, I wouldn't be by now."

The initially underfunded Dean, taking a page from Jimmy Carter's 1976 playbook, prefers staying in the homes of his supporters. "He's just cheap," O'Connor explained. The candidate's disdain for hotels meant that his traveling aide found herself consigned to the second-best available bedroom, which invariably belonged to the youngest child in the family. So she spent her nights sleeping on undersize single beds in rooms decorated with storybook mobiles, teddy bears and PlayStations. O'Connor, who has mastered the trick of packing for an entire week in a single carry-on bag, reveled in small luxuries, such as discovering that she was being upgraded to a foldout couch on a trip to Iowa.

In a presidential campaign, the first thing to go is memory, since the brain is ill-equipped to keep track of the ever shifting kaleidoscope of strange towns and strange beds. When CNN filmed me in Iowa before the 2000 caucuses for a Jeff Greenfield segment about journalistic geezers on the campaign bus, the question that left me comically sputtering with confusion was a simple query asking where I had been during the peripatetic prior week. O'Connor has developed her own way of coping with the amnesia that afflicts us all: She mails postcards from the edge. Whenever she arrives in a new place, she dashes off a postcard to her parents back in Vermont. "My parents are keeping all the postcards in a scrapbook they insist they'll give to me when I'm in the White House," she said during the early days of the campaign. "But I tell them to save them for when I'm so broke after we lose that I'll have to move in with them."

During this start-up period, Dean was both reluctant to hire staff since he would have to pay them and flattered that his self-created crusade was beginning to attract interest from Democratic operatives with actual campaign experience. But given a choice between penny-pinching and proven political talent, Dean's frugality won every time. As the candidate admitted to me in September 2002, "We're unlikely to get the people that everybody has read about in the *Washington Post* because we're going to be a come-from-behind insurgent campaign." To illustrate his point, he mentioned a recent phone call that he received from a political pro who told him, "You better talk to me soon, since I'm thinking of going with Edwards." In a voice thick with scorn, Dean said, "That's not a conversation we're ever going to have— that guy's an opportunist." Instead, Dean envisioned a staff who would mirror his own passions: "I want people to have some belief in me or the policies that we're talking about. I want people to be working for a cause, not just a paycheck."

The next month, October, Dean chose as his campaign manager Colorado political consultant Rick Ridder, a veteran of the Gary Hart and Bill Bradley presidential campaigns. Even though Dean had some national political connections from his days as president of the Democratic Governors Association, it was telling that he bequeathed the direction of his campaign to someone whom he met for the first time on a campaign trip to Colorado in July. But then Dean scorned most Washington-area consultants as mercenaries, an attitude that stemmed from the treatment he received as a client in his low-budget campaigns for re-election. The conspicuous exception to this disdain was Dean's longtime loyalty to the

Virginia media firm run by Joe Trippi and Steve McMahon, which had made the commercials for his gubernatorial races and signed on early for the presidential campaign.

But other than choosing up a campaign manager and a media-consulting firm, Dean—like a bridge player without a face card—stayed out of the frenzied bidding wars for political operatives after the 2002 elections. As a result, the Dean machine came together as the political embodiment of a Field of Dreams, not as the result of rigorous personnel planning. You could almost imagine a ghostly voice whispering in Dean's ear, "Build it and they will come." And so they did, one by one, pilgrims heading north, somehow sensing that something strange and wondrous was happening on the shores of Lake Champlain.

Take Courtney O'Donnell, who at twenty-seven had slaved in the penurious vineyards of losing 2002 Democratic campaigns from Janet Reno's gubernatorial primary in Florida to a hopeless Tennessee Senate race. Back in New York City after the election, she found herself attracted to a certain Vermont governor whom she had only seen on television. So on a snowy day in December, she drove to Burlington without an appointment or even the name of a contact person. "There was no one picking up the phones at headquarters and I didn't have a street address," she recalled. "All I knew from reading the papers was that it was located over a pub." Driving aimlessly around Burlington, she finally spotted a Dean sign on the building that the campaign then shared with the Vermont Pub and Brewery. After a few days volunteering in the tiny office, she stayed up until 3:00 A.M. constructing a set of charts for Ridder, who had just arrived in Burlington. The next day, after a fifteen-minute interview, Ridder hired her as his assistant, making O'Donnell the seventh paid employee in the Dean campaign. As Ridder said, "She answered all my questions, she had what I needed, so I was ready to hire her." She is now the campaign's deputy communications director.

Although richly emblematic of the Dean crusade, O'Donnell's story also captures the run-away-with-the-circus glories of presidential campaigns. Politics stubbornly remains the province of the messy life history, not the domain of executive search firms. In every campaign, plum jobs are awarded to people like O'Donnell who simply arrive at the right moment and demonstrate their competence and dedication. These opportunities are the political equivalent of battlefield commissions in the army—and they stand as a continuing rebuke to the right-scores, right-schools, right-friends rigidities of the American meritocracy.

Even in late February, after the candidate became the troubadour of the anti-war movement, the Dean campaign retained its eclectic hiring practices. In far-off Moab, Utah, thirty-one-year-old Matt Gross was working on a first novel and contributing to a political weblog (MyDD.com) when he was roused by watching Dean address the Democratic National Committee. "When I saw the DNC speech, I realized this guy's going to take off," Gross said. "If I wait until June, somebody's going to have my job." After a series of inconclusive phone calls to Dean headquarters seeking a low-level job in his original home state of New Hampshire, Gross left his wife, his two dogs and his pickup truck behind in Utah and flew to Burlington for a few days. "My only objective on day one was to make it past the volunteer coordinator," he recalled. A chance conversation with the Internet-obsessed Joe Trippi prompted Gross to mention that he had been writing regularly for MyDD. A fan of the website, Trippi immediately asked, "How soon will it take you to go back to Utah to get your stuff?" Gross, tall and thin with closely cropped brown hair, recounted this Moab-to-main-chance narrative as he sat at the computer terminal that is now his command post in campaign headquarters—the spot from which he, as content director of the campaign website, has helped transform the technophobic former governor into the Energizer Bunny of the Internet.

It would be a misconception to exaggerate the Mickey Rooney and Judy Garland let's-put-on-a-backyard-musical aspects of the Dean crusade. When it came to hiring for the top positions in New Hampshire and Iowa, the campaign operated within the contours of traditional politics. Although thirty-four-year-old New Hampshire Dean coordinator Karen Hicks boasts a standard political résumé (political director of Jeanne Shaheen's failed 2002 Senate campaign), she regarded her choice of a presidential candidate more as a calling than a cash transaction. Burned out after the Senate race, Hicks retreated to the Indian beaches of Goa in late November and December. "The process of being away and what was happening with Iraq was getting me pretty freaked out," she recalled. "I felt like I was coming back here almost in a time warp."

On her return, she had a series of conversations with the Kerry, Edwards and Gephardt campaigns about staff posts in New Hampshire. But Hicks realized that there were limitations on her choice of a candidate. "My value is my Rolodex," she explained, "and I couldn't get my friends to work for Gephardt." Still, the only presidential hopeful she unequivocally ruled out was Lieberman. Her reason for rejecting the Connecticut senator was both compelling and unique in the annals of the 2004 campaign: He once had her arrested! Working for the Naderite group Citizens Action in 1993, Hicks took part in a sit-in in Lieberman's office to protest the way he was dragging his feet on health-care reform. Lieberman responded by calling the Capitol police as Hicks and her group were dragged out while singing, "Say It Ain't So, Joe."

In early February, she briefly met Dean when he spoke to the state AFL-CIO. A few days later she had coffee in Hanover with Ridder, who almost instantly grasped that "she's a hotshot waiting to happen." He convinced her to ride around the state for a few days with Dean to get a feel for the candidate and the campaign. But there was skepticism in the Dean camp about entrusting New Hampshire to a woman who had never directed a statewide race. During their car talk, Dean never pressured Hicks to take the job. As she put it, "He's not a big sales guy." But the ambivalence cut both ways. Hicks was concerned about Dean's freewheeling, say-anything style that ran counter to the political dictates of message discipline. But she was impressed that Dean never flinched from a question in public or private. In the end, the whole thing just proved too irresistible. As Hicks said, "With Dean, it won't be hard to convince a friend that this is The Guy. I can organize my way to victory."

But even as Ridder was tapping Hicks, they were playing taps for the campaign manager in Burlington. The amicable divorce between Dean and Ridder evolved over the first few months of 2003; like most breakups, it was not triggered by a single cause. Part of the explanation involved differing strategic visions. Ridder, and to a large extent Dean, expected to run a small, stealthy campaign designed to achieve a Gary Hart–like breakthrough on the eve of the Iowa caucuses. Instead, in just a few dizzying months, Dean went from "Howard Who?" to "Howard Wow!"

Even though this Dean moment was partly created by his acerbic attacks on his rivals over Iraq, Ridder worried about creating lasting enmities with the party establishment, as Hart did in 1984. In contrast, Trippi, his replacement as campaign manager, reveled in the Dean spleen. Trippi had worked for Gephardt during the 1988 presidential season and displayed his incendiary style in Jerry Brown's 1992 scorched-earth primary campaign that bedeviled Bill Clinton until June. Even though the often disheveled Trippi and the buttoned-down Dean are stylistic opposites, they both come from the anger-management wing of the Democratic Party. Where Ridder wanted to court Democratic elected officials, Trippi was more inclined to shout, "Fuck 'em!"

Another important factor was what Ridder describes as Dean's "tight-fisted management style," which led him to complain to the candidate that he had been given "all the responsibility and none of the authority." Dean, accustomed to presiding over a governor's office that had fourteen employees, was slow to understand that he could not run the campaign from the backseat of a van in Iowa. "One of the difficulties I have with Howard is his willingness to let go," Ridder said, still using the present tense. But the candidate was also the political version of Scrooge McDuck. "When I presented Howard with a budget that had $6 million in overhead," Ridder recalled, "he just said it was way too high. He couldn't understand the salaries that people in politics were getting paid as professionals."

But Ridder also knowingly blundered into what may be the most dangerous place in Vermont—the spot between Dean and Kate O'Connor. On a certain level I don't fully understand O'Connor's reputation for internal ferocity, since as a reporter I have always found her to be engaging and rather self-effacing. But as Ridder recounted, "After I said to Howard in January that I wasn't sure what role Kate O'Connor could play in a presidential campaign, I wouldn't say that I was dead man walking, but I certainly was marginalized."

No one goes into Democratic politics for the money, but those who truly prosper are most likely to be media consultants. While pollsters and strategic advisers are usually paid a flat fee, ad makers also receive a portion (sometimes as much as 15 percent) of a campaign's TV buy. Even though presidential primary campaigns are more demanding, high-risk enterprises than free-spending Senate and gubernatorial races, it is safe to assume that the media-consulting firms for the leading Democratic hopefuls each stand to earn in the neighborhood of $1 million. (This is a guess, since the fees earned by consultants are camouflaged in the otherwise detailed expenditure reports that campaigns are required to file with the Federal Election Commission.)

This financial background is relevant in understanding Bob Shrum, the legendarily well-compensated roly-poly media consultant whose defection from Edwards to Kerry in February was treated in the Washington political community with the cosmic significance of Bill Gates leaving Microsoft. What Joe Klein, writing in *Slate,* called the "Shrum Primary" was a political fable with all the varying perspectives of *Rashomon.* There were grumbles from the Edwards camp that Shrum bolted after being told that his role would be limited to the behind-the-scenes task of making TV ads rather than serving as the public voice of the campaign. And cynics viewed Shrum's shifting allegiance as a measure of the political (and, yes, financial) viability of both Kerry and Edwards.

In quest of the Shrum version, I visited him in July at his new offices in Georgetown with panoramic views of the Potomac River. During our hour-long conversation, Shrum left the room to take phone calls from Kerry (just minutes before he delivered a major speech on homeland security) and the British Labor Party, another client. He took pains to show me a framed copy of the final draft of Bill Clinton's 1994 State of the Union Address, pointing out the last-minute changes that he had added to the text. Shrum's conversation was studded with references to his contributions to prior presidential campaigns: Ted Kennedy in 1980 (Shrum wrote his lilting "the dream shall never die" convention address), Dick Gephardt in 1988 (he and Trippi, a former partner, each take primary credit for the Hyundai ad that briefly revived the Missourian's campaign), and Gore's populist posturing in 2000.

Shrum, in short, was forthcoming about almost everything, save for many of the details of why he switched sides on the eve of battle. As the media consultant both for Kerry in his do-or-die Senate race against Bill Weld in 1996 and for Edwards in his 1998 maiden race, Shrum contended that he always stressed to both candidates that he would make no decision about his own plans until after the 2002 elections. He also emphasized that he never had a contract with Edwards for the presidential race. Still he acknowledged that he kept in close touch, mostly by phone, with Edwards during the crucial period in November and December when the North Carolina senator was wrestling with his White House ambitions. (Shrum's partner, Mike Donilon, was a frequent participant during the exhaustive deliberations in the Edwards living room.)

Ultimately, Shrum claimed, he went with Kerry because "he was the person who I thought would be the best president and have the best chance to win the general election." As Shrum told it, when he called Edwards from Chicago to inform him that he intended to move in a different artistic direction, "He was not happy about it. And for me, that was the hardest part of the whole thing."

Kerry, for his part, said that Shrum "knew that I was interested in his being involved, and it was really more his decision than mine." When Kerry hired Jim Margolis to make the ads for his unopposed 2002 re-election campaign, he told the media consultant that he might add someone like Shrum to the team for the presidential race. (Margolis confirmed this detail.) "I remember that conversation very well," Kerry told me. "I said, 'Will you have any problem with that?' And Jim to his credit said no and has not and does not. I think we have a terrific team as a consequence."

Edwards too may have benefited from Shrum's mid-course correction. As the presidential contender with the shortest political résumé, Edwards could have easily been portrayed—albeit unfairly—as the southern-accented mouthpiece for Shrum's script. But as winter glided into spring, Edwards was in the curious position of a candidate who had successfully lined up the money to pay for his TV commercials but had no one to make them. Lieberman, who had been dangerously slow to organize his campaign after Gore's withdrawal, faced an analogous situation. Carter Eskew, one of Gore's media consultants in 2000, was supporting Lieberman, but he preferred to play a backstage role rather than dedicate himself to long hours in an editing room cutting TV spots.

The upper echelons of Democratic politics form a small, inbred community. That's why it was not entirely surprising that Edwards and Lieberman gravitated toward the same two media consultants: Chicago ad-maker David Axelrod and Washington-based Mandy Grunwald, who created Clinton's 1992 commercials and performed the same role for a New York candidate named Hillary in 2000. Axelrod and Grunwald were interviewed by both senators—and they described the hiring styles of these would-be presidents in similar fashion. Lieberman, who talked with the media consultants alone, was jocular and decisive. Edwards, who convened a series of meetings that included his top advisers and his wife, was lawyerly, methodical and slow to pull the trigger. In the end, each candidate proffered one offer—to the consultant who provided the most natural fit.

Axelrod recounted his meeting with Lieberman at Chicago's Drake Hotel, where the senator was staying. "He was thoroughly engaging," Axelrod recalled. "I felt comfortable with him within five minutes. Part of it, to be frank, is that I'm a Jew from New York, and he's like a million relatives." The problem for Axelrod, who envisioned a campaign built around populist outrage about Bush's record, was that "I couldn't get past Lieberman's politics."

Things with Edwards, in contrast, clicked from the outset. "There was a lot of discussion about why he was running and what his world-view was and what my worldview was," Axelrod recalled. He was initially hesitant to make the drop-everything-else commitment to a presidential race. But he gradually abandoned his reluctance during a series of meetings in late March and early April. "I knew I was buying the stock low," Axelrod said. "People view Edwards as a long shot. And indeed he is a long shot, though I believe the opportunity is there." In early August—before any candidate but the now rich-as-Croesus Dean was on the air—Edwards began airing three exquisitely photographed Axelrod ads in which the candidate talked to the camera about his share-cropper grandmother, his mill-worker father and his dreams of economic justice.

Grunwald—one of the rare women playing a major role in the 2004 presidential race of the equal-opportunity Democratic Party—came to Lieberman recommended by fellow media consultant Eskew and pollster Mark Penn. Describing her interview with the Connecticut senator, she said, "He was disarmingly funny at the beginning of the conversation, got right into the substance of strategy—and forty-five minutes later said, 'I want you. I want to hire you.'" During the same period in early April, she also met twice with Edwards, one a large group meeting and the other a sit-down with the candidate and Elizabeth. Grunwald felt the meetings went well. She was intrigued by Edwards's obvious potential, but she began to worry a bit about working for a candidate who seemed to agonize over every decision. So Grunwald accepted the Lieberman offer. Afterward her sister, Lisa, a New York writer, told her, "So you wound up going to the prom with the nice guy that you probably should have been going with all along."

CHAPTER 6

Iowa and New Hampshire

What third-class railway coaches were to Mahatma Gandhi, Southwest Airlines is to Howard Dean during these early months of 2003. "If you get to the airport before we do, try to save us two places in Group A," instructed Dean aide Kate O'Connor. But as I arrive at the Southwest gate at Baltimore-Washington airport in the bleak pre-dawn hours of a January Saturday morning, I quickly spy Dean and O'Connor already clutching their oversize "Group A" early-boarding cards for the budget flight to Manchester, New Hampshire. As I join them, Dean looks up from reading the hockey news in the *New York Times* to gush, "I love Southwest. Because of Southwest, I've been able to spend three half-days in New Hampshire this week."

Dean sounds so enthusiastic, you could almost imagine him doing a commercial from the Oval Office: "Sure, I have Air Force One for my foreign trips. But as president when I want to move about the country, I fly Southwest." As Dean explains, every time he has to be in Washington, he flies back on Southwest via Manchester, holds a campaign event in New Hampshire and then makes the three-hour drive north to Burlington. This roundabout itinerary not only saves money but also boasts an inherent political logic, since nothing impresses the pampered voters of New Hampshire more than a candidate who shows up with the frequency of a UPS truck. You don't have to dangle a lamb chop in the window to attract the indefatigable Dean; he'll appear for the opening of an envelope, as long as it bears a Granite State postmark.

This morning Dean is a featured speaker at the quarterly meeting of the New Hampshire Democratic Party held in a Manchester elementary-school cafeteria decorated with crudely scissored paper snowflakes. Introducing the newly retired Vermont governor, state party chair Kathleen Sullivan says, "A year ago, people were saying that they didn't know him, but he's been here a lot. To win in New Hampshire, you have to cross a threshold so that people believe that you can be elected—and Governor Dean has crossed that threshold." When Dean starts off by reminding the 150 Democrats sitting on folding chairs that this is his twenty-third visit to the state since he began his uphill race for the White House, I find myself recalling Nelson Rockefeller's long-ago slogan in the 1964 Oregon primary. Mocking conservative rival Barry Goldwater's refusal to campaign in liberal Oregon, Rocky plastered the state with billboards pregnant with inadvertent double meaning: "He Cared Enough to Come."

After a wipeout in the 2002 elections, New Hampshire Democrats do not hold the governorship, either house in the state legislature or any seats in the congressional delegation. But this across-the-board minority status should not be equated with apathy. Judging from how often I see the same people at party events, I wonder how any of them manage to hold day jobs. Marathon runners spend less time training than New Hampshire Democrats devote to attending meetings and party functions. Take Beth Campbell, the first vice president of the Service Employees (SEIU) Local 1984, the largest union in the state. No candidate need ever face an empty room in New Hampshire because, at minimum, Campbell will be there. During the lull between Dean's speech and Dick Gephardt's arrival, I wander over to chat with this large,

enthusiastic woman who bird-dogs presidential candidates like an
autograph hound staking out the Oscars. "This is my drug," she
announces with a laugh. "I don't drink. I don't smoke. I don't do
illegal substances. But this is what gets me up in the morning."
Campbell, whom I met during the 2000 primary, is still searching
for a candidate who will make her "liberal heart go pitter-patter" as
Bill Bradley did last time. But she feels hamstrung by her union
position, which requires her to hold off formally embracing a candidate until the national SEIU meets in September. As she puts it,
"They asked us not to endorse, but I can flirt."

If Campbell is a seeker, Lou D'Allesandro is the sought. A former local college president (Daniel Webster) and basketball coach
in his mid-sixties, D'Allesandro is one of just six Democrats in
the state senate. Every time I come to New Hampshire with a
presidential contender, a closed meeting with D'Allesandro is an
inevitable part of the schedule. Back in August 2002, I cooled my
heels outside D'Allesandro's home in Manchester for nearly an
hour as John Kerry dropped by for a chat. In October, it was Joe
Lieberman's turn to have dinner with D'Allesandro. Now D'Allesandro confides that he and his wife will be treating Gephardt to
the family manicotti recipe this evening and—oh, yes—he's
slated to have dinner with Elizabeth Edwards next week on her
first solo visit to the state. "I'd love to see her run for president,"
he murmurs, conjuring up memories of the response that Hillary
Clinton first inspired during the heady days of the 1992 campaign. As for Dean, D'Allesandro says dismissively, "He's got
interesting ideas, but he's just not a player."

If D'Allesandro were in, say, the Ohio legislature and Campbell a
Colorado union official, the closest they would come to a presidential candidate would probably be the receiving line at an airport rally. New Hampshire and Iowa are so embedded in our
modern political mythology that it is easy to forget the inherent
injustice of a presidential selection system in which all voters are

equal, but some voters are more equal than others. The special status of these two states with the ethnic diversity of a reunion of *Mayflower* descendants (Iowa's minority population is 6 percent and New Hampshire's 4 percent) should be especially galling for the Democrats, a party so committed to affirmative action that its convention bylaws stress near-proportional representation for Native Americans and Asians/Pacific Islanders. The New Hampshire primary is hallowed by the weight of tradition dating back to 1916, but the Iowa caucuses were popularized by Jimmy Carter in 1976, who used this hitherto obscure delegate contest to jumpstart his outsider's march to the White House.

As a political reporter, I am prepared to offer a spirited defense of New Hampshire's outsize role in presidential politics. Nowhere else in the nation do voters display such fidelity to old-fashioned civic obligations. Once a pillar of rock-ribbed Republicanism, in recent years politically mercurial New Hampshire gave its four electoral votes to Bill Clinton twice. The 2000 Florida recount would have been moot had Gore not lost the state by just 7,000 votes to George W. Bush. (Connoisseurs of election maps may recall that New Hampshire was the only state north of the Potomac and east of Ohio to go Republican.) This state properly understands that without its presidential primary it would have all the global significance of, say, Delaware. Turnout for the 2000 Democratic and Republican primaries was an impressive 388,000, roughly two-thirds the number of voters who cast ballots in the November election. "If they ever do away with this primary," says D'Allesandro, stressing the virtues of personal campaigning, "we will have lost one of the few places in the nation where you can still do retail politics. It will be all image creation and television—and we'll never see a candidate again."

New Hampshire may be a living monument to participatory democracy, but what in God's name is the justification for making the Iowa caucuses the campaign equivalent of the book of Genesis? Okay, I will confess a New Yorker's testiness over dealing with restaurant closing hours in early-to-bed Des Moines—

Iowa is a state where any meal ordered after 8:00 P.M. is called breakfast. But there is also a wind-whistling-through-the-corn-fields emptiness to Iowa. Governor Tom Vilsack frequently cites this stunning statistic: More than two-thirds of Iowa's ninety-nine counties boasted more residents in the 1900 census than they do today. Not only does gray-haired Iowa have one of the slowest rates of population growth of any state in the union, but it also ranks second (to North Dakota, not Florida) in having the highest percentage of its population over eighty-five. Beyond these unrepresentative Grant Wood demographics, Iowa demands that presidential candidates lavish disproportionate attention on the abstruse details of agricultural policy and cravenly pledge allegiance to such parochial concerns as federal energy subsidies for corn-based ethanol.

The most damning indictment of the caucuses is that they do not inspire in most Iowans anything like the enthusiasm lavished on such heartland curiosities as a life-size sculpture of the Last Supper rendered in creamery butter at the State Fair. (This is not an eastern effete snob's comic conceit—I saw this milk-fat tableau with my own awestruck eyes in 1999.) The purported rationale for starting the presidential cycle in Iowa is that the caucuses are supposed to measure the intensity of commitment to a candidate. Unlike voters who make a five-minute trip to a polling booth or cast absentee ballots in a primary, caucus-goers must personally show up on a wintry Monday evening, listen to their neighbors debate party resolutions on everything from hog lots to whaling boycotts, declare their candidate allegiances in public and sit through enough parliamentary procedure to satisfy a high-school civics teacher organizing a model United Nations.

That's the theory, anyway. In reality, the caucuses are the kind of seventy-six-trombone hustle that would arouse the envy of Iowa brass-band huckster Professor Harold Hill. Iowa Democrats have never put on a shuck to equal the August 1999 Republican straw poll—an overhyped dress rehearsal for the caucuses that prompted candidates to squander so much money on buses, barbecue and big-name entertainers like Crystal Gayle that the effort prematurely drove Lamar Alexander and Elizabeth Dole from the race. Although the 2000 face-off between Gore and Bradley was Iowa's first spirited Democratic delegate contest in twelve years, the caucuses came across as an event mostly designed to fill the hotels and bars with reporters on expense accounts. On caucus night, January 24, every satellite uplink truck in North America seemed to be parked in Des Moines to broadcast the epic drama. The only thing missing was interested Democrats. Only 61,000 of Iowa's 500,000 registered Democrats cared enough to come.

For all my grumpiness about the unjustified political prominence of the Hawkeye State, I still felt compelled to fly to Des Moines in early October 2002 for the Democrats' annual Jefferson-Jackson Day fund-raising dinner featuring the presidential troika of Dean, John Edwards and John Kerry. For let's face it, if political convention decreed that the 2004 campaign began with a three-legged race in Enid, Oklahoma, I'd probably make the trip and then spend my time worrying that I was somehow missing the Big Story.

In politics, the unalterable reality is that Iowans are treated with the kind of deference that Manolo Blahnik might receive at a foot-fetishists convention. A conversation on this October weekend with Des Moines developer Harry Bookey—the leading early Kerry supporter in the state—underscored the point. As Bookey explained it, he had been intrigued with Kerry ever since he read the senator's 1997 book on narco-corruption, *The New War*. So with free time on his schedule during a July 2001 trip to Washington, Bookey cold-called Kerry's office and asked to speak to the chief of staff. The receptionist replied skeptically, "Who are you?" Bookey confidently responded, "Tell him that I'm a prominent Iowa Democrat." Seconds later, Kerry's chief of staff, David McKean, was on the line inquiring, "Do you want to have lunch?" The next step in this dance of recruitment was McKean

arranging for Bookey and his Washington-based daughter to have
dinner with Kerry the next month at a restaurant near Dupont
Circle. "At first Kerry was standoffish," Bookey recalled, "but
then he loosened up and we had a great time."

Dressed in jeans and a brown tweed jacket, Bookey was regal-
ing me with this story early on a Saturday morning as we sipped
our coffees at a crowded Starbucks on the ground floor of a converted 1910 Masonic hall in downtown Des Moines. This was not
just any Starbucks; it was the only purveyor of overpriced mocha
Frappuccinos in the entire state. This newly opened outpost of
mass-market caffeinated conformity was a proud symbol of the
way that progress (eventually) reaches Iowa—and Bookey was
the man who made it happen. With meticulous detail, he
described the harrowing ten months of negotiations with the corporate bean counters at Starbucks headquarters. Interspersed
with Bookey's real-estate saga were tales of his starry-eyed adventures in Iowa presidential politics. He began with the 1984 Gary
Hart campaign: "Carole King stayed in our house. And she's
someone who has sold more records than anyone." Bookey's losing streak continued with Paul Simon in 1988 and then Bradley.
Explaining his commitment to Kerry, Bookey said, "Having been
with Simon and Bradley, I didn't want to go with someone who
couldn't be a winning candidate."

Where Bookey is an enthusiastic amateur, Des Moines attorney Rob Tully, Edwards's major Iowa booster, is a political pro. A
former state party chairman and unsuccessful 1998 congressional
candidate, Tully got to know Edwards through their shared
involvement with ATLA (Association of Trial Lawyers of America). We were sitting on Tully's screened porch cradling our
single-malt Scotches and—to complete the manly cliché— puffing
cigars as he described his blunt conversation with Edwards at the
2001 ATLA convention in Montreal.

In the midst of a dinner with Edwards and a group of erst-
while supporters, Tully took the senator aside to say, "John, these
are all good people. They love you. But if you're serious, you've

got to start organizing now and start in Iowa." To emphasize his point, Tully told Edwards that he was going to utter two words to conjure up what can happen to a candidate who depends on personal popularity and charm rather than doing the small things that matter in Iowa. "Those words were," Tully said, savoring the drama, "John Glenn." (Despite spending more money than any other candidate in Iowa, the former astronaut finished an embarrassing fifth in the 1984 caucuses.) The next day Edwards told Tully, "Rob, I'm ready to do what you suggest and start now."

The trick for Edwards, Tully explained as he poured us another Scotch, is to remember that Iowa is a caucus and not a primary. "These are party regulars," he says. "This is a test of party strength. This is backroom politics that is conducted in the open." In deference to the sensibilities of the party faithful, Tully stressed to Edwards that when he campaigned in Iowa for the 2002 Democratic ticket he had to avoid the traditional politician's trap of always shouting, "Me, me, me!" Following this advice, Edwards in Iowa always emphasized the similarity of his life story and his values to those of Senator Tom Harkin and Governor Vilsack, both of whom were running for re-election. Tully believes that Harkin, an unsuccessful 1992 Democratic challenger to Bill Clinton, is the key to Iowa because he has the best political organization in the state. "John really needs to have a close relationship with Harkin," Tully said. "He needs to tap into Harkin." That was why Tully had adroitly arranged for Edwards to introduce Harkin at the Jefferson-Jackson dinner, even though it meant speaking near the end of the program.

The Beatles were probably right when they proclaimed, "Money can't buy me love," but Edwards didn't mind purchasing a little affection. His political action committee (PAC)—the maladroitly named "New American Optimists"—had loaned more than one hundred computers to the state party and had given every Iowa legislative candidate personalized campaign leaflets (which coincidentally featured Edwards's picture on one side) designed to fit over doorknobs for house-to-house canvassing.

This lavish, if self-interested, generosity was made possible
because Edwards's PAC, unlike those of his rivals, accepted
unregulated soft money contributions, mostly in the form of
$5,000 checks from trial lawyers. (The new campaign reform law
banning soft money did not take effect until 2003.) As then-PAC
director Steve Jarding told me back in September, amid signs that
he was falling out of favor with Edwards, "It is mind-boggling
to me that the other campaigns got caught up in the McCain-
Feingold mania and refused to use soft money. Why would you
ever leave money on the table?"

Sheila McGuire Riggs, the state Democratic Party chair, had no
problem with this income-transfer program from the trial lawyers
to obscure Iowa legislative candidates. During a chat before Saturday night's party dinner, she lauded Edwards in a tone that a
turn-of-the-last-century Iowa librarian might have used to praise
the beneficence of Andrew Carnegie. "When I hear the national
press talk about Gore and Gephardt," she said, "I'm just stunned
that they aren't aware of all that Edwards is doing here. I'll talk
back to the TV and say that they're missing things. It's subtle, but
Edwards is doing all the right things. He has figured out a way to
make his presence felt here without being here all the time."
(Riggs, after stepping down as party chair, became Bob Graham's
Iowa coordinator before ultimately ending up with Dean.)

Beyond such mercenary gestures, Iowa's political clout is
expressed in ideological ways as well. A prime illustration was
the way that Dean precipitously abandoned his lifelong belief in
unfettered free trade. As Dean recounted to me in September
2002, his epiphany occurred, conveniently enough, in the middle
of a breakfast meeting with Iowa UAW leader David Neil. "He
started talking about the hollowing out of our industrial capacity," Dean recalled. "You hear all this rhetoric from people who
are [representing] professional interest groups." But the conversation with Neil was somehow different for Dean. "I understood
what this human being was telling me and it was different from
[AFL-CIO president] John Sweeney telling me in Washington or

[AFSCME president] Gerry McEntee because it wasn't about [labor] business, it was about people. And all of a sudden, it clicked."

Looking out at the record crowd of roughly 1,500 sitting at round tables in the Polk County Convention Complex, I realized that this was one of the largest assemblages of Iowa Democrats who would hear the candidates in person before the 2004 caucuses. It was rare at this early phase for three White House hopefuls to share the same stage, even though the evening theoretically belonged to Harkin and Vilsack. Dean, for one, was keenly aware of the protocol that governs such joint appearances. Previewing the Jefferson-Jackson festivities, he said, "I'll probably leave out my lines about Democrats sounding like Republicans, since there's no need to directly antagonize these guys [Kerry and Edwards]."

While the Republicans, especially in the Bush II era, are the party of clockwork precision, the chaotic Democrats remain what they have always been—the Iowa dinner began forty-five minutes late. Listening to the speeches, I noticed how the presidential contenders shaped their personas to fit Iowa. Kerry, who had already announced that he would reluctantly vote for the president's Iraq resolution, still managed to coo dovishly: "You go to war not as a first resort, but as a last resort."

Dean, for his part, did the obligatory ethanol pander: "If we used 10-percent ethanol in every tank of gasoline, we'd reduce our oil bill substantially." But what roused the crowd, along with Dean's standard attack on invading Iraq, was his passionate embrace of pro-union trade policies. "Fair trade is more important than free trade," he thundered with the true-believer certainty of a recent convert. "You can see that in Clinton and Davenport and Dubuque. Our industrial capacity is being hollowed out because we are sending jobs to China..." His next words were drowned out by a roar of applause as union stalwarts rose to their feet to hail this kindred spirit from Vermont. But later in the evening, Dean endured the inadvertent indignities that are the lot of little-known presidential pretenders. Harkin, not once but twice, transformed the Vermont governor into a Watergate whistle-blower with lines like, "John Dean, I thank you for your great leadership on health care."

It was well past Iowa bedtime and empty tables dotted the hall when Edwards was finally allowed to take his coveted slot and declare his fealty to Harkin. Sensing the restlessness in the room, Edwards delivered a high-energy, arm-waving performance reminiscent of exercise videos as he declared, "I have seen Tom on the floor of the United States Senate with a backbone of steel—when it's just him and nobody else—no matter who he's fighting against. It can be the big drug companies, it can be the most powerful corporate interests in America." Afterward, a middle-aged woman standing near me offered this tartly worded verdict: "He must have been a cheerleader in college."

Once upon a time—that is, as recently as 1992—the presidential caucuses and primaries unfolded at a sensible pace that encouraged deliberation by the voters and, not incidentally, provided political reporters with a natural narrative arc filled with exciting reversals of fortune and dramatic comebacks. Back then, February belonged to Iowa and New Hampshire, which winnowed the field; the cluster of southern primaries in March known as Super Tuesday reduced the contest to an undisputed front-runner and a desperate challenger; the race was generally decided when the big industrial states such as New York and Illinois weighed in come April; and any remaining doubts were dispelled as California, Ohio and New Jersey went to the polls on the first Tuesday in June.

But then—hiss! boo!—the Republicans ruined everything in 1996. California jumped its primary to the first Tuesday in March in deference to the outlandish presidential fantasies of GOP Gov-

ernor Pete Wilson. New York moved up as well, as Al D'Amato
gamed the system to boost his Senate patron, Bob Dole. The
result was a slam-bang-thank-you-ma'am calendar that effectively truncated the presidential race from four leisurely months
to three pinballing weeks. This was politics reshaped to fit the
attention span of an eleven-year-old boy weaned on Mortal Kom-
bat video games and computer-generated movie mayhem.

Sadly, the leaders of both parties quickly learned to love this
new fast-forward primary schedule. No longer did they have to
worry about protracted and divisive primary fights filled with
snarling attack ads and belittling debate epithets. Instead of the
uncertainties of democratic decision, they now had de facto nominees by early March. And since the general election campaigns
of 1996 and 2000 were largely funded with soft money, the
unseemly haste of the primaries permitted both parties to concentrate their energies on raking in the five- and six-digit checks
that paid for the spate of TV spots that so elevated the political
dialogue.

It was a wonderful system unless, of course, you had the mis-
fortune to be a voter. In recent years, all the civics-book verities
about democracy seem to have been subordinated to the selfish
needs of a bipartisan $2-billion-plus-per-campaign-cycle, multi-
tentacled syndicate that might be called Politics, Inc. The central
beneficiaries of this closed-loop system are the political parties,
the consultants, the spin doctors, the imagemakers, the pollsters
and the local television stations that jack up their ad rates before
an election. The political press corps, so cynical about the motivations of most candidates, seems to be curiously uninterested in
the large financial benefit that their most indispensable sources—
the consultants—derive from free-spending campaigns. Now that
I have gotten that screed out of my system, we will return to our
regularly scheduled programming.

The Democrats, unlike the Republicans, have explicit rules
that protect the folksy rituals of Iowa and New Hampshire with
the political version of the Endangered Species Act. In 2000, the

Democrats retained their traditional rule barring any state, save
for the favored duo, from holding delegate contests before the
first Tuesday in March. Consequently, after Gore edged Bradley
in New Hampshire on February 1 (the earliest primary date in
history), the Democrats went dark for five weeks. On the Republican side in February, John McCain electrified the nation with his
lightning-round challenge to Bush in the South Carolina and
Michigan primaries—states where the Democrats were consigned
to the sidelines. As former South Carolina Democratic chairman
Dick Harpootlian recently said to me, "If Bill Bradley and Al
Gore had come in here and spent money, it would have been
dynamic for party building."

This history, arcane though it may seem, explains why the
Democrats most likely will have selected their 2004 nominee so
early in the year that most Americans will still be mistakenly
scrawling "2003" on their checks. In a classic example of fighting
the last war, the Democrats eliminated the South Carolina problem and the five-week gap that so bedeviled them in 2000 by
advancing the primary calendar by a month. Now for the first
time Iowa and New Hampshire are both in January, and other
states can freely hold their primaries and caucuses beginning
Tuesday, February 3. This scheduling decision, made by the
Democratic National Committee in early 2002, virtually man-
dated candidates such as Dean, Kerry and Edwards to start gun-
ning their engines before the voters went to the polls in the off-
year congressional elections.

Why this intemperate rush to judgment? Party chairman Terry
McAuliffe insists, "We have to get a nominee early." Yet the logic
behind his oft-repeated assertion remains elusive. There is no
risk this time of South Carolina Democrats being upstaged by the
Republicans, since North Korean plebiscites are more suspense-
ful than Bush's unchallenged renomination. With soft money
banned, the party fund-raising that is still possible by pushing
the margins of the new law can take place with the nomination
fight still undecided. As Bob Dole in 1996 and Al Gore in 2000

demonstrated, a presidential nominee selected months before the convention is a semi-unemployed vagabond with nothing to do other than listlessly campaign and endlessly mull his vice-presidential choice.

In McAuliffe's defense, he belatedly managed to impose some semblance of rational order on the Democrats' February frolic of primaries and caucuses, pressuring the state parties to fall in line. With the exception of the Michigan caucuses on February 7, the early campaign weeks will be confined to states with small enough populations that candidates do not automatically face bankruptcy by waging a media campaign. This is not to deny the system's inherent lack of deliberation—and the mind-numbing speed with which many of the Democratic dreamers will be forced to arrange vacations during which they can brood about might-have-beens. Theoretically at least, the presidential calendar allows candidates who are shut out in Iowa and New Hampshire one last chance to recover.

If midsummer conventional wisdom is correct (a highly dubious proposition), then Gephardt or Dean will win Iowa on January 19 and either Kerry or Dean will prevail in New Hampshire on January 27. My fellow reporters and I will immediately jettison parkas and boots as we head below the Mason-Dixon Line. South Carolina takes the place of honor on February 3, though it shares the date with four other primaries, most notably Arizona and Oklahoma and two caucuses (New Mexico is the one that matters). This fandango of Sunbelt delegate contests allows Edwards, Lieberman and Graham, who are all likely to finish out of the money in Iowa and New Hampshire, to construct credible scenarios for stirring comebacks.

There was a moment, though, when it looked like everything might come unraveled and the 2004 political calendar would prove Will Rogers's oft-quoted maxim: "I don't belong to any organized political party. I'm a Democrat." McAuliffe spent March 2003 beating back, with the aid of the national leadership of the UAW and AFL-CIO, a threat from Michigan to move its caucuses to January in defiance of party rules and the traditional prerogatives of Iowa and New Hampshire. Reflecting the Byzantine world of internal Democratic politics, a major factor in the equation was a failed drive by New Hampshire Republicans to approve a right-to-work law, which would have made the state anathema to labor. "Had they passed right-to-work," McAuliffe said during a May interview, "I would have lost a huge argument. What could I have said to defend a state that has a Republican governor and no Democrats in the congressional delegation?" In theory, the national chairman of an out-of-power political party has about as many divisions as the Pope. But for all his bluster, McAuliffe knows how to work the levers of power. Explaining the way he derailed the Michigan challenge while glossing over some of his hardball tactics, he laughingly said, "It took a lot of promises of good hotel suites at the convention and good seats on the convention floor."

The senator's aides were impatiently demanding that he leave immediately for his speech in Iowa City, but Tom Harkin had one more thing that he insisted on showing me. We had been talking politics over coffee on this mid-February Sunday morning in the tiny living room of the nine-hundred-square-foot shingled house in which Harkin grew up, the son of an Iowa coal miner. The senator—who recently restored this place redolent with childhood memories after acquiring it upon his brother's death—walked me to the back of the house to point out a small, nondescript bedroom that a weary traveler might grudgingly accept if the only alternative were sleeping in the car. "This is where we slept," Harkin said, referring to his brothers and sisters. "All six of us. Three to a bed."

The symbolism inherent in that 1940s bedroom goes a long way toward explaining Harkin, his populist values and the role that he may ultimately play in the Iowa caucuses. In an effort to focus the Democratic race on bread-and-butter issues such as jobs and health care, Harkin arranged a series of nine forums around

the state, which were broadcast on C-Span, giving each of the
nine declared candidates their own day to answer questions from
voters. The potential reward, when the forums concluded in September, was a Harkin endorsement. "I'm now the nine-hundred-
pound gorilla," he said in an uninflected tone that suggested that
he was merely stating the obvious. "I have the best organization. I
have the best list. I love Tom Vilsack, but he's never done the
nuts and bolts of politics."

Although Harkin's words were guarded on this frosty day,
even during the off-the-record portion of the conversation, it was
hard to detect much enthusiasm for Kerry or any sign that
Edwards's efforts to ingratiate himself were bearing fruit. Dean,
who had made the pilgrimage to this modest house in Cumming
the day before, appeared to intrigue Harkin—now that he could
remember the Vermonter's name. "A governor is different,"
Harkin said about Dean. "I saw it running in 1991–92 against
Clinton. People look on a governor as different than us [legisla-
tors]." But Harkin's encouraging comments about Dean's "nice
crisp message" did not necessarily portend a pre-caucus endorsement. "I've had a lot of people call me and ask me what to do,"
Harkin said. "And I tell them, 'Keep your powder dry.'"

Six months later in mid-August, as I chatted with Harkin on a
flight from Des Moines to Chicago, I could tell that the would-be
Iowa kingmaker was still far from striking a match to his powder.
The vacation-bound senator's major pre-occupation was his
annual mid-September "steak fry"—traditionally the biggest
Democratic event in Iowa—which this year would feature Bill
Clinton along with most of the Democratic class of '04. Aside
from state attorney general Tom Miller, who based on long-standing friendship was backing Lieberman, most prominent Iowa
Democrats have been slow to make presidential endorsements.
Chuck Todd, the editor-in-chief of the subscription-only on-line
daily political newsletter "The Hotline," captured the slow-to-gel
mood of Iowa Democrats when he wrote that only the "Gang of
5,000" activists were closely monitoring the pre-caucus jousting.

My trip to Iowa coincided with the State Fair in Des Moines, where this year the butter sculptures were secular rather than religious: a life-sized yellow cow and a grease-propelled Harley-Davidson. It was easy to revel in the hot-diggity corn-dog hokum of strolling down the midway with a glad-handing candidate, his entourage, several camera crews and a dozen political reporters momentarily liberated from any illusion that the Democratic race was a contest of ideas. This was a photo-op as old-fashioned as Calvin Coolidge donning an Indian head-dress for the cameras. Here the test of fire in your belly was what you put in your stomach. Lieberman, opting out of the traditional appearance at the pork pavilion, demonstrated his cast-iron gullet by cheerfully downing a mass-market, cream-filled cupcake that had been coated with batter and placed on the griddle. As he laughingly declared, "Anything I say for the rest of the day will be subject to the fried-Twinkie defense."

This was a week when all the serious Democratic contenders made pilgrimages to the heartland. Even though Dean was now powered by what the original George Bush back in 1980 called "the Big Mo," I was the lone reporter who trailed the candidate, traveling in a borrowed van with the vanity license plate "MCFUN" to a late-night appearance at a tiny public library in the hamlet of New Hartford. How small was the library? Well, I have more books in my dining room, though I can't begin to compete with New Hartford when it comes to the collected works of Zane Grey.

The sixty-five mostly gray-haired Democrats—an impressive turnout in this rural Republican county—who heard Dean deliver his standard stump speech lustily cheered lines like "Of all the people leading in the polls, I'm the only one who didn't support the president's war in Iraq." But applause did not equal caucus commitments. I watched Dori Jurgensen, a college biology instructor from nearby Denver, as she punctuated virtually every Dean sentence with an approving nod. But she declined to take the final step of signing the Dean pledge card that she cradled in her hand. "We're just starting to think about who to support," she said. "I'm not ready to commit."

Edwards, in contrast, toured Iowa in an over-sized bus, the kind of vehicle favored by country-music stars and John McCain in the 2000 primaries. Speaking to forty Democrats on a supporter's front lawn in Waverly, Edwards exuded passion about his plan to mandate health-care coverage for the nation's twelve million children without insurance. That might seem like standard-issue Democratic rhetoric except for what happened next. "We're going to do something about twelve million kids," he said, before cutting himself off mid-sentence as he belatedly noticed the arrival of his wife Elizabeth and their two small children. "Oh, they're here," Edwards burbled. "This is my family." He completed his speech with three-year-old Jack clinging to his waist and Emma Claire, now five, periodically venturing forth in a valiant but vain effort to dislodge her brother.

Over the last quarter century, I have shared campaign buses with drunks from British tabloids and hymn-singing supporters of Pat Robertson in 1988. But never, until now, had I experienced the romance of the road in the company of two small children. As soon as we pulled out on the Edwards bus, Jack, exuberantly pointing out the window, announced, "Daddy, a playground!"— and seemed mystified when we didn't immediately brake to a halt for a ride on the swings. Reviewing the day's schedule a few minutes later, Edwards mentioned that he would be making an appearance at a house party to raise money for an Iowa legislative candidate. That prompted Emma Claire—in a dazzling display of the eternal innocence of children—to ask in a puzzled tone, "Daddy, what's a fund-raiser?"

New Hampshire Democrats, unlike their Iowa counterparts, are not afflicted with Indecision 2003. The website "politics NH.com" has been charting the candidate preferences of 105 leading Granite State Democrats—and only 37 of them remained undecided by mid-August. But those on the fence were certainly noticed.

It is a truth universally acknowledged that an uncommitted New Hampshire Democrat in possession of political influence must be in want of telephone calls. Consider Terie Norelli, the assistant Democratic leader in the New Hampshire State House, who hosted a series of receptions at her home in Portsmouth for the candidates, including one for Edwards in late May. During the week following the North Carolina senator's appearance, Norelli received calls from Edwards, Dean and Hadassah Lieberman. "Edwards definitely is hard sell," she said, comparing phone techniques. "It was 'This is John Edwards, I definitely need your help.'" In contrast, she explained, "Howard Dean was more friendly. It was 'I'd like to have you involved.'" She never returned the Lieberman call since Norelli described the senator as "way too hawkish for me."

As for Beth Campbell, the SEIU official, her liberal sentiments were drifting toward Gephardt, but Dean had proven to be her most faithful gentleman caller. During one conversation when Campbell was obviously afflicted with a bad cold, Dean even volunteered to make a bedside medical visit. On another occasion in the spring, Campbell was at her state job in Concord, dealing with stray dogs and other animals, when the telephone rang. The conversation went like this:

CAMPBELL: Animal Population Control Program.
CALLER: Is this Beth?
CAMPBELL: Yes.
CALLER: This is Governor Howard Dean.
(A brief exchange of pleasantries)
CALLER: Will you endorse me?
CAMPBELL: No, but thank you for asking. (Pause) Governor, you know better than that. I can't endorse until my union does.

As we sat in a booth at Pappy's Pizza in Manchester in late May, Lou D'Allesandro was mulling his status as the last remaining uncommitted Democratic state senator. Originally on this Friday, D'Allesandro was slated to have breakfast with Kerry and lunch with Lieberman, but both were unexpectedly trapped in Washington by Senate votes. "I want someone who I can believe in and trust. I'll tell you in all candor," he declared gesturing toward his heart, "I'm not looking for anything. I just want a president who has not only compassion but common sense."

Then, as an exercise almost more for his own benefit than mine, D'Allesandro worked his way through a process of elimination. Dean was still dismissed as someone who won't survive the long haul. "The one thing that Kerry presents that's objectionable—and that's his patrician attitude," he sniffed. "He can't seem to get rid of it." The state senator, a moderate Democrat, was attracted to Lieberman's views but troubled by his style of self-presentation. "I think Lieberman plays up the religious role too much," he complained. "If Gore thought he was good enough to be vice president, stop thanking God."

Two straws were left, since Graham did not factor into these calculations. "The most likeable guy in this race is Edwards," he said, radiating enthusiasm for the first time in the conversation. "Of all these guys, he's the sleeper. This guy can explode. He can battle Bush on likability and credibility." It would be a coup for Edwards, running just ahead of an asterisk in most New Hampshire polls, to snag such a major figure in the largest city in the state.

If only politics were that simple. But then there was Gephardt, who phones D'Allesandro at least once a week. "My loyalty to Gephardt is that he's always been very good to me," the veteran politician said with just a tinge of sadness in his voice. "He's done everything I've ever asked. That's important in this business."

And so D'Allesandro held off—waiting for that elusive flash of certainty. On his sixty-fifth birthday in August, the state senator received phone calls from Kerry and Edwards. Lieberman sent a letter, while Dean and Gephardt dispatched staffers to attend the birthday festivities. Having once dismissed Dean as irrelevant,

D'Allesandro was belatedly warming to the former Vermont governor: "Dean has surprised everyone. He's resonating with people because he's very direct." Then came a brief whirl with Wesley Clark before finally, in October, D'Allesandro ended up where he always wanted to be—endorsing John Edwards for president. Through it all, D'Allesandro remained keenly aware that his current importance to a would-be Democratic president was greater than that of Tony Blair or Jacques Chirac. And he knew full well that it was only because he resides in a magical place called New Hampshire.

CHAPTER 7

The Candidates in Wartime

It's not exactly Buck Rogers in the twenty-fifth century, but there is a tone of science-fiction incredulity in Howard Dean's voice on this late January morning as he gleefully describes his latest technological breakthrough. After a round of breakfast interviews (George Will and myself) and a post-breakfast meeting (a Steelworkers executive), Dean has established a traveling salesman's command post in an armchair in the basement lobby of Washington's Four Seasons Hotel in Georgetown. With the *New York Times* on his lap and a cell phone in his hand, Dean announces that he is about to dictate a press release. For a candidate who travels without a computer, this is cutting-edge stuff. As Dean proudly explains, "I read the papers, call the office and we're on the news cycle in ninety minutes."

In his enthusiasm, Dean provides a hint of what he might have been like as a nine-year-old boy in Manhattan who had just discovered the mischief-making potential of prank phone calls. It's all so easy. You just dial, dictate and insinuate your criticisms in another candidate's news story. Just yesterday Dean previewed this technique after John Kerry delivered a major foreign-policy address assailing the Bush administration's "blustering unilateralism" in its headlong rush to war over Iraq. Dean, the most out-spoken dove in the Democratic aviary, responded by composing a tartly worded press release claiming that he was "thrilled" that Kerry is finally echoing his concerns "about the White House's unilateralist foreign policy." Of course, Dean couldn't resist pointedly adding that he—unlike Kerry—had opposed the presi-dent's congressional Iraq war resolution that was approved by Congress last October. In his *Los Angeles Times* story on the Kerry speech, Ron Brownstein obligingly awarded Dean's cri-tique a walk-on role, but added that the sarcastic press release represented "one of the first criticisms aimed by one Democratic presidential candidate at a potential rival."

With this Iraq attack on Kerry, Dean has found a medium to match his message. Watching Dean master the rat-a-tat of quick-response campaign press releases is a bit like sitting on the copy-desk next to William Randolph Hearst as he composes his first screaming yellow-journalism headline. It all seems like harmless fun and games until, before you know it, you're in the middle of the Spanish-American War.

Okay, the Dean-Kerry feud has not yet inspired dirty-faced newsboys to scream, "Remember the *Maine!*" But with both New England candidates competing for the same upmarket Demo-cratic constituency, it amounts to a real war. The quarrel mirrors divisions in the Democratic Party that go all the way back to the anti-war furies of the 1968 primaries. During that tempestuous year, the real cleavage on the left was between the purist parti-sans of Eugene McCarthy and the pragmatic politics personified by Bobby Kennedy. That Democratic dilemma endures: How do you weigh dewy-eyed idealism against partially flawed electabil-ity? In his righteous anger, Dean can be seen as the spiritual descendant of McCarthy, while Kerry never shies away from wrapping himself in the Kennedy myth.

Two weeks later, Dean was in Iowa, a state where caucus-going Democrats are so dovish they make Mahatma Gandhi seem bellicose. Colin Powell had just come before the United Nations

Security Council in early February to deliver the Bush administration's case against Saddam Hussein. But here in the heartland, Democrats were bristling with no-war-for-oil fervor. This was Howard Dean's moment—the maverick candidate was transformed from an ego-tripping outsider to the embodiment of a cause. Not since Vietnam had an insurgent Democrat become so identified with a single transcendent issue so early in the presidential campaign cycle. Dean's original dream was built around lighting an Iowa prairie fire. But the blaze was slated to erupt in early 2004, not eleven months before the caucuses.

Arriving in Des Moines, Dean again chided his tongue-tied rivals by declaring, "I think there are a lot of folks dancing around on this one because they voted for the resolution and now they're trying to figure out what to say." That night in Ames at the Story County Democrats' annual soup supper (no, I don't recommend the cream of mushroom), Dean won standing ovations without resorting to souped-up rhetoric. Something big was happening when an audience rose for thirty seconds of thunderous cheers in response to uninflected lines like this: "We ought not to resort to unilateral action unless there's an imminent threat to the United States. And the secretary of state and the president have not made a case that such an imminent threat exists." But at the back of the room, Dean adviser Joe Trippi, making his first trip with the candidate, sounded a cautionary note about premising an entire campaign around anti-war fever. "You don't know how it will play out," Trippi said nervously. "What if we win the war in three days and three guys have bruised knuckles from going over a wall? What if everybody then forgets that they were against it?"

After the dinner, I headed off with a group of Dean aides to a raucous sports bar, the only place we could find in Ames to get a Saturday night drink. Struggling to hear above the din, I listened as Trippi, the media consultant who was soon to become campaign manager, explained the difficulty in getting Dean to accept the tedium of an all-purpose stump speech. "Howard's problem is that he'll get bored with the same spiel and he goes off in an entirely new direction," Trippi said. He cited Dean's riff, which I had heard often, that America faces the danger of becoming another Argentina in forty or fifty years if we keep running unsustainable deficits. For Trippi, the problem was that voters didn't want to hear dire prophecies about America becoming "a second-rate nation." When Trippi pointed this out to Dean, the candidate promised to banish the offending phrase from his lexicon. So in his next speech, the ever obedient Dean warned that America risked becoming "a third-rate nation."

A presidential contender spends more time visiting college campuses than an itinerant drug dealer because nowhere is it easier for a candidate to gin up a respectable-size audience. But there was nothing ersatz about the crowd of roughly three hundred students and faculty members waiting for Dean the next afternoon in the student lounge at Grinnell College. These weren't the curious but the already converted, eager to see the object of their anti-war ardor. While the smattering of nose rings and hair colors never seen in nature spoke to a twenty-first-century sensibility, the red beanbag chairs that dotted the room sparked nostalgic memories of the 1960s. Dean's speech was also something of a throwback as he triggered a rolling thunder of applause by angrily declaring, "If we're going to send our children, your age, and our grandchildren to die in Iraq, the president has got to do better than Saddam is an evil man."

For all his crowd-pleasing critique of the administration's facile arguments, Dean was walking a tightrope on Iraq. If he took even a small step to the right, he would tumble off his anti-war perch as the only serious Democratic contender loudly opposing a go-it-alone invasion. But if he veered further left, he risked plunging into the McGovernite black hole reputed to doom dovish Democrats to irrelevance.

That helped explain why Dean disappointed the militants during the question period at Grinnell by stressing that he was not a disciple of the war-is-not-healthy-for-children-and-other-living-things school of international relations. "Remember," he declared, "I did not say that I would not use unilateral force against Saddam. What I said was 'He is not an imminent threat to the United States.'" Unilateral American action would be justified, he argued, if Saddam ever acquired nuclear weapons or if it were proven that he was sharing chemical or biological weapons with terrorist groups.

On the ride to the next stop, Dean tried to define the larger stakes in this Democratic donnybrook over Iraq. "I think the war is emblematic of a lot of differences," he said. "There is a restlessness in the Democratic Party over exactly what I talk about, which is not trying to be all things to all people." Then he took the unorthodox step in challenging the political legacy of the man who, despite it all, remains the nation's most popular Democrat. "What a lot of people learned from Bill Clinton is that if you accommodate and you co-opt, you can be successful," Dean argued. "And Bill Clinton was very successful. But that role doesn't work for everybody, and it's not the right time for it anymore. It's a new time to be blunt, to be direct, and to stand up for what you believe. That's really the fault line—and the war is a piece of that."

Sure, there are other fault lines among the Democrats on issues such as health care and trade. But there is a wisp of the theoretical to these disputes over domestic policy, since any Democrat in the Oval Office would have to completely revise his proposals before submitting them to a Congress that is likely to be Republican-dominated. But Iraq remains tangible, immediate and real. It is the Rorschach test by which all would-be presidents must be judged.

The trick is to make sense of the patterns. Based on their ideological predispositions, voters could see in the candidates what they chose to see. With the conspicuous exception of Dean and to a lesser extent Bob Graham, all the leading contenders can be said to have used the war to toughen their national-security credentials and to demonstrate that even wimpy Democrats can be warriors. But if you turn the ink blots, you can reach a different conclusion. The Democrats—again excluding Dean, Graham and sometimes Kerry—proved that the shell-shocked party could pander to the gung-ho, trumpet-blaring excesses of Bush foreign policy without ever sounding a note of skepticism. Another twist and it was all about politics—and under this cynical reading, only Dean, the hawkish Joe Lieberman and the idiosyncratic Graham ever publicly expressed their honest opinions.

Even after the war was over, Iraq played havoc with Democratic harmony. It was not just the continuing American casualties, the AWOL alert for Saddam's elusive weapons of mass destruction and the Bush administration's comically inept efforts to explain how gremlins inserted sixteen deceitful words about African uranium into the State of the Union Address. For the Democrats, Iraq became a metaphor for something larger. In late July, Dick Gephardt, presumably seeking political cover for his flag-waving support for the war, delivered a blistering speech in San Francisco attacking George W. Bush for manhandling the peace. "When President Bush landed on an aircraft carrier and declared victory in Iraq, I think he chose the wrong backdrop for his photo-op," Gephardt said. "If you ask me, if he really wanted to show us the state of affairs in Iraq, he should have landed on a patch of quicksand." A few days later, Lieberman went after Democrats like Gephardt—and of course Dean—by warning, "Some in my party threaten to send a message that they don't know a just war when they see it and, more broadly, are not prepared to use our military strength to protect our security and the cause of freedom."

I cannot write about Iraq without admitting my own biases. As a dove, though one who was sympathetic to the human-rights case for working with the United Nations to eventually oust Saddam, I came down close to the Dean side of the debate. In hindsight, Dean's repeated argument that Saddam presented "no imminent threat" looks prescient now that no one can credibly argue that Iraq was secretly preparing to nuke Cedar Rapids. But for all my dovish plumage, I also respect Kerry's early contention that the unilateral nature of the war represented a failure of Bush administration diplomacy. In New Hampshire, three days after the first cruise missiles landed in Baghdad, Kerry said that if he were president he would have waited another forty-five days to try to reach a diplomatic consensus at the United Nations. He made a similar statement in Iowa in late July: "It would have been my preference to work another thirty days with other nations to try to resolve it." The current military and financial burdens of reconstructing Iraq would obviously have been far less onerous had the administration worked longer and harder within the Security Council.

A Democratic wag cleverly pointed out that a major reason why Dean turned out to be so right on Iraq was that he was the only leading candidate who never received a top-secret intelligence briefing. All the congressional Democrats—even Graham, who voted against the Iraq resolution—shared the belief that Iraq was poised to launch its arsenal of chemical and biological weapons. But none of them, not even Graham or John Edwards, who served on the Senate Intelligence Committee, were privy to the internal disputes between the CIA, State Department and the Pentagon over the validity of the evidence. The Iraq war was Bush's mega box-office cinematic epic, a *Saving Private Ryan* for the twenty-first century, and the Democrats in Congress were reduced to the role of uniformed extras on the beaches at Normandy. Only Lieberman was as gung-ho as Bush to go to war, even with ambiguous intelligence information and only Tony Blair as an ally.

Political reporters, myself often included, have a tendency to elevate clichés into immutable laws that have governed elections since Pericles's first campaign in Athens. Within the echo chamber of the Invisible Primary, it is easy to fall into the trap of believing that if three campaign consultants working for different candidates all make the same argument, it has to be true. And nothing in politics invites more blather than the presumed weakness of the Democrats on foreign policy.

Oh Lordy, how many times have I heard pollsters claim that the 2004 Democratic nominee must be able to neutralize the president's national-security credentials. By this exacting standard, a Dean victory in the primaries would presage a fifty-state wipeout and an Edwards nomination would unleash scathing attacks on the ability of a one-term senator to match Bush's mastery of the intricacies of foreign policy. Even Gephardt's quarter century on Capitol Hill may not measure up to the president's globe-girdling greatness. This oft-repeated equation would prematurely narrow the Democratic field to an unabashed hawk (Lieberman) and a certified war hero (Kerry) with a possible opening for the former chairman of the Senate Intelligence Committee (Graham). Casting it in self-serving terms, Lieberman argued during May's South Carolina debate that the voters are not going to elect "anyone who sends a message that is other than strength on defense and homeland security."

As the right fielder on the Democratic nine, Lieberman has to stress his purported electability. But there is something dangerously simplistic to the notion that so far in advance of the election, the Democrats' help-wanted sign must read, "Only Hawks and Heroes Need Apply." Like stock-market mavens and budget analysts, the political community assumes that all current trends will continue in straight-line fashion until the election. In truth, not even Dick Cheney can confidently predict the national-security environment in the fall of 2004 or even which countries Halliburton will win federal non-competitive bidding contracts to rebuild. Beyond the obvious foreign-policy uncertainties, like the number of body bags coming home from Iraq, there is also the unanswerable question of how the victorious Democratic nominee will demonstrate that he is prepared to lead the nation in perilous times. Sandy Berger, Clinton's national security adviser during his second term, sounded like Lieberman when he said, "The American people are not likely to elect anyone in 2004 who is not as tough or tougher than these guys [in the White House]. That's the threshold." But Berger, who is quietly advising most leading Democrats, recognizes that toughness is often measured through personal qualities rather than explicit policy positions. A vigorous performance against Bush in the debates, for example, may register a higher reading on the 2004 toughness meter than the candidate's two-year-old statements on war with Iraq.

But the Democrats seem no more willing than the fractious Iraqis to settle for permanent peace. Appearing before a group of young Democrats in New York in mid-May, Lieberman was hissed and dissed for his pre-war pro-war stance. The Lieberman camp seemed more comfortable with Old Testament eye-for-eye justice than those new-fangled gospels about turning the other cheek. That same week in May, the centrist Democratic Leadership Council, whose CEO, Al From, is one of Lieberman's staunchest backers, unleashed a scathing attack on Dean—a foreshadowing of the bitter charges to come. A memo signed by From and mild-mannered DLC president Bruce Reed bluntly stated, "What activists like Dean call the Democratic wing of the Democratic Party is an aberration: the McGovern-Mondale wing, defined principally by weakness abroad and elitist, interest-group liberalism. That's the wing that lost 49 states in two elections, and transformed Democrats from a strong national party into a much weaker regional one."

Hey, guys, tell us what you really think. With its venomous assault on the Democratic Party's standard-bearers of two and three decades ago, the DLC memo brought to mind the famous put-down of the Bourbon monarchy of Louis XVI: "They have learned nothing and forgotten nothing." The same, alas, can be said of the Democratic Party as it perpetually searches for new venues in which to refight the Vietnam War.

The response from the Democrats in Keene, New Hampshire, was so electric that Kerry never got to finish his sentence. On this summer day in August 2002, the Massachusetts senator was talking passionately about energy independence. "We need to create renewable energy," he thundered, "so that we never again have to send young men and women abroad to die..." A wave of applause drowned out Kerry's efforts to offer a final phrase that could have been "in Iraq" or "in the Middle East." But none of the party activists cared about Kerry's interrupted syntax. They knew that he had just expressed his full-throated opposition to the president's determination to unleash a new war against Saddam Hussein.

Or had he? In the car afterward, I casually mentioned to Kerry that I was impressed by the way that he tapped into the growing fervor of the anti-war movement. The senator looked at me in non-comprehension as if I had just started speaking in tongues. "That was all backward looking," he said with exasperation in his voice. "It was about Kuwait. It has nothing to do with weapons of mass destruction."

For me, this was an emblematic moment that underscored the danger of making glib assumptions about Kerry's foreign-policy beliefs. His views, particularly on Iraq, were complex, subtle and politically tinged—and often the shadings got lost in translation, opening him up to charges by both Dean and the press of two-faced duplicity. "I think Kerry's enormously thoughtful on these issues," said Jim Steinberg, the deputy national security adviser during Clinton's second term. "He may know foreign policy better than anyone in the Senate. But does it cohere into a world view? The big challenge for Kerry as a candidate is to take his wisdom and his world view and turn it into a compelling message."

There were moments when Kerry's twin passions for politics and foreign policy became comically entwined. In Maine, a week before the 2002 elections, Kerry was on his cell phone with his scheduler in his Boston office. He was talking animatedly about the details of the day he was scheduled to devote to campaigning for Shannon O'Brien, the Democratic candidate for Massachusetts governor who was trailing badly in the polls. Suddenly, in the middle of a discussion of the logistics of a planned rally, a new thought crossed Kerry's mind. "When we're done," he said to the scheduler, "can you get me Kofi Annan on the phone?" Much to my disappointment as a potential eavesdropper, the U.N. secretary-general was temporarily unavailable.

That afternoon at a small Democratic fund-raiser in Bangor, the senator was pressed to justify his recent controversial vote in favor of the president's Iraq resolution. His answer was revealing, both for its endless outpouring of run-on sentences and for its core of difficult-to-summarize logic. "It was one of the toughest votes that I've cast," Kerry began, "because votes are yes and no. But my vote was not yes or no, nor does the issue lend itself to yes or no." This was the moment when I wondered whether Kerry was about to update Humpty-Dumpty and declare, "When I cast a vote, it means what I choose it to mean, nothing more nor less."

Instead, Kerry was still working up to his answer: "The president has the power to decide if there is an imminent threat to the United States." At that moment, a cell phone went off to the eerily apt tones of the *William Tell Overture*. Without missing a beat, Kerry cracked, "They're summoning us to the attack. The charge!"

After the laughter subsided, Kerry slowly moved toward the nub of his argument: the weapons of mass destruction and "Saddam Hussein's failure to live up to the international community's standards." After offering lengthy quotes from both his speech on the Senate floor before the vote and an op-ed he wrote for the *New York Times* in September, Kerry finally, mercifully, said, "My vote was cast in a way that made it very clear, 'Mr. President, I'm voting for you to do what you said you're going to do, which is to go through the UN and do this through an international process. If you go unilaterally, without having exhausted these remedies, I'm not supporting you. And if you decide that this is just a matter of straight pre-emptive doctrine for regime-change purposes without regard to the imminence of the threat, I'm not going to support you.'"

Okay, try fitting that on a bumper sticker or into a thirty-second TV commercial. This prolix style was Kerry's albatross all through the run-up to war. Despite vocal claims to the contrary, his underlying position remained consistent every time I subsequently heard him explain it on the campaign trail. Stripped of the verbiage and most of the conditional clauses, he supported an invasion of Iraq to remove Saddam's weapons of mass destruction as long as it was launched in concert with a broad-based international coalition, preferably under U.N. sanction. But Kerry never mastered brevity. At an outdoor rally in Columbia, South Carolina, in early February, Kerry responded to a three-word shouted question—"What about Iraq?"—with a six-minute answer that even included a rambling aside about his efforts on behalf of Vietnam veterans.

If his Vietnam service gave Kerry a political credibility that most of his rivals lacked on national-security issues, his Janus-like role in that thirty-five-year-old war had distinct similarities to his stance on Iraq. As Kerry put it at a house party in Nashua, New Hampshire, in late March, shortly after the war began, "I'm the only person running for president who has fought in a war and actually fought against the war I volunteered to fight in because I found it wrong." That was Kerry, hawk and dove in a single lanky body.

It was a shame that heart surgery prevented Bob Graham from emerging as an active candidate until after the Iraq war was over. What voters and reporters missed was the potentially comic motif of the gray-haired Florida senator totally befuddling dovish Democratic audiences.

While Dean railed against the blank-check congressional resolution, Graham was one of only twenty-three senators to actually vote no. But his damn-the-polls-full-speed-ahead reasoning was quirky. Unlike the peaceniks, Graham was a gung-ho supporter of unilateral military action against terrorism. He just believed that

Iraq could wait until after we destroyed al-Qaeda and went after groups like Hezbollah in Syria. "Graham's position was in some ways a courageous one because a lot of Democrats thought it but didn't say it," said Steinberg, now the director of foreign-policy studies at the Brookings Institution. But Graham's Baghdad-on-the-back-burner beliefs didn't fit into any of the ideological cubbyholes that define the Democratic Party. How do you categorize a senator who was simultaneously as hawkish as Lieberman and as fretful as Dean?

In mid-January, as he was still mulling the merits of entering the Democratic fray, I dropped by to chat with Graham in his Senate office. "Chat" may be the wrong word, since our conversation turned out to have all the intimacy of a split-screen TV interview, owing to Graham's penchant for launching into a monologue, oblivious to any reportorial questions. Part of the distancing was physical: The senator and I were separated by his desk, which was roughly the size of the flight deck on an aircraft carrier. Any second, I expected the president to zoom in for a tail-hook landing.

When Graham finally paused to exhale, I managed to breathlessly squeeze in a question about Iraq. In his methodical fashion, Graham, who has just ended his ten-year tenure on the Intelligence Committee, ticked off his three dominant fears about the impending war. First, Graham said, there was the danger that Iraq would "use chemical and biological weapons against the attacking troops." Second, there was risk that Saddam would launch "his twenty to twenty-five Scud missiles with chemical and biological warheads against Israel." And, third, the war would prompt Saddam to break his "long history of non-involvement with religious fundamentalist groups," creating a 75 percent risk (according to intelligence estimates) of a new wave of terrorist attacks against Americans here or abroad.

Graham spoke in the apocalyptic tone of Cassandra warning of Greeks bearing gifts, but he lacked her uncanny ability to foresee the arrival of the Trojan Horse. Looking back on this January interview, I cannot help recalling the confident fashion in which Graham offered his dire but incorrect predictions about Saddam's intentions to use chemical and biological weapons and his ability to launch Scuds against Israel.

How much of this history is relevant in choosing a president? Since a president's judgment in the Oval Office ultimately matters far more than his issue stands during the campaign, it can be argued that the conclusions the Democrats derived from ambiguous information about Iraq represent some of the best clues available about the mind-set they would bring to the White House. But it is difficult to keep score. For example, does Graham win points for his skepticism about the war or lose them for his seemingly credulous acceptance of CIA estimates regarding the Iraqi arsenal?

As an active candidate, Graham quickly discarded his courtly ways to excoriate Bush with a fury that makes Dean seem like Dale Carnegie. Projecting a sense of personal betrayal, Graham denounced the administration for its "Nixonian stench of secrecy." During a July press conference before an NAACP candidates forum, the Florida senator carried the Nixonian parallel to a new extreme: "If the standard of impeachment that the Republicans set for Bill Clinton, that a personal, consensual relationship was the basis for impeachment, would not a president who knowingly deceived the American people about something as important as whether to go to war meet the standard of impeachment?"

The last-angry-man tenor of Graham's remarks appeared to be less political posturing than a symbol of the liberation of a long-shot candidate with nothing to lose by speaking his mind. His campaign manager, Paul Johnson, said judiciously, "His vote on the war with Iraq helps with some people and hurts with others." But Johnson laughed when I asked if there was anything scripted about Graham's statements about the president's deceptive statements about Iraq. "The whole notion of full disclosure and what did they know and when did they know it—and the whole idea of the Nixonian stench coming out of the White House—those things would have been said regardless," Johnson conceded. "We haven't sat down and plotted it out."

A reporter types some lines so often that they become devoid of meaning. Take the phrase "the hawkish Joe Lieberman." Lieberman so personifies Democratic ferocity on national-security issues that it is easy to forget that he once flew with the doves. As a young Yale Law School graduate in New Haven in 1968, he turned against the Vietnam War and backed the presidential candidacy of Bobby Kennedy. But gradually he moved to the right on foreign policy, though the transformation was almost invisible, since Lieberman was fixated on state politics.

All that changed when he ran against liberal GOP Senator Lowell Weicker. "In 1987 and early 1988, no one knew what Joe's views were on foreign policy," recalled John Droney, who was then the state party chairman. "He had been quite progressive on social issues and everyone assumed, since he couldn't be that complex, that he'd have progressive views on foreign policy."

Even after he arrived in the Senate in 1989, Lieberman was pigeon-holed as a Jewish Democrat from Connecticut, a pedigree suggesting that he couldn't be very conservative. That supposition lasted until the Senate Democrats began plotting strategy in the fall of 1990 on how to respond to the first President Bush's determination to go to war with Iraq without congressional sanction. With puckish glee, Lieberman recounted a meeting that Majority Leader George Mitchell convened with a dozen Senate Democrats. Lieberman had to leave early, and, as he got up to depart, Mitchell pressed him on his views. "I totally agree with you that this is war, and he should come to Congress for authorization," Lieberman replied. "But, George, I want you to know that when he does, I'm going to support him." As Lieberman described it, the response from his fellow Democrats was "one of those mouths-drop-open silences."

We were (surprise!) riding in a van in New Hampshire, soon after the second Bush declared victory in the second Gulf War. Curious about his transformation into "the hawkish Joe Lieberman," I had been pressing him on whether there was a triggering event for his rightward ideological migration. Lieberman freely conceded that his hard-edged views on crime were shaped by the breakdown of law and order in New Haven in the 1970s (his house was burglarized twice)—and even laughingly agreed that on this issue he fits the model that a conservative is a liberal who's been mugged.

But on military matters, it was not like Lieberman caught Saddam with mask and gun carrying his television set out to the getaway car. "I read a lot," Lieberman said, groping for an explanation for the sea change in his attitudes. "I was very moved by my heroes like Teddy Roosevelt, Churchill and Harry Truman. Nothing unusual there. But those were all people who believed in strength and in using strength to protect security." Even Lieberman knew that he was being vague, so he tried again by conjuring up another hero: "John Kennedy stood for, in my opinion, a real internationalism, but a kind of muscular internationalism."

That's the thing with Lieberman; you keep running into these blind alleys. Desperate for a shred of specificity, I asked Lieberman—that Bobby Kennedy backer in '68—whether he was for George McGovern in 1972. It was a relevant question since Lieberman's supporters at the DLC had been deriding Dean as the second coming of McGovern. The resulting dialogue with Lieberman was akin to an old-time radio drama in which the hero has amnesia. "No," he said tentatively, before adding in a puzzled tone, "why can't I answer that question?"

I suggested that a Freudian might use the word "repression" to explain his forgetfulness about McGovern. "Maybe I didn't get too actively involved that year," Lieberman mused, as he did the dog paddle in the waters of memory. "Who else might I have been for?" Ed Muskie? Hubert Humphrey? Somehow I didn't think that Shirley Chisholm was ever Lieberman's kind of candidate. But none of these names aroused Lieberman out of his coma. "It's weird," he said. "I can't remember."

Richard Nixon, McGovern's opponent in that 1972 election, expressed the belief that the country didn't need a president to run domestic policy, since a competent cabinet could handle the job for him. But in foreign policy, Nixon said, a president is indispensable. This was admittedly an extreme view that fit Nixon's Republican sensibilities. But some Democrats veer toward the opposite end of the spectrum. Unlike the other leading Democrats, Iraq-war supporters Gephardt and Edwards conveyed the impression that foreign policy was something that you had to get through in order to have the freedom to concentrate on domestic issues.

Maybe I'm becoming as forgetful as Lieberman, but if either Gephardt or Edwards expressed a single original foreign-policy thought during the long run-up to war with Iraq, I can't remember it. This was not to say that they were silent or vague. In early October 2002, Gephardt negotiated with Bush the final wording of the congressional resolution endorsing an invasion—and then, to the consternation of House Democrats, appeared (with Lieberman) at a White House pep rally in support of passage. Although Edwards, a co-sponsor of the president's resolution, took a far less prominent role in the congressional debate and ducked a last-minute invitation to the White House, he too enlisted early in the on-to-Baghdad brigade.

Yet in private conversations and during public appearances, I picked up a persistent sense that the first major war of the twenty-first century failed to arouse the passions of either pro-war candidate. Some suspect that Gephardt, who voted against the 1991 Gulf War, had made the calculation that supporting the

Iraq war was good politics—and then was chagrined to find himself on the wrong side of the Democratic fault line. With Edwards, never much of a world traveler before he was elected to the Senate, it was more subtle. After he won a politically useful seat on the Senate Intelligence Committee in early 2001, Edwards was shrewdly advised by Sandy Berger to pay particular attention to terrorism. The North Carolina senator did his homework, convened briefings by experts and developed a veneer of expertise. But you get the feeling that with Edwards this is all book learning; his views seem to be based more on borrowed concepts than on real-world experience.

What was intriguing about both candidates was the dramatically different ways they chose to present their pro-war views to skeptical audiences of Democratic activists. Granted, style has an annoying way of trumping substance in political coverage. But in this case, Edwards's and Gephardt's stylistic differences were far more revealing than the intricacies of their foreign-policy decision making.

The North Carolina senator consistently presented himself as a determined truth teller seeking to win plaudits for his honesty rather than his ideological orientation. If Bill Clinton could denounce Sister Souljah to a black audience in 1992, then Edwards could take on Saddam Hussein in Iowa. You could almost see Edwards calculating: I'm so likable and so nice that I can get away with expressing an unpopular viewpoint as long as no one thinks I'm hiding anything.

On the eve of the invasion, Edwards faced down angry chants of "No war! No war!" at the California state Democratic convention, declaring, "I have the responsibility to have the backbone to tell you directly what my position is." Speaking to an Iowa forum organized by dovish Senator Tom Harkin in the midst of the war, Edwards didn't mince his words: "I believe in this cause. I believe that we're doing the right thing. I know that there are a lot of you who disagree with that. But I believe it is the right and just thing to do." For Edwards, it all came down to Saddam's purported—and now discredited—nuclear-weapons program. "He believes he is entitled to dominate the Arab world, and his ticket for getting there is not chemical and biological weapons, but nuclear weapons," Edwards said. "He can never, ever be allowed to have a nuclear capacity. It's been my position for a long time. It's still my position, and I stand behind it. Period."

Gephardt, to the end, clung to the illusion that somehow the U.N. Security Council would saddle up and save America from a go-it-almost-alone war with Iraq. Not since Woodrow Wilson and the League of Nations had a Democrat placed so much faith in the international community. On a Saturday in mid-March, just four days before the Iraq war began, Gephardt was in Concord, New Hampshire, pounding the drums and sounding the trumpets on behalf of his signature cause: health care. Leaving a plant store where he had just met with the employees, Gephardt was confronted by two anti-war protesters holding an emotionally potent sign: "Our Son Is a Marine—Don't Send Him to War for Oil." Pressed to explain his pro-war position, Gephardt kept talking about his belief in working through the Security Council. One of the protesters asked, "What if the U.N. says no and George Bush says yes?" With his voice dripping with earnest sincerity, Gephardt replied, "I don't want anybody to go to war."

An encounter in the parking lot of a garden store in New Hampshire will never be confused with the serene deliberations of the Council on Foreign Relations. But Gephardt repeated that unrealistic proposition, a stance that was belied by every newspaper headline, at a reception that evening at the home of Peter Burling, the Democratic leader of the New Hampshire state house, who later endorsed him. Asked about Iraq, Gephardt expressed a dreamy, otherworldly view of the recalcitrant Security Council. "Still tonight," Gephardt said, speaking of Bush, "he's trying to get the U.N. lined up. And I hope and pray that he still can. And for those who have given up hope, I urge you to remember that when 1441 [the original Security Council resolution that passed 15–0] was being put together, there was no hope before it got put together."

Listening to Gephardt advocate peace on the eve of a war that he had voted for, I was reminded of a medieval mathematician trying to square the circle. You knew that the endeavor was sheer logical folly, but you had to reluctantly admire his persistence in trying.

The Iraq war became a character test for Howard Dean. He deserves plaudits for his position, which has stood the test of time. But the ungoverned way that the former governor some-times expressed it got him into trouble. As the drums of war reached a crescendo in mid-March, Dean attacked Kerry and Edwards before the left-leaning California Democratic conven-tion for pretending that they were against the war. Kerry could be rightly derided for never uttering the word "Iraq" in his speech, but Edwards, who later received a handwritten note of apology from Dean, unequivocally reiterated his support for the looming invasion.

Another embarrassing moment came in mid-April, a few days after Baghdad fell, during a debate sponsored by the Children's Defense Fund. At one point, Dean offered this grumpy assess-ment of Saddam's ouster: "We've gotten rid of him. I suppose that's a good thing." Rarely have two innocent-sounding words like "I suppose" revealed so much about a candidate. The com-ment—which Dean later unapologetically defended on *Meet the Press*—illustrated the downside of the Dean difference: the can-didate's stiff-necked stubbornness.

The yogurt hit the fan for Dean in late April. *Time* magazine's Karen Tumulty wrote a brief item mentioning that Dean, while visiting the Stonyfield yogurt factory in New Hampshire, said, "We have to take a different approach [to diplomacy]. We won't always have the strongest military." Objectively, Dean was right: America's military prowess is unprecedented and—unless we have entered into what will be known as the Rumsfeld Century—probably cannot be sustained forever. But politically, Joe Trippi had seen the potential danger back in January when he objected to Dean's oft-repeated refrain that another half century of mega-deficits could transform America into a "second-rate nation."

Now that the war was over—and Kerry no longer felt as defensive about his hard-to-explain vote in favor of the Iraq resolution—the senator's camp could finally hit back. Under the signature of communications director Chris Lehane, the Kerry team rushed out an intemperate press release charging that Dean's comments about America's military power raised "serious questions about his capacity to serve as Commander-in Chief." This wasn't the normal jousting of the Invisible Primary; this was the kind of go-for-the-jugular attack that campaigns launch on the eve of the New Hampshire vote. The Kerry thermonuclear response signaled that the Democratic race had already entered its mean season. Hard to believe that just three months earlier in January, Dean had been joyously describing his newfound ability to hurl press releases into the maw of the twenty-four-hour political news cycle.

CHAPTER 8

The Reverend Al

Al Sharpton is forcing me to confront my prejudices. As a New Yorker, I am prejudiced against him because I keenly recall the vitriol and vituperation of this agitator in clerical garb as he echoed the false rape charges leveled by Tawana Brawley. As a political columnist, I am prejudiced against vanity-driven candidates like Sharpton, Carol Moseley Braun and Dennis Kucinich, who deliberately clutter up a presidential race that they have no chance of winning. So I have been following a personal policy of malign neglect, stubbornly ignoring Sharpton and the rest of this no-hope, all-hype contingent on the off chance that someone, anyone, might offer them a TV cable show as an inducement to drop this ridiculous pretense of running for president.

But now in early February in Des Moines, my interview with state Democratic chairman Gordon Fischer ends just minutes before a scheduled Sharpton press conference at party headquarters. It feels ludicrous to drive off in a fit of pique. Jettisoning principle (a familiar occupational hazard), I add another warm body to the Sharpton welcoming party of a dozen local reporters and three television cameras. A pre-press-conference conversation with *Des Moines Register* columnist Rob Borsellino leads to the agreement that our joint membership in the opinion-mongering trade demands that we pose a few Tawana Brawley questions.

Borsellino goes first and immediately finds himself in a no-win argument with Sharpton over the simple statement "You came to national notice during the Tawana Brawley case." Sharpton angrily, and accurately, insists that his initial star turn on Action News came a year earlier during the 1986 protests over a racially motivated murder in the Howard Beach section of Brooklyn. Moments later, I follow up with a softer-worded question premised on the $65,000 civil judgment assessed against Sharpton (and belatedly paid by the reverend's supporters) for defaming a prosecutor as a rapist. Trying to make my point without triggering a second shouting match, I ask in a soothing tone, "Why can't you simply say that you're really sorry that you were wrong in the Tawana Brawley case?"

As I quickly discover, Sharpton is a living rebuke to the adage that you can catch more flies with honey than vinegar. He comes right back at me by declaring, "I don't have the right to say to a young lady that she's lying if she says that's what happened and a hospital says that something happened to her." Then Sharpton irrelevantly veers off into a replay of the Central Park jogger case in which the rape convictions were overturned because of DNA evidence. "What if I told those young men in the Central Park case to apologize," he says, "and now we find out that maybe they were right when they said they didn't do it." Standing there with what I hope is a skeptical expression, I momentarily debate re-entering the fray. But this is Iowa, a place not known for its rambunctious press conferences. So I hold my tongue as a perky TV reporter asks Sharpton—a political figure whose involvement with the soil has hitherto been limited to picketing Korean green-grocers in black neighborhoods—to give his views on farm policy.

Two weeks later, Sharpton won repeated standing ovations at the mid-winter meeting of the Democratic National Committee with clever jibes like claiming that Bush was "the ultimate bene-ficiary of a set-aside program—the Supreme Court set aside a whole election." Unlike his early mentor Jesse Jackson, whose inspirational cadences reflect the moral fervor of the pulpit, Sharpton excels at breathing new life into the nearly moribund tradition of political humor—suggesting to the DNC that anyone but Bush could find Osama bin Laden since "he has made more videos than any rock star in Hollywood." It was easy to grasp why the Democrats could not resist the temptation to cheer Sharpton's lines, such as his dismissal of trickle-down Republican economics: "We never get the trickle, we just get the down." But whether they knew it or not, the 443 members of the DNC were empowering Sharpton by legitimizing him as a leading Democratic orator. The more credibility that party leaders award to this self-created preacher-politician, the more difficult it will be to deal with inevitable demands for, at minimum, a prime-time speaking role at the Democratic Convention.

The logic behind the party leaders' embrace of Sharpton seemed obvious, albeit misguided. They devoutly pray that he will respond to these goodwill offerings by behaving like a good trouper when it is time to coalesce around the de facto nominee. Party chairman Terry McAuliffe told me in early May—underlining the message that he delivered to all the presidential contenders—"I've said to Sharpton that you run and you energize the base and then on March 10, if you're not the nominee, you get out."

The choice of that precise departure date was not accidental. The relentless front-loading of the primary calendar suggests that the presidential race will probably be over after March 2, when a mind-numbing twelve states (including California, New York and Ohio) hold delegate contests. If there is any lingering doubt, it should be dispelled on March 9, when Democrats in Florida and Texas weigh in at the polls. McAuliffe's legitimate fear is that a no-chance candidate like Sharpton will end up behaving like those Japanese soldiers on isolated Pacific atolls who held out for years because they didn't get the message that the war was over. (Neither Kucinich nor Moseley Braun is likely to pose a similarly disruptive threat. For all his strident posturing, Kucinich exists within the traditional political universe as an Ohio congressman. Moseley Braun, the other African American nominally in the race, appears to be doing virtually nothing beyond gracing the dais at multi-candidate forums.)

Although it seems bizarre, now that he has graced the covers of *Time* and *Newsweek*, Howard Dean originally was the presidential contender who went out of his way explicitly to warn McAuliffe that he planned to scrap for the nomination until the Boston convention, heedless of the delegate count or the sentiments of party leaders. That was Dean's blunt message when he met with the party chairman in Vermont in late July 2002. At the time, McAuliffe said to him, "You will get out, Howard. This isn't about you. It's about beating George Bush." Dean, back in September 2002, explained to me the theory behind his planned bitter-end strategy: "Sometimes you nominate somebody because he's the favorite and has lots of money and then you have buyer's remorse." Dean cited the 1976 examples of Senator Frank Church and California Governor Jerry Brown who won a series of late primaries because of Democratic discomfort with presumptive nominee Jimmy Carter. "If I don't win," Dean said, "I'm likely to be the Frank Church and the Jerry Brown of 2004. I just wanted to give Terry fair notice that this was what was going to happen."

How Quickly They Forget Department: Dean was asked by Larry King in August 2003 about a report in *U.S. News* of an unspecified I'll-never-drop-out conversation with McAuliffe. Even though Dean himself first told me the story in a tape-recorded interview—and McAuliffe later confirmed the details—the former Vermont governor denied everything on CNN. "Terry McAuliffe has certainly never had a conversation like that with me," Dean flatly declared. "I checked with my campaign, and I never heard of anybody he had that conversation with in my campaign." Maybe it was temporary amnesia under the TV lights, maybe it was Dean dissembling, but this tiny episode left me feeling unsettled about the candidate I probably agree with the most on the issues.

By the time of the Democrats' first televised debate in South Carolina in early May, I was beginning to feel uncomfortable with my stiff-necked refusal to acknowledge Sharpton in other than cursory fashion. As boycotts go, this was not exactly up there with Save the Whales. So I arranged an interview following Sharpton's pre-debate appearance before the South Carolina Democratic convention. Despite the cavernous hall at the state fairgrounds and erratic acoustics, Sharpton roused that midafternoon crowd out of its torpor with a speech that encapsulated his challenge to the Democrats: "The way to move a donkey is to slap the donkey. I'm going to slap the donkey 'til the donkey kicks and we kick George Bush out of the White House. I'm going to slap the donkey!"

Minutes later, we were in the candidate's car heading for what a local supporter promised was the best soul food restaurant in Columbia. I asked Sharpton to explain his provocative slap-the-donkey rhetoric. "To motivate people you have to have sound policy," he said, "but you also have to have phrases they can relate to. And all the way up the aisle today after I spoke, every other person said to me, 'Slap the donkey.'" Crushed in the back-seat with Sharpton's aides, I obligingly nodded as this self-appointed donkey slapper launched into his routine rap about the need to mobilize "new voters, disaffected voters, young voters." As Sharpton put it, "The hip-hop generation, a lot of them don't even know these guys [the other candidates] and they don't trust career politicians."

Reflecting my new suck-up style, I mockingly suggested that the hip-hop generation—with which I was so familiar—had been eagerly following everything in Dick Gephardt's career. It got the desired laugh as Sharpton responded, "You said it, I didn't." At this point, our local guide discovered his favorite soul food restaurant was closed and suggested a detour to another eatery with a less memorable menu. "I ain't eating anyway," Sharpton announced, "so it doesn't have to be good."

Curious how the candidate would respond, I passed on McAuliffe's expectation that Sharpton would obligingly withdraw from the race after the early March primaries anointed a nominee. "I appreciate Terry wanting to strong-arm people to support me on March 2 or March 9," Sharpton responded, savoring his own joke. "But we should let democracy run its course. Clearly, at the end of the convention, we should all support the nominee, but I don't think we should try to infer bossism before that. A lot of people want to go to the convention for the person they voted for. And I don't think we should turn them off as we try to turn them on." His use of the word "bossism"—a New York City political epithet dating back to the days of Tammany Hall— signaled that the dewy-eyed Democratic dreamers who assume that the new mainstream-model Sharpton would settle for a confetti-drenched hug from the nominee at the end of the Boston convention were in for a rude awakening.

As I discovered, Sharpton is more than just a poseur with James Brown hair and custom-tailored suits. Confounding my one-dimensional image of his candidacy, Sharpton out of nowhere offered me a gift-wrapped set of insights about the other Democratic contenders. Calling on his backstage observations from a half dozen multi-candidate forums, he observed, "The ones who are the most comfortable have been Lieberman, Gephardt and I. Probably because Lieberman and Gephardt have run nationally and are used to it. Me, because I've always been in the middle of some kind of give-and-take and controversy. The others seem a little nervous and trying to find their way."

Smiling broadly, Sharpton went on to describe watching the anxious first-time candidates rehearse by "trying to cram down that last leather-bound looseleaf binder." In contrast, he said, "Joe Lieberman kind of laughs and chuckles. He and I probably disagree more on policy stuff than anybody in the race, but he has a congeniality, a comfort level, because he has done this before. And he's a nice person. Gephardt is the same way." After Dean put out an over-the-top press release attacking Gephardt's health-care plan, Sharpton whispered to the congressman at a candidates forum a few days later, "And you thought that I'd be the disruptive one."

About then, we arrived at Bert's Grill, a pretty good soul food restaurant with a great slogan: "When You Can't Get Home to Mama Come to Bert's." No-food-for-me Sharpton and aides Frank Watkins and Marjorie Harris loaded their plates with fried chicken before beginning a relaxed session of debate preparation. Watkins, who was Jesse Jackson's top adviser during his 1984 and 1988 presidential races, began instructing Sharpton—"There will be one and a half million retiring teachers in the next two years"—when a restaurant patron wandered over to their table and introduced himself as Daryle Lucas. For the next five minutes, Lucas delivered a passionate, fact-laden defense of the conspiracy theories of former Georgia Congresswoman Cynthia McKinney, who lost a 2002 re-election primary, in part, because she suggested that the Bush administration failed to prevent the September 11 attacks because it stood to profit financially from the war on terrorism. After Lucas finally excused himself to head for the men's room, Sharpton said to his luncheon companions, "People underestimate these folks."

I had been hovering on the periphery of the conversation as I waited for a taxi, mostly to get a sense of how Sharpton readied himself for a debate. Spying my notebook, Lucas on his return decided that I was a prime target for a reprise of his pro-McKinney rant. Trapped in a corner with an African American conspiracy theorist who had the intensity of the Ancient Mariner, I attempted to change the subject by asking about his views on the presidential race. "I assume you're for Sharpton," I suggested, aware of the reverend's presumed appeal to black voters in South Carolina. After making sure that Sharpton wasn't watching, Lucas shook his head no. "You know the guy who I want to see

on the Democratic ticket?" he asked in a tone designed to elicit
surprise. "It's John Edwards. You know he'd beat Bush. He's a
trial lawyer, the stage is his home, he knows theatrics and dra-
matics. John Edwards is the white Jesse Jackson of politics. He's
that fluent in his speech."

Sharpton was right: People underestimate the mainstream
political loyalties of these folks.

Okay, I will admit it, I was reluctantly softening toward Sharpton, just as I have in the past toward other talented humbug
artists dabbling on the fringes of politics. (Modesty and a keen
sense of retrospective embarrassment prevent me from quoting a
few columns I wrote about Pat Buchanan around the time he was
winning the 1996 New Hampshire primary.) So journalistic mar-
tyr that I am, I set up a second interview with Sharpton in Des
Moines in late June. This time our meeting place lacked the local
color of Bert's Grill; we were at a cluttered breakfast table in the
coffee shop at the Renaissance Savery Hotel, a few hours before
Sharpton was scheduled to participate in yet another multi-
candidate Democratic cattle show in nearby Newton.

The day before, at a meeting of Democratic state party leaders
in St. Paul, Minnesota, there was talk of trying to arrange a few
presidential debates that would exclude the minor candidates. I
was dubious that any Democrat boasts the courage to stand
between Sharpton and a microphone, but I felt compelled to ask
him about this putative effort to consign him to oblivion. "If you
look at the most recent CNN poll," he said, "I'm ahead of
Edwards, I'm ahead of Graham, I'm ahead of Dean." (A late May
USA Today/CNN/Gallup Poll indeed showed Sharpton at 7 percent, even with Edwards, and ahead of Dean and Graham.) "So
one of the interesting things to me in this campaign is how do
you decide first-tier candidates," Sharpton said, relishing the statistical quandary for the Democrats. "Because, according to the
polls, I'm a first-tier candidate. Now they say, 'We don't think

Sharpton can be elected.' But the question becomes, if I can't be elected, and these guys are lower than me in the polls, then what makes them electable?"

Maybe it's a symptom of (campaign) trail fever, maybe it's a narcotic reaction triggered by overdosing on applause, but even candidates like Sharpton concoct private victory strategies. So I had to listen to his loving rendition of the primary schedule with an emphasis on that period in early February when lily-white Iowa and New Hampshire give way to states with large minority populations such as South Carolina, Missouri and Michigan. "If the polls are in any way correct," he said, "we can be, if not the nominee, a very serious deciding factor." All I could think about was a Superman comic book from my childhood in which a cosmic trickster from another dimension gets elected mayor of Metropolis by magically making the hands of all the voters slip as they were pulling the ballot-box levers. That's the only way we will ever hear Sharpton's acceptance speech at a Democratic Convention. Sensing my skepticism, Sharpton added, "Let me say in answer to your real question, I will be at the Boston convention and I will be in every primary all the way through." I made a mental note to send McAuliffe a box of antacids and a container of headache powder.

My fascination with Sharpton was beginning to flag, so I moved in a different artistic direction and asked him whether the campaign was fun. "I always have fun," he said with uncharacteristic brevity. Well, in the hierarchy of your fun life, how does this rate? "It's tedious work," he said. "I don't want to downplay that. But when you say are you having fun, it's up there." Then, to underscore how far he has come from his days as a street corner rabble-rouser mouthing off to a lone TV camera, Sharpton said it twice more, savoring every syllable, "It's up there. Yes, it's up there."

That afternoon in Newton, Sharpton had the crowd laughing with glee as he declaimed, "Bush can't even find the weapons of mass destruction that he claimed that he had evidence of. But at least he's being consistent, since I can't find the votes that made him president of the United States." But my mind wandered during the questioning of the serious candidates (John Kerry, Dick Gephardt and John Edwards), who had reached that level of artistry in which they reflexively responded to any query with an unrelated string of practiced catchphrases. Asked about Bush's education record, for example, Edwards within seconds was talking about the glories of a nation where "the son of a mill worker can run against the son of a president of the United States."

The mostly gray-haired audience in the high-school gym was dominated by UAW members petrified that the local Maytag plant will close. Trade agreements like NAFTA may be an abstraction to most voters, but here in central Iowa they symbolize the ease with which good union jobs can be shifted to Mexico with the stoke of an uncaring executive's pen. No one pandered to the crowd like Kucinich, who vowed that his first act as president (ha!) would be to repeal NAFTA. I found myself struggling with equal-opportunity guilt over my instinctive avoidance of Kucinich, this short, left-wing vegetarian firebrand with slicked-down black hair.

Didn't he warrant a brief whirl on my dance card? So I listened as the former failed mayor of Cleveland railed against the iniquities of the Bush administration. "This is not their land," he declared, "this land belongs to you and me. And I can't think of any better way to conclude this than to ask you to send that message to the Bush administration and all of America as we recapture who we are." Then, to my gape-jawed horror, Kucinich began singing, "This land is your land, this land is my land . . ." By the time the off-key Kucinich got to the "Gulf Stream water," I vowed that life was too short to bother probing the essence of this troubadour of political irrelevance.

Al Sharpton was enough for any political reporter.

CHAPTER 9

In Which the Candidates Define Themselves

Eli Attie, a young coproducer of *The West Wing,* looks like every other Hollywood writer as he pulls up in front of the Four Seasons Hotel in Los Angeles. Under Attie's arm is the telltale badge of his trade: a sixty-page printout on three-hole script paper held together with fasteners. The industry-savvy hotel parking attendant immediately grasps the implications of this sheaf of paper and calls out, "Good luck with your script meeting."

The early February 2003 script meeting has everything to do with the West Wing (potentially), even if Attie has momentarily put aside his commitment to President Bartlett. Attie, who was Al Gore's chief speechwriter during the 2000 campaign, is about to reenter the real-life world of presidential politics. The TV writer's sixty-page "script" is really a compilation of a Democrat's policy positions and stump speeches—printed out on the only paper used in the fax machines of *The West Wing.* And the candidate who will be joining Attie for a drink at the Four Seasons is far more Heartland than Hollywood.

Dick Gephardt, that straight-arrow Midwesterner whose TV viewing habits revolve around satellite broadcasts of St. Louis Cardinals games, is a man of tribal loyalties. His favorite wordsmith during his long congressional career was Attie, who got his start in politics writing fiery speeches for Gephardt during the combative days when Newt Gingrich and his revolutionary cadre had seized the Capitol. So it should not have been surprising—though it was to Attie—when Gephardt phoned in early January to say, "I'm running for president, and I'd love it if you'd write my announcement speech."

The announcement speech is the most overt act of self-definition in any presidential campaign. This is the moment when the candidate first stands in the spotlight to enunciate the themes, the issues and the message designed to carry him to the nomination. Attie understands his responsibility: "There isn't another moment until your convention speech when you're judged on having presidential-level rhetoric." But Gephardt needed something more transcendent than just sonorous words to explain why he is seeking the presidency after failing in four successive congressional elections to become Speaker of the House. To a far greater degree than his rivals, Gephardt demands redefinition. He must become something more than that familiar figure from Capitol Hill railing stridently, but vainly, against the GOP legislative agenda. As Steve Elmendorf, his congressional chief of staff, put it back in December, "Gephardt has to come out of the box with a message that is some combination of big and new. He will not be successful if people view him as inside the same congressional box that he was in. If he comes across like that, his opponents are going to paint him as the second coming of Bob Dole."

But how do you reinvent white bread? Gephardt is never going to be credible masquerading as raisin bread with cinnamon swirls, let alone pretending to be an authentic hand-rolled croissant. Sure, you could revamp the packaging, gussy up the label with a fancy logo and emblazon the loaf with a catchphrase: "New and Improved!" But Gephardt's image problems would not be solved with such snappy sales gimmicks. The challenge is to find the words that would present the candidate as the best possible version of Dick Gephardt—words that would remind

Democrats why, despite the allure of gourmet bakery products, they still crave white bread.

In his *West Wing* incarnation, Attie resides in a world where, as he describes it, "the music swells as you're making big decisions about the fate of the country." Attie is about to help make big decisions about the fate of Dick Gephardt. But there is no orchestral accompaniment, aside from the clinking of ice cubes and the murmur of nearby cell phone conversations, as he sits down with the candidate and LA-based media consultant Bill Carrick. The quick drink turns into a leisurely dinner with an animated Gephardt quizzing his former staffer about the writer's life far from the madding press releases. Only gradually does the topic veer toward the February 19 rollout speech in St. Louis, which Attie has been intermittently working on after a preliminary brunch with Carrick. Some things are obvious: Gephardt's life story has to be organically connected to his quarter century in Washington. The candidate intends to lambaste the Bush record, but in a "holistic way," a favorite Carrick phrase. Gephardt wants to stress that government must provide a way for people to succeed on their own—a concept that Attie dubbed the "Fourth Way" in contrast to Bill Clinton's "Third Way" between liberalism and conservatism. The most vigorous debate is over Gephardt's insistence that the speech contain specific policy proposals (the Big Ideas that Elmendorf referred to). Attie initially resists but eventually bows to the guiding principle of all successful political ghostwriters: It's his speech—not yours.

After the dinner, planned as Attie's only face-to-face meeting with Gephardt, the writer is left blessedly alone to produce the speech. While the drama of the part-time speechwriter hunched over his computer is undoubtedly electrifying, we will reluctantly turn our gaze elsewhere—to Carrick, the bearded South Carolinian who was the campaign manager for Gephardt's failed 1988 presidential race. The media consultant quickly put together the ultimate Gephardt home movie, both to assist Attie and to provide grist for the campaign's pollster: just the candidate in a suit and white shirt sitting in front of an unadorned blue backdrop responding to Carrick's questions. As Carrick explained, "I thought we ought to get Dick on tape just talking about the issues that he wanted to talk about and his own personal involvement in them."

Instead of the flag-draped razzmatazz of a thirty-second spot, the thirty-minute edited version of that performance offers a sidewalk engineer's tour of a presidential campaign as a construction zone. All the raw material is here—Gephardt's steely determination, the political career assembled brick by brick, the concrete policy positions—but it is all stacked around the gaping hole of an unfinished excavation. Some of the building blocks are starkly personal. Gephardt talks in a clipped but emotional tone about his son's brush with death: "1972. Matt was diagnosed with terminal cancer. Complete shock to us. We had no idea that there was anything wrong with him ... That was devastating to us." But in politics, autobiographical details must carry a larger message—so, on the tape, you can hear Carrick gently prodding, "What did you learn from that about the health-care system?" Taking his cue, Gephardt talks about the other, less fortunate, parents he met at the children's cancer center who were struggling to pay for chemotherapy without health insurance. "I will never forget the terror in their eyes," he says. "It should not happen to anyone in this country."

But Gephardt recounted another aspect of his personal story in a manner that redefined the word "soporific." His advisers knew they had to turn his lengthy congressional career into an asset—otherwise, as Carrick believed, "we will have malpracticed." But the candidate's words on the tape cry out for radical surgery. Gephardt may have spent half a lifetime in Congress, but his flat, uninflected description of the experience conjures up Bob Dole without the humor, Lyndon Johnson without the earthiness: "I became Majority Leader in 1989 and Minority Leader in 1995 ... I learned a tremendous amount from that experience. I learned the issues. I learned what you can pass and what you can't pass. I learned a tremendous amount about foreign policy."

Gephardt's advisers were vexed by another section of the tape.

It comes when the candidate, with his hand over his heart, tries to crystallize the unifying theme of his campaign. "My philosophy is that we're inter-dependent, tied together, and we've got to help everybody succeed so we can all succeed," he says. "The Republicans think we're all separate and you've got to take care of yourself. I don't believe that." Carrick stage whispers, "The Martin Luther King quote." Like a veteran actor responding to his prompter, Gephardt obligingly recites, "As Martin Luther King once said, 'I can't be what I ought to be until you are what you ought to be.'"

For a presidential candidate to be what he ought to be, he, of course, requires a pollster. Enter Ed Reilly, Gephardt's 1988 pollster, who had been working primarily for corporate clients in New York. To test-market the themes of the announcement speech, Reilly took the Carrick tape, chopped it into bite-sized segments and showed it to ten focus groups in Iowa, New Hampshire and South Carolina. Like the rest of Team Gephardt, Reilly had a hidden agenda: to convince the candidate to get rid of what Carrick called "this inter-connectedness shit." Gephardt had been using the "we are all tied together" passage to end his stump speeches and now wanted to give it a starring role in the rollout address. As Reilly explained, "In any campaign, you have that list of bad ideas that come up from the candidate, his spouse, his family, the fund-raisers. It's not worth the pain to blow these ideas out of the water yourself. You let the focus groups do that."

Beth Campbell, the New Hampshire SEIU official, once again played her Zelig-like role in presidential politics. When Campbell heard that union members were needed for an unspecified political focus group, Campbell eagerly volunteered even before she learned that the session would pay $75. The eight-person mid-February group grope in Londonderry began with a general discussion of leadership before the facilitator asked for initial impressions of Kerry, Lieberman, Edwards, Dean and, yes, Gephardt. Then Campbell and Company watched the Gephardt tape in three-minute chunks as the moderator paused after each snippet to ask the group to discuss what they had just seen and to rate it on a 1 to 5 scale. One segment, in particular, triggered an enthusiastic response: Gephardt talking about inter-connectedness. The group's final exercise was to draw a picture of Gephardt. Campbell sketched the candidate with a union insignia on his shirt and an arrow pointing to his face with the legend "No eyebrows."

So much for research. Campbell's focus group was not an aberration: Gephardt's homily about inter-connectedness scored well everywhere. A rueful Carrick admitted, "All of us cynical guys were wrong. That was all Dick. Shame on us that we missed it." Before the St. Louis speech, Reilly also conducted a national poll for Gephardt. "It was just a temperature check," Reilly explained. "I used the poll to see if you didn't have a false positive or a false negative." Attie, however, was sheltered from the hurly-burly of polls and focus groups as he worked on the speech draft. Carrick sent him the Gephardt tape, which the speechwriter mined for the section on the family. Attie, for example, lifted virtually verbatim the candidate's description of the financial plight of one of his two daughters, Kate, an underpaid teacher. But Attie, who had written about Matt's cancer before, neglected to use Gephardt's description of "the terror in the eyes" of the parents without health insurance in the speech text he submitted on February 13, just six days before it was scheduled to be delivered. Carrick, in a rare intrusion, pointed out that the missing line had the imprimatur of the focus groups. Attie obligingly wove it into the fabric of the speech.

Dick Gephardt had practiced the speech with a TelePrompTer three times: in snowbound Washington over the weekend and in St. Louis on the morning of February 19. But moments before he would stride onto the flag-draped podium erected in the packed gymnasium of his old elementary school, the candidate was overcome by emotion. Gephardt could not bear to watch the speaker who was introducing him: "If every voter would know him as I do, we'd win in a landslide." It was his son Matt, now married and living in Atlanta. So many memories revolve around Matt, the child who was special to Gephardt in so many ways that he cannot articulate. It was not just cancer. It was also the long years that Gephardt and his wife, Jane, worried that Matt would be psychologically damaged by his childhood ordeal. Gephardt also carried the burden of his mortally ill mother, Loreen, about to turn ninety-five and enfeebled by a heart ailment and afflicted with lung cancer. She was here to watch a kickoff of her son's campaign—but would not live to see its win-or-lose conclusion. But such tearful ruminations had to wait. As Matt concluded, "Ladies and gentlemen, my father, Congressman Richard Gephardt," the grinning and waving candidate, with Jane by his side, entered his childhood gym for his Big Moment.

The speech started slowly with memories of Mason Elementary School before Gephardt hit his trademark autobiographical riff: "My dad was a milk-truck driver, a proud member of the Teamsters . . . My mother was a secretary. Neither of my parents finished high school. They didn't have much money." Then an initial quick flick at his focus-grouped theme song, as Gephardt said, "We're all bound together. We're all members of the American family." Gephardt gathered energy as he moved into his familiar role of partisan battler decrying the Bush economic record. The lines were good: "I believe in what you might call trickle-up economics," a trope that Attie had lifted from a 1995 speech that he wrote for Gephardt. Radiating union-hall passion, the candidate declared, "I'm running for president because I've had enough of the oil barons, the status-quo apologists, the special-interest lobbyists running amok in the White House."

It was not the second coming of William Jennings Bryan —an I-can't-believe-I've-misjudged-Dick-Gephardt speech that vaulted him into the Democratic pantheon. But it was good, very good, right at the outer limits of what Gephardt could ever hope to achieve. Gephardt told Matt's story, this time describing one set of parents without health insurance and how he would never "forget the terror in their eyes." He used Matt as a bridge to introduce his road map to reach the Democratic version of the Holy Grail: a bold and expensive tax-credit proposal to provide health insurance for all workers. Gephardt went on to launch the other arrows in his quiver of policy proposals from portable pensions (yawn) to a global minimum wage (it tested well in focus groups). Finally he was back at the Martin Luther King quote and how "we're all bound together. If a child doesn't have health insurance, we pay the price when she shows up at the emergency room. If a child drops out of school and joins a gang, or goes on welfare, we all pay the price of violence, dependence and indulgence."

In this throng of longtime supporters standing ovations came cheaply, since there were no chairs. After forty minutes, as his audience began rocking back and forth to ease leg strain, Gephardt still hadn't discussed his congressional career or directly confronted his shopworn, creature-of-Capitol-Hill image. Then it came with a rush—and instead of prattle about the "tremendous amount" that he had learned, there was Attie's speechwriting artistry. "I'm not going to say what's fashionable in politics," Gephardt said, raising hopes of surprises ahead. "That I'm a Washington outsider, that I couldn't find the nation's capital on a map, that I have no experience in the highest levels of government." After a one-sentence nod to experience, Gephardt reached the Promised Land—the passage that would define his candidacy. "I'm not the political flavor of the month," he said. "I'm not the flashiest candidate around. But the fight for working families is in my bones. It's where I come from. It's been my life's work."

During the first months of 2003, the Democratic contest was not yet the horse race it would later become with the consultants and the handlers spurring their mounts toward the finish line. What this early phase resembled more than anything was an old-time vaudeville circuit with the candidates playing the same houses in places like Manchester and Des Moines, but on different nights. After these tours of "the sticks," the presidential contenders would be summoned back to Washington for a joint appearance, the equivalent of playing the Palace for impresario E. F. Albee and all the leading critics. The NARAL convention in late January—a command performance that underscored the sway of abortion-rights activists over the Democratic Party—was the first time that the entire presidential field (then a manageable six-pack) shared the same stage. After NARAL came another big event: the two-day convocation in late February of the Democratic National Committee. These 443 automatic "superdelegates" to the 2004 convention heard speeches from every member of the presidential field (now a full nine-man baseball team of ambition), save for the recuperating John Kerry (prostate cancer) and Bob Graham (heart surgery).

By chance, Gephardt was to speak to the DNC just two days after his announcement speech. Even if anti-war sentiments were not rising to a crescendo, this would be a tough crowd for the hawkish Gephardt to woo. DNC members felt affection for Gephardt, but they pragmatically viewed him as a failed congressional leader rather than an onward-to-victory-in-November presidential nominee. For Gephardt to have a chance to succeed, that skepticism had to give way to a reinterpretation of his political persona. The magic charm of the St. Louis speech would seem like a short-lived conjurer's trick if the candidate followed up with a faltering performance to the DNC. For Gephardt, it was repeat or retreat.

The candidate, who had just returned to Washington after a quick rollout tour to Iowa, New Hampshire and South Carolina, was upbeat. In his congressional office the morning of the DNC speech, Gephardt confidently announced that he was comfortable enough with the twenty-minute condensed version of his announcement speech to operate without a prepared text. "I think we should just wing this thing," he said. Carrick argued for the

TelePrompTer: "Dick, you've been on the road and you're tired. This will help you keep focused." Gephardt responded dubiously, "Are you sure?" The candidate's other advisers were Tele-PrompTer true believers. So Gephardt rehearsed with the ubiquitous device that looks to the uninitiated like twin see-through music stands, but allows a speaker to follow a projected text as his gaze rhythmically shifts from left to right. An aide rushed the computer disk for the TelePrompTer over to the Hyatt Hotel on the other side of Capitol Hill, the site of the DNC meeting. But there was a slight hitch—when Gephardt arrived at the Hyatt, just minutes before the speech, an apologetic DNC staffer announced that the disk was incompatible with the TelePrompTer system. Moments later, in the elevator heading down to the ballroom where the DNC was assembled, Carrick joked, "Well, Dick, maybe you're right. Maybe you ought to wing the speech."

Gephardt is not Bill Clinton, who flawlessly improvised during a State of the Union Address when the wrong speech was inserted into the TelePrompTer. Although there were a few boos because of his Iraq stance, Gephardt did well with a speech text consisting of a few phrases hastily scrawled on the back of a press release. Because Gephardt knew his message, his self-confidence was compelling, even if the speech lacked the polished precision of Attie's prose. There were a couple of minor snafus. Only after Gephardt detailed his health care plan did he backtrack to talk about Matt's cancer and to recall "the terror in the eyes" of the other parents. He got away with announcing flatly, "My ideas come from twenty-six years in the U.S. House of Representatives. I learned a lot from those years." Still, he ended with a flurry of passion as he declared that his success in life, as the son of a milk-truck driver, underscores the truth that "we are all bound together." With his voice rising and his syntax falling by the wayside, Gephardt declared, "I want to be a president in that Oval Office who every day I walked into that office what I have in my heart and my mind is the aspirations and the dreams and the potential of people like me."

Like so much during the Invisible Primary, the ripple effects from the Gephardt announcement address and his ad-libbed DNC speech were subtle. Gephardt media adviser Laura Nichols said proudly, "In the span of a week, we went from old face to seasoned and experienced." But it was more complex than that. In an effort to reach beyond traditional political settings, Nichols booked Gephardt in early March on the *Daily Show* on Comedy Central. After thirty minutes of friendly political banter, host Jon Stewart turned to Gephardt and said with surprise, "Let me tell you something honestly. I had no idea that you had this kind of passion in you. You have fire in your belly, sir. I watch you on C-Span and [here Stewart adopted a deliberate monotone] it's just bill no. 5–14–3." Bingo! That second look, the notion that this veteran legislator was more than just another blue suit on C-Span, was what Team Gephardt had been questing for all along.

From the days of the born-in-a-log-cabin mythology that helped elect William Henry Harrison in 1840 to the small-town-boy portrayal of Bill Clinton as "the man from Hope" in 1992, presidential candidates have hawked their humble beginnings to suggest that only rutted roads lead to the White House. No line is more important in defining Gephardt's political persona than his proud boast "My father was a milk-truck driver." It's his calling card. It's his way of forging emotional bonds with the voters that conveys the implicit message: "I, and I alone, instinctively understand your struggles, your values and your aspirations."

The problem for Gephardt is that he is not alone in claiming such a populist pedigree. John Edwards possesses an equally glittering up-from-the-working-class heritage, which he brandishes to full effect: "My dad worked in a mill all his life, and my mother's last job was working for the post office." The youthful-looking North Carolina senator does not dwell on the $25-million fortune he made as a trial lawyer. He glides over this pesky detail as he strains to create a linkage connecting his parents, his hard-scrabble legal clients and his goals as a politician. He can be heavy-handed with these I'm-fighting-for-people-just-like-you claims. When he declared his own candidacy in early January 2003 with a nonstop round of TV interviews, Edwards was like a wind-up toy mechanically repeating the script, "I want to be a champion for regular people, the same people I fought for my whole life, people like my own family where I was the first to go to college, where my dad worked in the mill..." Edwards's use of the phrase "regular people" was so incessant that it inspired mocking comparisons to a TV pitchman hawking a new over-the-counter remedy for constipation.

But what about Democrats not lucky enough to be born with a workingman's tin spoon in their mouths? One of the curiosities of the Democratic race is that three leading contenders (Lieberman, Kerry and Dean) all attended Yale University during the 1960s, an educational institution not normally confused with City College. In fact, if Kerry wins the Democratic nomination and runs against fellow Yalie George W. Bush, it will set up the first all Skull and Bones election in American history, a political event certain to send conspiracy theorists into a frenzy of speculation about the hidden machinations of the power elite. Social class is laden with inherent contradictions when it is brandished in Democratic politics. Voters revere the memories of patrician presidents named Roosevelt and Kennedy, even as they crave a candidate who's just like themselves.

Lieberman, the son of a Connecticut liquor-store owner, can rightfully claim to be the product of the meritocracy. That message is emblazoned in oversize lettering on his campaign website: "I feel as if I have been blessed to live the American Dream." When Lieberman formally announced his candidacy in mid-January on a stage at his alma mater, Stamford High School, he said proudly, "It was here [in Stamford] that my parents Henry and Marcia—themselves children of immigrants—worked their way into the American middle class and gave my sisters and me the opportunities they never had."

More than most reporters, I instinctively understood the symbolism behind Lieberman's decision to kick off his campaign surrounded by a melting pot of long-ago high-school classmates. Five years younger than Lieberman, I attended a similar high school in nearby Norwalk. Back in that era, public schools in small Connecticut cities like Stamford and Norwalk came close to replicating the fabled ethnic diversity of a World War II infantry platoon as students named Rooney, Vizi, Cunningham and Shapiro all shared the small classroom. Later, when I talked about Stamford High School with Lieberman, he said, "It was a powerful experience in the diversity and unity of America for me. Most of my friends were not Jewish, but there was no bias. I never experienced a single act of anti-Semitism in my entire youth." The high-school experience was so idyllic for Lieberman that he actually likened it to the old sitcom *Happy Days*. Referring to his classmates who provided the backdrop for his announcement speech, Lieberman said, "The real-life Fonz was actually up there on stage with me."

Autobiography is a bit trickier for Dean and Kerry, candidates whose prep-school classmates were more likely to have trust funds than to be nicknamed "The Fonz." Dean, who grew up on Park Avenue as the descendant of a long line of WASP stockbrokers, handles the problem by rarely referring to anything that happened before he attended medical school. Unlike his rivals, Dean draws his entire campaign narrative from adult life, from his twin careers as a doctor and a governor. With Dean, it's never where I come from. It's always what I have done.

Kerry, whose pre-campaign political action committee (PAC) was called the "Citizen Soldier Fund" defines himself through the duality of his Vietnam experience, the yin and yang of a young medal-draped navy officer who returned home to lead anti-war protests. Flying back to Boston in late October 2002, after a campaign trip to Maine, Kerry began musing about what it would have been like to grow up in a blue-collar Boston suburb like Lynn or Revere. "There are times when I really say to myself that I missed something," confessed the well-born senator, whose father was a diplomat and whose mother belonged to a Bostonian family with a lineage almost worthy of conversation with the Lodges and the Cabots. "Because I didn't have a neighborhood like a lot of kids did. I moved around. But I've made up for it. I've learned a lot about what that was, what that means. I have respect for it. Affection for it. But I can't live there. I'm not going out and pretend. I'm not going to talk about farming in some place because I once dug a hole in a garden."

The question came at the end of a late February interview with Gary Hart, that Banquo's ghost from the 1980s who was toying with becoming the tenth Democrat to enter the presidential fray. The former Colorado senator—who came so close to winning the 1984 nomination and still carries the painful memories of the 1987 sex scandal that derailed his second bid for the presidency—was now sixty-six, and his gray hair had begun to thin with age. But his intellect and his seriousness of purpose remain formidable. Hart had rightfully earned a reputation as a seer. He co-authored the prescient mid-2001 report that warned of terrorist attacks on America. The former senator and I had been talking for an hour about old campaigns and new terrorist threats in the dark bar of Washington's Hay-Adams Hotel, just a short walk across Lafayette Square from the White House of his then-and-now dreams. At the end of the conversation, Hart asked in a soft voice, "Do you think I'm crazy thinking that this period ought to be the ideas period?"

I was embarrassed by the intersection of his earnestness and my world-weariness. My encounter with Hart was already tinged with guilt, for I rode with the press posse that hunted him down for the crime of sailing to Bimini with Donna Rice aboard a boat named *Monkey Business*. I also felt protective of Hart's wispy fantasy that ideas still matter in politics and that his hard-won wisdom about foreign policy and defense strategy could earn him a respectful hearing in the clotted Democratic field. But I couldn't honestly tell him what he wanted to hear. I couldn't portray the early stages of the 2004 Democratic race as a noble struggle of policy arguments with party activists and the press providing a rapt audience. In presidential politics there is a vast chasm between what ought to be and what is. Ideas, aside from the deep rifts over Iraq, were no longer how serious candidates defined themselves. And a grudging acceptance of that reality may have contributed to Hart's subsequent decision not to run.

It is not that the Democrats have collectively decided that, in an age of Bushian platitudes, intellectual rigor is an impediment to power. Most of the leading presidential contenders have followed Bill Clinton's 1992 pre-primary strategy of delivering what are billed as "major policy addresses" to undergird their campaigns. From a Kerry speech on "Citizenship and Service" to a Lieberman presentation called "Creating Factories of the Future" and an Edwards oration about "Revitalizing Rural America," the candidates have not deliberately shied away from substance. In August Edwards released a sixty-five-page booklet of his detailed issue prescriptions entitled *Real Solutions for America,* clearly modeled after Clinton's 1992 collection, *Putting People First.*

Now for the problem: Democrats sound eerily alike on most domestic issues. Instead of zesty policy debates, it's bring in the clones. The candidates all stoutly oppose the Bush tax cuts for the wealthy and want to use the budgetary savings to provide health care for uninsured Americans. They worship at the shrine of Clinton-era balanced budgets and angrily decry the fiscal recklessness of the Bush administration. For the Democrats, energy independence is a sacrament and affirmative action is the birthright of the disadvantaged.

There are differences at the margins—distinctions that are sure to be exaggeratedly portrayed in attack ads as symbolic of character flaws as the primaries draw closer. Dean and Gephardt, for example, stand alone in their determination to roll back virtually all the Bush tax cuts, instead of docilely supporting fiscal relief for the middle class. The candidates' health-care plans can be neatly arranged in newspaper charts by the magnitude of their ambition: Gephardt's $200 billion-a-year tax-credit plan lies at one end of the spectrum and Edwards's $53 billion-a-year child-centered proposal at the other. But pardon my refusal to portray these varying approaches to health care as a titanic struggle for the soul of the Democratic Party. Forgive my reluctance to become bogged down in a debilitating debate over the proper tax rate for a family of four in Phoenix with $57,000 in income, a small 401-K plan and two children in middle school. For after too many campaigns and too many position papers that were forgotten after the election, I cling to the stubborn belief that these minor programmatic disputes reveal little about how any of these Democrats would govern as president.

What most primary voters will remember is that all the Democrats sound alike in excoriating the Bush economic record and earnestly pledging that when they are elected parents will no longer have to lie awake at night worrying about how to pay for a doctor's visit for a sick child. The duplication in the candidates' agendas for the nation's future is so great that you can almost imagine vendors roaming the early primary states shouting, "Hey, cold beer, peanuts, position papers! You can't tell the players without a scorecard." During the same week in mid-March 2003, three White House aspirants made major addresses delineating their prescriptions for the nation. So here's a snap quiz to deconstruct the Democrats. Step into your isolation booth, furrow your brow as the band plays "thinking" music and identify which candidate offered these predictable policy maxims:

1.   "I want an economy in this country where we create jobs that don't move offshore. I want an America that has health insurance for everybody."

2. "Energy independence is critical to the long-term national
    security of the United States."
3. "Before September 11, this administration's central
    domestic policy was budget-busting tax cuts for the
    wealthy. Today, even as the bill for those tax cuts contin-
    ues to climb ... and families are struggling to make ends
    meet, what is the administration's central domestic pol-
    icy? Budget-busting tax cuts for the wealthiest Ameri-
    cans."

I'm sorry, time's up. The correct answers are (1) Howard Dean,
(2) John Kerry and (3) John Edwards. But these words could just
as easily have been spoken by Joe Lieberman or Dick Gephardt or
Bob Graham. It's all so random. That's the fun of playing Deconstruct the Democrats: The Game of Interchangeable Oratory.

Why this barrage of boilerplate? There's a two-word explanation: Bill Clinton. The forty-second president transformed the
Democrats into the party of fiscal responsibility; his most glittering tax cut was the dramatic expansion of the Earned Income Tax
Credit (EITC), which freed working Americans a notch or two
above the poverty line from any federal income-tax burden. Clinton's most galling failure, of course, was the congressional rebel-
lion against his 1994 health care plan. So it was inevitable that
any Democrat running for president in 2004 would cleave to the
Clinton record on the budget and taxes, while lifting high the
soiled banner of health-care reform for all Americans. But Clinton also bequeathed something else to his party: issue advisers.

Whenever a major "new ideas" speech loomed on the horizon
in the early days of the campaign, a Washington-based candidate
would invariably instruct his staff, "Talk to Bruce and Gene."
That's Bruce Reed, who was Clinton's chief domestic policy
adviser, and Gene Sperling, the former White House economic
coordinator. Veterans of the 1992 campaign and all eight years of
the Clinton administration, they are the Gilbert and Sullivan of the

Democratic Party, effortlessly composing witty and tuneful variants on familiar party themes. Reed and Sperling are equal-opportunity policy mavens, dispensing unpaid policy guidance to any serious candidate who seeks it. Reed, now the president of the Democratic Leadership Council, laughingly described their role in helping the candidates frame their opening-gun speeches on the economy: "We provided a number of people with the same lack-luster advice. There was a similarity to the arguments they all made, but that probably would have happened even if Gene and I had called in sick that day." But there was a yawning ideas gap, stemming from too many candidates needing to make too many speeches. Calculating that the major contenders each required a minimum of five major domestic policy addresses, Reed wondered, at the risk of sounding immodest, "How can we fuel twenty-five speeches when Gene and I have maybe five big ideas?"

The Democratic candidates are a bit like the Israelites who were handed a Holy Writ to guide them in their wanderings through the political desert. Instead of the Ten Commandments, it's the playbook from the 1992 Clinton campaign. You can hear echoes of the only two-term Democratic president since FDR in the words of all of them, most notably those of work-hard-and-play-by-the-rules Clinton disciple John Edwards. Appearing before the DNC in February, Edwards began his speech with a classic Clintonian conceit: "Across America, every day, most people go to work believing that hard work will earn them a chance to get ahead. Every day, they try to do the right thing for their families and on the job, because they believe that's more important than making a quick buck." A leading Democratic consultant put it like this: "In one way or another, all the candidates are still using some version of the rhetoric that Bill Clinton introduced in 1992. The exception is Howard Dean, who has a very blunt, apolitical way of speaking. Dean has found fresh language and a new way of talking about things that, at least, is different."

* * *

Howard Dean was exasperated. Meeting with his Burlington-based campaign staff in late January to plot out his travel plans, he moaned, "What's happened to the schedule? It's out of control." The last-minute invitation to appear before NARAL symbolized Dean's need for a body double. It's madness: Iowa on Sunday, Vermont on Monday, a three-minute speaking slot at the NARAL convention in Washington on Tuesday, then a pre-dawn flight to New Hampshire on Wednesday morning for a long-planned appearance at a retirement home in Nashua. Not even the most desperate traveling salesman, Willie Loman with his bulging sample cases, would tolerate this itinerary from hell. The candidate exuded a palpable reluctance to juggle his travel plans to accomodate NARAL. Dean can be stubborn, but this time his staff got its way.

On the day of the speech, Dean's mood failed to improve when his direct flight from Burlington to Washington was canceled, forcing him to make a mad dash to change planes in Philadelphia. Needless to say, the harassed doctor-turned-governor-turned-presidential candidate didn't spend long hours revising speech drafts and honing his rhetoric in front of a TelePrompTer. Instead, the unflappable Dean limited his preparation to a few minutes in the holding room at Washington's Omni Shoreham Hotel, the site of the gala dinner honoring the thirtieth anniversary of *Roe v. Wade.* Dean followed his standard practice of jotting five key points on a stray piece of paper, punctuated by a single word to remind him of an illustrative anecdote.

The first group visual of Campaign 2004 came as the candidates emerged from the holding room in the order of their speaking positions. Edwards, looking like he was inwardly rehearsing his rhetoric, strode out first, followed by Al Sharpton, Lieberman and Gephardt. Then came the six-foot-four Kerry with his arm draped over Dean's shoulder, maybe eight inches beneath his own shoulder, the Mutt and Jeff of the Democratic Party. As Kate Michelman, the president of NARAL Pro-Choice America, introduced the six Democrats, Gephardt staffers distributed to reporters a prepared text of his remarks. The Missouri congressman, who entered the House in the 1970s as an opponent of abortion, was the only candidate expected to make news. He would offer a sober explanation of his gradual "change of heart and mind" on the issue, as "my eyes were opened ... by friends and colleagues and by strangers, women I didn't know and would never meet again, and by members of my own close family."

But what opened the eyes of the 1,500 abortion-rights stalwarts at the Shoreham were speeches by Sharpton and Dean. The rambunctious reverend from New York, a protest candidate reveling in his sudden elevation to Democratic responsibility, roused the rafters with sure-fire lines like "It's time for the Christian Right to meet the right Christians." When he stepped to the microphone, Dean began by declaring, "I'm going to talk to you as a governor and a doctor." But he soon let rip with a full-throated attack on the Bush administration: "This government is so impressed with itself in promoting individual freedom, they can't wait to get into your bedroom and tell you how to behave." The audience cheered lustily as Dean thundered, "We don't want the government telling us how to practice medicine! The practice of medicine is none of the government's business!"

Okay, Dean was preaching to the converted. But then he abruptly lowered his decibel level and changed his tone. "Let me tell you a story," he said, his voice beckoning the audience to move a little closer to the fire for a good yarn. "As many of you know, I am a doctor and an internist. One time, a young lady came into my office, who was twelve years old. She thought she might be pregnant. We did the tests, and she was pregnant. She didn't know what to do. After I talked to her for a while, I came to the conclusion that the likely father of her child was her own father." Dean paused to allow the tension to build as his rapt listeners contemplated the realities of life in small-town Vermont. Then as his voice filled with angry indignation, Dean delivered his devastating applause line: "You explain that to the American people who think that parental notification is a good idea." By the time Dean finished his eight-minute speech, which was interrupted by applause seventeen separate times, the shock troops of the abortion-rights movement were waving glow-in-the-dark table decorations to light his way toward the White House.

It is almost unprecedented for a single evening during the Invisible Primary to transform a candidacy. But, make no mistake, that was exactly what happened to Dean with his almost canceled NARAL speech. Afterward, Howard Fineman, *Newsweek*'s influential political correspondent, was prompted to write, "I came away from the annual National Abortion and Reproductive Rights Action League dinner the other night with one conclusion: Howard Dean is going to be a player." Suddenly Dean was no longer a former governor from the land of Ben and Jerry, but a plausible rival to Kerry, Gephardt, Edwards and Lieberman. It took a day or two for Dean to grasp the implications of his Cinderella transformation, but he eventually got it. "What those dinners do is that they establish me as a serious candidate," Dean told me three days later during, yes, another trip to Washington. "People have never heard of me before. Then they hear about me from other people, but they don't see me. And when they see me, they realize this is a serious candidacy. Once they realize it's a serious candidacy, because they like the message, they're now free to help."

There was only one flaw in this upbeat narrative. Dean's sad-eyed story about the pregnant twelve-year-old girl was partially deceptive. Worse, Dean didn't fully comprehend how he compromised his credibility by editing and over-simplifying the tale. I will confess that an influential figure in another presidential campaign prompted the questioning of Dean about his NARAL narrative. But when he was asked about what Paul Harvey would call "the rest of the story," Dean said, "I don't want to talk about it. It turned out that the father wasn't the father. But I can't say too much about this because it will lead to an exposure of the girl, which is absolutely wrong."

My desire, obviously, was not to intrude on anyone's privacy.

But I was stunned by Dean's admission that the central salient detail of the anecdote dramatically brandished before NARAL to expose the folly of parental notification (that the girl was impregnated by her father) was incorrect. As Dean explained, "It turned out that she was improperly [sexually abused], but not by her father. Not that I knew at the time." But he did know it when he retold the tale to NARAL. I wondered, as I often do when I catch a candidate embellishing the truth, whether I was being too harsh and judgmental. This was not the equivalent of Ronald Reagan continually citing a fictional "welfare queen" driving around Chicago in her Cadillac. This was also not George W. Bush reciting sixteen deceitful words about African uranium in his State of the Union Address. Something awful did in fact happen to this twelve-year-old girl. For his part, Dean conceded, "I've thought about not using that story any more, though it's so powerful, because I don't want this girl exposed and that could happen."

Self-definition is a tricky affair in presidential politics. The same autobiographical stories that attract voters can, when viewed from another perspective, repel them. It's simpler when campaigns revolve around issues. You can parse position papers and cost-out policy proposals. But the 2004 Democratic race is about personal history and character—and there is no official source like the Congressional Budget Office to rate the candidates based on what they consciously choose to reveal about themselves. Does it matter that Dick Gephardt is a milkman's son and John Edwards's father started as a mill worker? Should we admire John Kerry because he fought in Vietnam, or is the essence of his appeal his later anti-war fervor? Is voting for Joe Lieberman the only way to ensure the survival of the American Dream? And what of Howard Dean, who dramatically demonstrated with a single story both his Marcus Welby-as-politician appeal and his preference for powerful narrative over the literal truth?

Every political leader is a prisoner of his own life experience.

But what a presidential campaign cannot reveal is whether the illustrative tales that candidates tell the voters are the same stories that will be reverberating in their minds, if and when they find themselves brooding alone in the Oval Office. For that is the most elusive truth of all: who the candidates truly are when they are out of the view of the adoring throngs and the ever-inquisitive reporters.

CHAPTER 10

In Which the Candidates Remain Themselves (Despite All Efforts to Package Them into Something Else)

Any Jewish male, with the possible exception of Philip Roth, can identify with Joe Lieberman's tone as he describes his eighty-six-year-old widowed mother, Marcia. Lieberman, of course, projects a good son's love coupled with pride at her live-alone independence: "She works hard to do almost everything. I told her she remains an inspiration in that sense." But there is also a flicker, just a flicker, of boyish Mom-do-I-have-to annoyance, especially when the topic turns to food.

Lieberman and I are in the backseat of his van, that familiar venue for political interviews, on a glistening New Hampshire Monday morning in late April. On the floor next to Lieberman is the ultimate campaign survival kit—a brown paper bag stuffed with Passover rations that his mother pressed on him (you can hear her saying, "Take it with you, Joey, you look thin") after a holiday visit to his childhood home in Stamford, Connecticut. Reaching into this maternal brown bag, Lieberman becomes the first presidential candidate in the proud history of American democracy to ever offer me—or quite possibly any reporter—matzos, saying, "This will probably inhibit your ability to ask serious questions." And then gesturing to an unopened box of kosher-for-

Passover macaroons on the seat next to him, Lieberman adds, with a hint of private amusement, "We also have sweets."

Even during a backseat interview, the senator is a gracious host. But that's Lieberman's style: so amenable, so affable and so damned elusive. It isn't that he bristles with defensiveness or even ducks questions. Rather, Lieberman blesses virtually every query with the same empty compliment, "That's interesting," and then frowns with momentary concentration as he frames his careful answer. With Lieberman, there is a circular quality to the reporter-candidate exchange, since every Q and A brings you right back to where you started. I have been at this game too long to believe that you can achieve anything close to intimacy with a man who is running for president. But I do nurture the conviction that enough time in the backseat of a van and enough off-the-news conversations can produce a level of insight that goes beyond the self-confident certainties of a candidate's sales pitch. Yet here I am, my mouth gummy with matzos and my lap filled with crumbs from the bread of affliction—and the always friendly Joe Lieberman is testing my faith in my reportorial wiles.

Maybe I am unused to a presidential candidate with Lieberman's medium-cool temperament. He's neither pompous nor soporific; his wry-with-corned beef sense of humor prevents him from being equated with über-hawk Scoop Jackson, the 1976 presidential contender often described as so boring he could douse the fire during a fireside chat. At the start of our conversation, I mention to Lieberman that I noticed a hidden religious motif to his Easter Sunday appearance on *Face the Nation,* since he shared the broadcast with a fellow Jew, Bush foreign-policy adviser Richard Perle. Lieberman immediately cracks, "John Edwards is going to do Yom Kippur." But what if Edwards, like John Kerry, discovers he has Jewish ancestors? With a chuckle, Lieberman says, "He seems to be sticking with what we know about him."

For all his Good Humor Man persona, Lieberman, more than any Democrat running, embodies the locker-room sports cliché

"Don't get too high or too low. Just take it one game at a time." Interviewing aides and family members about Lieberman's mood on that fateful mid-December day when Al Gore pulled out of the race, I was struck by similar tales of the senator's well-modulated calm. As his son Matt put it succinctly, "There was no 'Yippie!'"

I repeat Matt's comment to Lieberman, not to glean fresh anecdotes about Gore's withdrawal but to get a better fix on his personality. "Temperament," Lieberman responds, "it's interesting. That day I felt a combination of excitement and seriousness because this was it. I was now faced with this awesome responsibility. So I wasn't jumping up and down. Part of it may have to do with my respect for Al Gore."

Okay, I suggest, maybe that's an atypical example. Lieberman, munching one of Mom's apples, is still mulling the earlier question. "There is no question that I have a more even personality," he concedes. "But I can get high." Somehow, I sense, this is not a coded reference to drug-addled youthful escapades. "I get angry about things. I get happy about things," Lieberman defiantly insists in his soft, slightly quavering voice. "I'm having a great time. It's very demanding, but I'm enjoying it and I do feel a sense of mission and purpose."

At that moment, inflamed with mission and purpose, Lieberman arrives at the high school in Derry, where he will be speaking to a current-events class. As the van pulls to a stop, Lieberman offers a final thought: "Here I am with the opportunity to run for president and to try to make a difference on a scale that I honestly never imagined that I would get a chance do. It's great." Unlike Tony the Tiger who always roared, "It's Gr-r-r-eat!" as he hawked Kellogg's Frosted Flakes, Lieberman pronounces the word "great" without a hint of inflection.

All of us—ordinary voters and out-of-the-ordinary political reporters alike—cannot resist reducing presidents and pretenders to cartoonish caricatures. Ronald Reagan was a dim-bulb actor reading a presidential script; George Bush (good ol' 41) quested after the presidency simply because it was the missing line on his résumé; Bill Clinton, governed by his libido, squandered his enormous talents to his outsize appetites; and George W. Bush wanted to be president both to avenge and transcend his father. Granted, there is an element of truth to these crude portraits, but they also obscure far more than they explain. Both in cocktail-party chatter and daily political coverage, we brandish these facile interpretations with all the subtlety of a pre-schooler trying to jam a round peg into a square hole. Just hit the point harder, we reflexively think, and maybe it'll fit.

I understand the allure of such armchair psychiatry, even if most analytic interpretations come closer to fraud than Freud. The powers that we bequeath to a twenty-first-century president are inherently frightening, whether it is the ability to obliterate Saddam Hussein's regime with minimal congressional oversight or the authority to imprison Americans as "enemy combatants" without a public trial. For all the hype and hoopla of a presidential campaign, the choices that voters make are fraught with unimaginable consequences—and they know it.

Who in their right mind feels comfortable basing this decision solely on gauzy thirty-second commercials and poll-tested speeches that obedient candidates read off the TelePrompTer? Who can derive lasting insight from newspaper charts dutifully listing the candidates' health-care plans? Rightfully suspicious of media manipulation and yet supinely dependent on television and the press for information, voters are desperate to cut through the phoniness of a presidential campaign in search of larger truths about the character of the candidates. Any glimmer of authenticity—a sepia-toned childhood photograph, a brief televised glimpse of a frowning spouse, a flippant remark during a debate—becomes incorporated in an overarching theory, becomes a building block of air castles filled with psychological speculation about the candidates. Even the smallest details can be fraught with symbolic significance. Howard Dean's buttoned-down Brooks Brothers shirts. The brief flap over whether Edwards was chewing gum onstage during the NARAL convention or whether, as his aides insisted, it was a breath mint. Or the bigger brouhaha prompted by John Kerry's too-effete-to-eat request for Swiss cheese, rather than the authentic Cheez Whiz, on his Philly cheese steak sandwich.

With our psychological bent, those of us in the press vans can be described as forever Jung. So much campaign coverage involves listening (to variations of the same speech) and watching (the smiles, the laughs, the handshakes and the back slaps) from afar. When you spend your days with your nose pressed up against the toy store window, you inevitably start wondering about the secrets hidden in the backroom. Journalists know just enough biographical details about a candidate to connect the dots in a graphic that may lack artistic precision but appears close enough to reality for daily deadlines.

As the self-appointed guardians of the entrance to the Oval Office, reporters are constantly alert for any character trait that smacks of Nixonian weirdness or suggests that maybe this guy shouldn't be entrusted with nuclear weapons. That's why the press during the 1980s was so merciless toward Gary Hart—that's why so much was made of his name change (from Hartpence) and his conflicting accounts of the year of his birth. This time around, the *Boston Globe* tried (unsuccessfully in my view) to paint John Kerry as two-faced for sometimes failing to contradict the easy assumption that anyone with his last name had to be Irish. Similarly, nothing makes Bob Graham's advisers more nervous than a protracted discussion of the color-coded notebooks (which I quoted from earlier) that he uses to record the flotsam and jetsam of his public life. Sadly, it doesn't take much of a journalistic leap to go from these quotidian details to psycho-babble about Kerry's identity disorder or Graham's anal-compulsive behavior.

For all my uneasiness about the shock (therapy) troops of the press marching off to cover a campaign carrying analytic couches on their backs, I recognize that a candidate is far more than a walking set of position papers. For me, the relevant distinction is between psychology and temperament. No reporter or profile writer knows enough to plumb a politician's inner psyche, but journalists are equipped with the observational skills to describe his personality and draw conclusions from it. It's the difference between unknowable causation and visible effects. A candidate will spend days huddled with his handlers deciding how to best portray himself on the campaign trail, choosing which biographical snippets to stress and which policies to peddle. But a presidential contender's basic temperament remains an innate and immutable quality that defies the mind-clouding powers of even the most adroit political image makers.

Franklin Delano Roosevelt stumbled onto something of lasting political import when he came before the 1924 Democratic convention to hail New York Governor Al Smith as "the Happy Warrior of the political battlefield." The Happy Warrior sobriquet was lifted by speechwriter Samuel Proskauer from a William Wordsworth poem, and initially Roosevelt dismissed the reference as too literary. But as FDR himself went on to dramatically demonstrate, Americans want their presidents to be jaunty and optimistic, rather than dark and brooding. In modern times, Richard Nixon and maybe Lyndon Johnson are the only exceptions to this Iron Law of Presidential Positivism.

Personality may not be destiny—or the ebullient Hubert Humphrey would have defeated Nixon in 1968. But in presidential primary politics, temperament matters more than any other factor beyond the direct conscious control of the candidates. Voters may not be able to decipher which of the candidates secretly felt inadequate as a child, but they can judge personality. If you were to rate the serious 2004 Democratic contenders on an upbeat-downbeat grid, the enthusiastic John Edwards would easily win the Happy Warrior award as the spiritual descendant of Al Smith, followed by the sublimely confident Howard Dean and the ever-smiling Dick Gephardt. At the other end of the scale are the stiffly senatorial Bob Graham and the long-faced John Kerry. As for Joe Lieberman, he is exactly where his uninflected personality puts him—squarely in the middle.

Like so many in Lieberman's immediate orbit, the crisply efficient Clarine Nardi Riddle goes back a long way. Back to the late 1970s, when Lieberman was a leader in the Connecticut state senate and she was his legislative counsel. When Lieberman went on to become state attorney general, she became his deputy before succeeding him in that office when he was elected to the Senate in 1988. After stints as a Connecticut state judge and a trade-association executive in Washington, Riddle rejoined Lieberworld in early 2003 as the senator's congressional chief of staff for the duration of the campaign. Despite, or maybe because of, her long experience as Lieberman's alter ego, Riddle resorted to all too familiar imagery in describing his workaday personality. "Joe is a wonderful person to work with because he's so even-keeled," she says. "You're not diverted by someone who has highs and lows in temperament."

We were talking behind closed doors in Riddle's interior office as anxious staffers visibly paced in front of a glass wall in hopes of attracting the attention of the senatorial stand-in. But I was not about to yield my seat for the press of congressional business. I had come to see Riddle because I had been toying with a notion about Lieberman. My conceit was that he had developed a public style that used affability as a weapon to keep the intruding world at a safe distance. Like any reporter in the grips of a big theory, I was searching for evidence to fortify my gut instincts. That's why I sprang to attention when Riddle said, "When I first worked for Joe in 1979, he was so quiet that when we talked about bills, I'd have to do all the talking."

It all fit. Lieberman used to be shy and quiet, and the humor is now all part of the facade of the public man. Riddle, though, had scant patience with my insistent theorizing. To her, Lieberman was simply blessed with a good sense of humor. "He enjoys connecting with people," she explained. "Humor is one of the ways that he connects. It's one of his ways of drawing the world closer." Maybe closer, but not too close. Robert Frost might have been speaking for political reporters when he wrote, "Something there is that doesn't love a wall." So I left Riddle's office, still stubbornly convinced that Lieberman uses humor more to wall people out than to draw them in—to safeguard his privacy by deflecting probing questions with a deft quip.

But temperament isn't hereditary, at least in the Lieberman family. Feisty and funny, ditsy and dedicated, Rebecca Lieberman is endlessly exasperated by snap judgments about her father's bland public image. Rolling her eyes in remembrance, she recalled a dinner at an Italian restaurant in Manhattan's Greenwich Village where the couple at the next table began loudly handicapping the Democratic field. She was enraged when she overheard their smug pronouncement: "Lieberman's too conservative. He has no personality." As she put it, "I wanted to go over there and shout at them, 'How could someone with no personality have a child with this much personality?'"

Few reporters would dare ask a candidate's wife a question this blunt. But campaign consultants operate free of the social constraints that govern the work lives of journalists, and media consultant Tad Devine, in the midst of taping commercials for her husband's 1998 Senate race, asked Elizabeth Edwards, "Why did you marry him?" Instead of the usual prattle about a twinkly smile or a good heart or love at first sight, she responded with an answer that captured the essence of Edwards's political appeal: "I married him because he was so optimistic."

Those of us blessed or burdened with an Eastern European Jewish heritage may find it hard to imagine what it must be like to go through life feeling, as Mary Martin did, "When the sky is a bright canary yellow, I forget every cloud I've ever seen." The ancestors of cockeyed optimists didn't live in shtetls. But for a presidential candidate, what a gift of the gods. Imagine waking up every morning fired up with the faith that today you'll raise $100,000, work out the kinks in your health-care plan, corral that elusive endorsement and rouse campaign audiences to a fever pitch. Imagine what it must be like to believe that the inevitable setbacks in a campaign are momentary detours on the road to fulfilling your destiny. But it's more than inner self-confidence. When radiating from a presidential candidate, optimism is contagious; it is the essential quality that convinces voters that, hey, he really means it; maybe this time we'll get a president who does something for me.

TV coaches can teach a candidate how to smile on cue and even how to feign sincerity. But optimism isn't learned behavior; it is bred within the fiber of your being. Edwards has spurned instruction in the black-box arts of projecting well on a twenty-seven-inch screen. But put him in a small room with real-life voters on the right day and it's akin to watching Clarence Darrow address a jury. That's optimism talking. As Elizabeth put it, "John's viewpoint, and it's become the viewpoint in our marriage, is that if there's a problem, you do whatever you need to do to solve it. It's not that it's insoluble and you moan and groan. It's just if there's a problem, you do something about it." So simple, so easy and so baffling to us born pessimists. (A prime illustration of this mindset was Edwards's go-for-broke decision in early September to stop hedging his bets and to unequivocally rule out running for re-election to the Senate in 2004.)

Edwards attributes what he calls his "relentless optimism" to his parents, Bobbie and Wallace, and their mantra that "there's nothing you can't overcome with hard work and knowing who you are." We were sitting in his Senate office and his eyes were rimmed with dark circles from continually getting three or four hours' sleep a night—the pitfalls of relentless, seventeen-hour-a-day fund-raising and living in a household with two small children. Describing his life as an upward arc of unimaginable accomplishment, Edwards began, "Growing up in our family, it was a big thing for me to go away to college. A big thing." He originally enrolled in Clemson on a football scholarship, living with his grandparents in South Carolina, before dropping out after one semester to return home to attend North Carolina State. He majored in textiles—yes, textiles—on the assumption that he would eventually join the management team at a mill. As Bobbie Edwards told my wife Meryl in a 2001 interview, "That's the practical side of him. He wanted something to fall back on."

There were job offers after he graduated, but Edwards wanted to go to law school, a leap he made with the aid of student loans. "When I became a lawyer," he continued, "I remember talking to my parents about how I wanted to be one of the best lawyers in North Carolina, thinking that probably was not reachable, thinking that was not a realistic goal." He began contemplating a political race before his son, Wade, died. "When I decided to run for Senate, no one had ever heard of me. After a lot of hard work, that worked out," Edwards said, glossing over the detail that it was mostly a self-funded campaign. "And the same thing has happened with respect to the presidential race. Each of these steps has been a great surprise."

Listening to this oft-told tale of a seemingly charmed life, my gaze kept returning to Wade's Outward Bound pin in the lapel of Edwards's suit jacket. How, I wondered, does he manage to project a sense of hope for the future after the death of his son? That was the kind of traumatic event that turns any man into Job railing against a merciless God. When Meryl wrote a magazine profile of Edwards in early 2001, Elizabeth told her, "The kind of carefree happiness that we had before is forever gone from our lives. We will never have it back." But as I watched Edwards's smiling face, I also remembered that a *Washington Post* writer recently reduced him to tears by pressing him about his dead son. Such intrusiveness wasn't my natural game, though I did feel compelled to hesitantly mention Wade in the interview. Edwards responded in a quiet, controlled voice, "I just don't think that's something that, even in private, I want to talk about."

I honored his reticence, certain that Edwards would never emulate Al Gore in using the death of his sister from lung cancer to frame a political argument about smoking in a speech to the 1996 Democratic Convention.

Don Marquis—the 1920s newsroom bard who chronicled the sayings of a cocksure cockroach named archy who couldn't reach the shift key on the typewriter—once wrote, "an optimist is a guy/that has never had/much experience." Say what you will about John Edwards. Complain that at age fifty he still comes across as jejune. Sniff that he has no business running for the White House after a Senate career of such brevity and flickering achievement. Grump that he is the willing captive of the trial lawyers who are funding his campaign. But never, ever say that his optimism is based on a lack of real-life experience.

Any interview with a presidential contender during the Invisible Primary involves an elaborate ritual of information sharing, since the contours of the race are so amorphous that both candidate and reporter are looking for validation of their instincts. But none of the candidates is more attuned to the nuances of political gossip than John Kerry. Which was why, with deliberate name-dropping intent, I mentioned to Kerry during a conversation the morning after the campaign's first debate (sponsored by the Children's Defense Fund in mid-April) that I had dinner afterward with fellow columnists Maureen Dowd and Joe Klein. "Wow, I'd like to be a fly on that wall," Kerry said, leaning forward in his armchair in his Senate office. My point in pricking Kerry's how-am-I-doing curiosity was to spark his reaction to a comment by a Midwestern friend of Joe's, a non-political novelist who just happened to be in Washington on her book tour. Having never seen any of the candidates in person prior to the debate, the novelist observed that the tall Massachusetts senator had struck her as a "sad sack." So with that comment in mind, I asked Kerry bluntly, "Are you a happy person?"

Kerry responded, as most of us would, "Absolutely. I'm a happy person." Then he paused, intrigued, and inquired, "Why did that come up? Did somebody suggest that I wasn't a happy person?" Airbrushing last night's dinner conversation, I mention that a non-columnist at the table thought that Kerry came across as "sad." (The telltale term "sad sack" seemed too cruel to repeat.)

God knows, Kerry was entitled to his downcast moments. In the prior six months, he had endured the death of his mother, Rosemary, and surgery for prostate cancer, the same disease that killed his retired diplomat father, Richard, in 2000. As if Kerry's "Annus Horribilis" were not complete, the *Boston Globe* in February 2003 revealed to both the world and Kerry himself that the senator's paternal, Jewish-born grandfather had shot himself in ghoulishly public fashion in the men's room of Boston's Copley Plaza Hotel in 1921.

But in a presidential race, a candidate cannot easily admit to vulnerability. So, reacting to my deliberate provocation, Kerry tried to frame his answer in political terms: "Is there some sadness in my life? Sure. But ask anybody who hangs around with me in my free time. Yes, I'm a happy person. But I'm also a serious person, who gets frustrated when things that ought to be happening and are possible don't happen. It makes me angry. Like kids last night [referring to the Children's Defense Fund]; it makes me angry that kids are neglected."

Most politicians would have left things there. No one can get into trouble seeming depressed over the plight of abandoned children. But even as the conversation drifted toward more predictable political topics (Kerry's pique at Howard Dean), the Lincolnesque senator was clearly troubled by the notion that he projects a sad visage. Being characterized as aloof was something he could handle; in his February press conference announcing his prostrate cancer, Kerry joked that the doctors were planning to remove his "aloof gland."

But being called sad was different in referring not to his mannerisms, but to his essence. It may also speak to the reality that his heritage on his paternal side was not Boston Brahmin, but prone-to-depression Central European Jewish. Kerry tried to explain that he really was not that complicated a person, at least to himself, even while acknowledging that he might be puzzling to some. "Partly, it's because I like to hold on to parts of life that sometimes politics doesn't want to let you hold on to," he said, in a reflective tone that seemed closer in spirit to two guys in a bar late at night than a formal interview. "I like to create a little zone of privacy, where you can be who you are and go off and veg and relax and not have a public piece." Belatedly recognizing the obvious truth that running for president is to privacy as burlesque is to modesty, Kerry added, "I know what's involved in this thing."

Still, it gnawed at him that a woman he never met perceived him as hangdog. Maybe it was ego; maybe the word "sad" resonated with something his handlers had told him, but Kerry was determined to find a safe explanation for his image problem. "It's funny," he said, harking back to the debate, "if you want to know the truth about yesterday, I didn't get to exercise. I was pissed off that I had to go straight to the thing. She might have picked up on that. I thrive from being able to touch life during the day. Give me one half hour outdoors during the day to be able to run around with the sun in my face, the wind, and I'm a new human being." Finally, Kerry was at peace. The problem did not lie in his nature, but in the nature of his exercise regimen. If only the voters could see him with the wind in his hair on his Harley, if only they could see him in a wetsuit with a surf board (as he was pictured in *Vogue*), then they could understand who he really is and they could appreciate his hard-earned, late-in-life happiness.

My sense of Kerry is shaped by the time I spent with him in the shadow of his mother's impending death in the fall of 2002. Every presidential candidate is a canvas for our projections, so perhaps inevitably, I came to see Kerry not as a graspingly ambitious politician but as an embodiment of the fragile fabric of mortality that we all confront, even amid the hurly-burly of a presidential campaign.

During a late October campaign trip to Maine, Kerry mentioned that he and his daughters had recently carried a tree fashioned from vibrant, multi-hued autumn leaves to his mother's bedside. "My mom helped me appreciate them," he said. "I'm a nut for fall foliage." Now in his office, five months after the funeral, Kerry said, "I wish my mom had hung around for longer, but it was her time. We were blessed with an enormous period of good-bye. It was very gentle, very touching and very meaningful."

The rhythms of political careers mean that men often seek the presidency at an age when they are grappling with the death of a parent. While Dick Gephardt should have been planning his presidential campaign in December 2002, he spent much of the month in St. Louis tending to his ailing mother, Loreen. She had lung cancer, and Gephardt faced the agonizing decision of whether an aggressive course of treatment was appropriate for a woman in her mid–nineties. During an interview in mid-March, Gephardt described in an almost inaudible voice what her doctors had recommended: "She's too old. It won't help. It will just put her through a lot of torture." Gephardt was tormented by his inability to return to St. Louis as often as he would like. "You want to be there for your mother," he said. "It's part of life. Everybody goes through it." (Loreen Gephardt passed away two months later at ninety-five.)

Howard Dean too had gone through it. In August 2001, Dean's father, a retired stockbroker also named Howard, died at eighty. That same month, Dean chose not to seek another term as Vermont governor, a decision that soon led to his impetuous bid for the White House. Back in 1974, Howard Dean's younger brother Charlie, possibly a CIA agent, perished under mysterious circumstances in Laos. Subsequently Dean jettisoned a Wall Street career to attend medical school.

Hearing these twin stories, a Viennese analyst might run his hand over his Vandyke beard and murmur, "Interesting. Very interesting." Dean, however, denied an overt connection between these deaths and his unorthodox career moves. Admittedly, the back of a van in Iowa, surrounded by four campaign aides, was not the ideal arena for an intense round of psychological probing about hidden motivations. "I'd probably have to go into analysis to figure out why," Dean said, "but it's not something that conscious." He paused to contemplate the evidence. "Okay, this is interesting," he conceded. "My brother dies, and I switch careers and go to medical school. My father dies, and I take on the big prize. It's an interesting coincidence, worthy of discussion, but no light is likely to be shed on it in five minutes or an hour." Since we are just twenty minutes away from a rendezvous with the Washington County Democrats, the Lucy Van Pelt "Psychiatric Help 5¢" booth officially closed.

Despite incessant coverage of the presidential race, the fact that three leading Democratic contenders have lost parents in the last two years is never discussed in print, not even as a way to explain a candidate's occasional dour mood or to put the ordeal of campaigning for president in a larger human perspective. No other subject is off-limits for political reporters—not sexual escapades, youthful drug use or medical history. But parental death has long been a taboo topic. For all the keyhole coverage of the Clinton presidency, the deaths of the president's mother and Hillary's father in the mid–1990s were noted only in passing. For all the ridicule heaped on Al Gore in 2000, it was hard to find a mention that this was the first campaign that the vice president waged without his father, Albert Sr., watching from the wings.

The same November day that Rosemary Forbes Kerry's obituary ran in the *Boston Globe,* the major political news in the paper was the rumor (later confirmed) that Teddy Kennedy would jilt his protégé Edwards to back Kerry for president. Reporters had no problems badgering Kerry with questions about his health, both before and after his prostate surgery. But the death of the candidate's last surviving parent passed almost unnoticed. What

is the explanation for this unusual degree of journalistic reticence? It's possible that mourning in America still commands the
last vestige of old-fashioned privacy. But my own theory, and it is
offered tentatively, is simply that most political beat reporters are
still in their thirties, too young in many cases to personally
understand how the mid-life loss of a parent can tilt one's inner
world off its axis.

If I were forced to describe Kerry in a single word, it might be the
soft, autumnal adjective "wistful." Traveling with Kerry, I kept
picking up the sense that he is someone who constantly gazes out
the window, thinking about the private might-have-beens of life
and fate. At a Kerry event in New Hampshire, I found myself
chatting with Herb Church, the candidate's English teacher at St.
Paul's. Asked to describe his former student, Church said, "He
was not the sort of a guy who had a wildly colorful [prep-school]
career. He was not a hell-raiser. He was a very solemn young
man."

These days, that solemnity has a musical accompaniment—
the cherry and rosewood Spanish guitar that Kerry carries with
him for relaxation on the campaign trail. If Bill Clinton's saxophone was a symbol of exuberance, then Kerry's mid-life fascination with mastering the classical guitar suggests a more subdued
inner nature. Climbing aboard Kerry's chartered jet in Maine in
the fall of 2002, the first thing that caught my eye was a book
entitled *Guitar for Dummies*. Later Kerry explained sheepishly,
"Someone just gave it to me." Listening to Kerry play—and I'm
the last one to judge musical talent—I was struck by both his
intense concentration and the mournful quality to the music,
whether it is a melody from Segovia or a slow, sad-eyed rendition
of the Beatles' "Yesterday." Kerry's fingernails are a bit elongated
on his right, guitar-strumming hand, but I was surprised when he
said at one point, "People think I'm weird because the nails on
one hand are longer than the other." Presidential candidates are

allowed to find a soothing refuge in playing the classical guitar, but they are never supposed to self-consciously muse aloud about being judged "weird."

Kerry came to Maine to campaign for doomed Democratic Senate candidate Chellie Pingree. Riding in a van somewhere near Bangor, Pingree explained that she was aided in her fundraising by all the wealthy Democrats who once attended summer camp in the state. That prompted Kerry to recall that his parents packed him off to camps in New Hampshire and Nova Scotia. "That summer in Nova Scotia," he said, "I fell in love. I was eleven or twelve. And I still think about it. Isn't it awful?" At the end of the day, as the candidate was fixing me a Scotch on the plane (no stints in the pilot's seat this time), I asked about the mysterious girl from summer camp. Slightly embarrassed, Kerry admitted that he never mustered the courage to speak to the object of his affections—it was all rapture from afar.

There are two types of moments in politics: genuine ones and those when the cameras are rolling. Tape recorders, which candidates tend to regard as far more obtrusive than old-fashioned notebooks, also distort events even as they provide a faithful vocal souvenir. My own reporting technique in covering presidential contenders is to alternate between notebook and electronic record, since I crave the spontaneity of a conversation delineated by hastily scrawled notes and also relish the recorder's ability to reproduce long, multi-claused sentences. Although it was not my original purpose in frequently switching from nineteenth-century technology (notebook and pen) to twenty-first-century technology (an Olympus digital, downloadable recorder), I began to find it revealing how the candidates reacted to my choice of mode to replicate their words.

Howard Dean, to my surprise, often seemed uncomfortable when the recorder was off, as if my not taping (okay, digitizing) symbolized a fluid, ill-defined relationship and undermined the reality of his unorthodox campaign. Kerry, in contrast, sometimes viewed the recorder as his mortal enemy, akin to waving a cross in front of a vampire. Part of his reaction may simply have been the innate caution of a veteran politician, but my brandishing the recorder may also have said to Kerry, "The fun's over. Now I have to work at crafting my answers."

All of this is a way of saying that Kerry Unplugged comes across as a more intriguing political figure than his digitized alter ego. With little exposure to the candidate before the current campaign, I never fully understood why he is so widely perceived as haughty and distant. More than any Democratic contender, even the exuberantly outgoing Edwards, Kerry is a hands-on candidate, a toucher, who revels in the momentary tactile contact of a hand on the shoulder, a tap on the arm—and, for friends and fellow Vietnam veterans, a bear hug. In private, with the recorder off and the notebook closed, he can be surprisingly candid and astute in his analysis of his rivals for the Democratic nomination. But in a formal interview session, it quickly became, "Here's the thing about John [Edwards]. John's been running around saying— no, wait, this is off the record ... "

Andy Stern, the national president of the Service Employees (SEIU), encountered Kerry at that workingman's Mecca, the World Economic Forum, which was held in New York in February 2002. As they talked, Stern bluntly asked Kerry how he could get over the impression that he is too cold and too distant to win the nomination. "He had a whole I'm-not-aloof speech," Stern recalled. "He gave me his whole snowboarding, windsurfing, motorcycle-riding side." It seemed to have worked. As Stern put it a year later, "When you get to know him personally, he's a different kind of guy. You can talk to him like you're sitting in your living room."

Political reporters, like psychiatrists, cannot shrink from the age-old therapeutic question: Can people change? Both groups, bearded Freudians and bedraggled Broders alike, have a vested professional interest in answering in the affirmative. Journalism is not normally considered a "helping profession," but those of us in the press pack are as dedicated to inspiring sagas of personal growth as our couch-bound counterparts. What is the point of enduring the endless campaign season, all those bus rides and tarmacs at two in the morning, if we can't chronicle how a politician (a Bobby Kennedy, a John McCain) dramatically changes before our very eyes? Professional cynicism is momentarily put aside as we dutifully type the clichés about "maturing" candidates and presidents who "grow in office."

So what then are we to make of the new, approachable Kerry? No less an authority than Jim Jordan, Kerry's campaign manager, suggests that much of this is learned behavior. "John Kerry's improvement as a political performer in the last four years is breathtaking," Jordan said. "I recognize that people don't change in their late fifties. But Kerry has developed the political skills to connect with people and charm them quickly. A lot of it is craftsmanship: how to deliver a better speech, how to write a better speech, how to work a room."

Direct-mail consultant Ron Rosenblith, whose ties to Kerry hark back to the anti–Vietnam War movement, made an analogous point. "As a thirty-two-year friend," Rosenblith said, "there has been a process under way to make him more realistically ready to make this race. Part of it is the marriage to Teresa [in 1995]. Part of it is himself. It's been a long march for the guy who came to the Senate in 1984 as John 'Live Shot' Kerry."

But to Rosenblith, it was far more than Kerry simply learning to mask his ego-driven, publicity-hound ways. "He came back from Vietnam having seen terrible things and having watched comrades die," Rosenblith pointed out. "It was very hard for him to open up emotionally. You could be his friend, and he wouldn't open up emotionally. But time heals all wounds—and a supportive environment heals all wounds. John today isn't the person I knew thirty-two years ago." As an example of Kerry's transformation, Rosenblith pointed to his friend's recent willingness to greet him with such uncharacteristically emotional phrases as "big hug" and even "I love you." Rosenblith also stressed the reverberations from the back-to-back deaths of Kerry's parents. "He had to go through some serious emotional stuff," Rosenblith said. "Is it psycho-babble? All I know is that John's more comfortable in his own skin."

The same could be said with justice about any of the leading Democratic contenders. Lieberman, Edwards, Gephardt, Graham and probably even the tightly coiled Dean all seem to have a comfort level with who they are and who they're not. But for Kerry, unlike most of his rivals, it has taken a long pull to get there. He appears to have weathered the self-contained storms of middle age and has reached safe harbor aware that his internal ballast has shifted during the voyage.

Kerry freely admitted, "I went through a period where I wasn't very happy," referring to the tumultuous years surrounding his divorce in the mid-1980s. And he added, "Anybody who has been through a divorce and doesn't tell you it's hurtful is insensitive." But that was long ago. As the fifty-nine-year-old senator put it in a reflective voice, "Maybe you cross that great divide with being fifty years old. Suddenly you see things differently and feel things differently—and things that used to bother you don't. And life is fixed. It's all there. I like it, very much. It's a comfortable place to be emotionally."

More than his stance on the issues, more than his fund-raising, more than the imagery of his TV ads, Kerry's political fate will be dictated by his ability to communicate this new-found comfort and ease with himself. He never will be Kerry the Cuddly. And it's not that he has to bound onto every stage or warble ecstatically about the joys of finding himself amid the world-famous delights of Cedar Rapids, Iowa, on a cold winter's night. But on the cusp of a difficult election, Democrats crave a candidate they can, well, warm up to. It makes no difference whether the candidate's inner fires radiating external warmth were kindled at birth or whether the long smoldering embers only began to burn brightly in midlife. What matters is the glow—and the desire of the voters to see their dreams reflected in it.

CHAPTER 11

Visions of the White House

No matter what the calendar says, the 2004 campaign began for me on a rainy weekend in late June 2002 as I followed John Edwards on an eastward trek across southern New Hampshire ending up on the seacoast in Portsmouth. Presidential politics proceeded at a languorous pace back then, as potential candidates like Edwards gently unfurled their sails to the wind hoping to catch the breeze on their initial voyages of discovery. Yet etched in my memory is the sheer joy that Edwards derived from the act of campaigning and his intense curiosity about how each sentence he uttered was perceived in this ultimate political test market. He brimmed with eager conviction that a presidential race would be a glorious adventure and that its presumed success, after a single term in the Senate, would represent the fulfillment of his pre-ordained fate.

Now, nearly a year later, we are back in Portsmouth on the wet, cold Saturday of Memorial Day weekend. Nearly seventy Democrats—who have been waiting over half an hour for Edwards to make his belated appearance—are shoehorned into state representative Terie Norelli's living room. The crowd is so thick that an Edwards aide with an obstructed view is holding a

digital camera high over her head in an effort to decipher from
the resulting pictures who has turned out on this damp afternoon. As we wait for Edwards to speak, I strike up a conversation
with Barclay Jackson, a telecommunications lawyer who is
already restless about the many candidates and the long wait
until the primary. "Why don't you get them all in a room and
decide on somebody and just go after Bush?" she asks. "I do
think that it's more important to get a candidate who can win
than somebody who's perfect." As Edwards, dressed in a lavender sweater and black slacks, finally emerges into view, Jackson
hints at her personal definition of electability as she gushes,
"He's so cute."

Edwards continues to fascinate me, despite his minuscule
standing in the polls. His inchoate potential suggests a dramatic
denouement to his presidential ambitions—either a stunning
come-from-behind triumph or one of the most precipitous flame-
outs in recent political history. Edwards is a candidate still in
flux, changing and developing as he races along an arc of possibility that could end in the White House or with a return to practicing law in Raleigh. Standing there poised to speak, appearing
far younger than a man at mid-century should, Edwards knows
how far he has traveled already. Earlier in the day, as we discussed his evolution as a candidate, he told me, "There's no
question that I'm different. I've gotten better. Some of it is a comfort and ease."

Edwards has matured as a candidate. Gone is the cornpone
style with its painful references to "North Carolina and New
Hampshire common sense." Gone too are the complex run-on sentences that ramble through a thicket in search of a predicate. His
delivery is crisp, confident and filled with passionate scorn for
that Republican in the White House. "They think we're soft and
nice, and we'll let them run right over and through us," Edwards
begins in an effort to demonstrate that he's tough enough to play
in the center ring. "And we're going to prove that they're wrong in
2004. Because we're going to take this fight right at this guy."

But what remains consistent about Edwards is his soft-edged southern populism built around his autobiography and his oft stated belief "in an America where the son of a mill worker can actually beat the son of a president for the White House." That practiced line wins rousing applause from New Hampshire Democrats who cling to their own patriotic myth that the civic-minded residents of a tiny New England state can pick the next president.

Harking back to his lonely days after Christmas on the beach in North Carolina debating whether to run, Edwards says, "This is personal for me. This is not some message that some consultant came up with. This is my whole life." Win or lose, Edwards is determined to test his belief that autobiography is destiny. For all his detailed position papers, he is out there with a shoeshine and a smile peddling not his ideas but himself. At every turn, he stresses the personal nature of his crusade, sometimes overdoing the effort to prove that the words he utters are the embodiment of his own beliefs rather than the artifice of his political handlers.

A year ago, Edwards was surprised by how often New Hampshire Democrats pressed him with questions about John Ashcroft's assault on civil liberties. Now it is embedded in his stump speech. "Finally," he says, "a subject that the people in Washington tell me that you have to be careful in talking about— this could be dangerous politically." You can feel a sense of expectation in the room as Edwards continues, "As long as I am a candidate for president of the United States and when I am president of the United States, I will champion this cause. We cannot, in an effort to protect ourselves, in an effort to fight a war on terrorism, let people like John Ashcroft take away our rights."

The burst of applause sets up Edwards's final appeal as he tries to close the deal and convince these desperate-for-victory Democrats that he's for real. "I have so much energy and passion, you have no idea," he says as his North Carolina accent seems to thicken with the implicit I-can-win-in-the-South message. "It drives me seven days a week—sixteen, eighteen hours a day—

because at the end of the day, it's not about me, it's about us."
With his aides carefully watching the clock, Edwards takes a
handful of questions before he departs with a flurry of handshakes.

Unlike the early trips to New Hampshire when his speeches
earned him little more than muted applause from the uncommitted, this time Edwards wins converts. "I'm sold," says Barclay
Jackson, who was probably ready to sign on at hello. Though she
adds, reflecting both her historical grasp of eighteenth-century
New England theologians and the novelty of her candidate preference, "I still want to call him Jonathan Edwards."

This is the obvious moment to offer a paean to the enduring
vibrancy of American democracy as it plays out every four years
in Portsmouth living rooms. Here in New England, where American liberty took root, here on the seacoast so close to where the
Pilgrims landed, here in the state in which Eugene McCarthy top-
pled a sitting president, here where Bill Clinton promised New
Hampshire voters that he would remember them "until the last
dog dies," here where Maytag repairmen and telecommunications lawyers, each with the precious gift of a single vote—
enough, enough already!

Don't get me wrong. I still love New Hampshire living rooms.
They remain that rare oasis in the parched desert of twenty-first-
century American politics. But all idylls must come to an end.
Listening to Edwards's now polished refrain and picking up the
premature impatience of New Hampshire voters, I begin to get a
premonition of how fast events are rushing on, how soon the
soft-edged possibilities of the Invisible Primary will give way to
the hard-sell certainties of the TV commercials.

How I dread the coming air wars, that other insidious version
of living room politics. It won't be long before TV sets in early
states like New Hampshire begin blaring out the phony catchphrases and the empty slogans—the endless variants on the

shop-worn Democratic pledge "I will fight for you." And then the
gauzy images and the uplifting music will inexorably yield to the
attack ads, as a scrum of well-funded Democrats battle for traction in a crowded field. Obscure congressional votes will be
exaggerated into traitorous betrayals. Small differences in health
care plans will be magnified beyond recognition in a cynical
effort to prove that rival Democrats (yes, Democrats) want to
undermine Medicare and Medicaid. The campaign that began so
placidly with six appealing serious candidates will likely degen-
erate into a snarling sea of invective featuring offscreen announc-
ers with ominous voices, grainy photographs and blown-up,
red-circled, out-of-context newspaper clips. How sad, how ugly
and how inevitable as the Democrats choose their nominee.

Yes, in the beginning, there was one candidate, one car and
one reporter. But in the end, there will be one Democratic nominee, armies of deadline-driven reporters waiting for a gaffe or a
stumble, motorcades that snake across the landscape like freight
trains, dozens of anxious Secret Service agents murmuring dark
forebodings into their headsets and cheering crowds penned up
behind rope lines. This traveling circus, this frenetic caravan,
this hydra-headed beast will symbolize the nature of success in
America. It is the American way to take something that started in
an intimate, innocent spirit in Iowa and New Hampshire and
transform it into something elephantine, cynical and synthetic.

Come the fall of 2004, as the general election campaign against
George W. Bush heads into its syncopated showdown, the gos-
samer memories of New Hampshire living rooms will seem like
phantoms from another era, like black-and-white photographs
from the 1950s showing Dad in his suit, Mom in her housedress
and the kids in Davy Crockett caps all clustered around the family's brand-new Buick with tail fins that almost reach out to
embrace the sky. True, the Democratic nominee will be the same
person that he was a year or two earlier, the same amalgam of
dreams, drive, discipline and sense of destiny. But the trappings
of his candidacy will have changed beyond recognition; he will

be enveloped in a retinue of aides fantasizing about their West
Wing offices, sycophants plotting to snare plum embassies, and
the occasional friend along to help the nominee maintain his san-
ity. Nothing in his life will be spontaneous; everything down to
his twice daily shaves and his cherished exercise breaks will be
scheduled. Even as he jets across the country, he will be overcome by the sameness of the routine and the claustrophobia of
the bubble. His life will be reduced to the confines of the campaign plane, motorcades along Secret Service–secured, carless
highways and mind-numbingly repetitive speeches, delivered to
crowds that have lost their individuality and have become little
more than a blurry sea of faces.

Yet if he is successful in his quest to make the proper noun
"Bush" synonymous with the compound adjective "one-term,"
the Democratic standard-bearer will look back on his race for the
White House—both its humble beginnings and its frenzied
finale—as a curiously carefree interlude, a time when his only
real responsibility was to act out the tightly scripted role of a
presidential candidate. During the campaign, none of his decisions will send soldiers into battle or the dollar into free fall on
the international currency markets. Instead the candidate will
exert his authority by rewriting a paragraph in a speech, arguing
over the text of an attack ad and rehearsing his ad-libbed comebacks for a presidential debate. In the annals of lonely guy decision making, none of this qualifies as heavy lifting.

But, for the moment, the presidential campaign is still being
played out in the modest confines of Terie Norelli's living room.
That's why a single confident phrase embedded in Edwards's
Portsmouth peroration startles me: "When I am president of the
United States . . ." It seems impossible to make the imaginative
leap between this engaging man in a lavender sweater and someone who on a wintry afternoon in early 2005 might, just might, be

placing his left hand on a Bible held by the chief justice of the
Supreme Court and taking the oath of office as the forty-fourth
president of the United States.

Despite all my years covering presidential campaigns, I cannot
get over the weird disconnect between the familiar rituals of the
campaign trail and that overly fortified white mansion on Pennsylvania Avenue. The long and arduous race for the presidency
always feels like an end in itself, an enterprise designed to cli-
max with the back-slapping, bear-hugging, champagne-drenched
ecstasy of a victorious election night. For all its single-minded
intensity, presidential politics seems closer in spirit to a sporting
contest than a transfer of power that will bequeath to the victor
globe-girdling military and economic authority. The obvious parallel is to major league baseball, where a World Series triumph is
followed by a four-month respite of awards banquets and
endorsement contracts; then the new season magically begins
with spring training.

It is hard to picture Edwards or any of his leading Democratic
rivals in the White House. This is not a tribute to Bush's political
invulnerability. Rather, it is a reflection of the failure of our collec-
tive imagination to envision any flesh-and-blood president other
than the incumbent or his immediate predecessors. Even the
sainted President Bartlett of *The West Wing* is a New England version of Bill Clinton with his oversize appetites air-brushed away to
achieve liberal wish fulfillment. Back when I was devouring political novels as a teenager during the Kennedy-Johnson 1960s, every
fictional president was either a handsome, young former senator
with a rich and controlling father or a ribald, ruthless former congressional leader with a Texas twang. When even novelists cannot
transcend our limited supply of presidential archetypes, it suggests
an almost royalist reluctance to commit psychological regicide and
mentally dethrone our current leader.

The conventions of political journalism contribute to this arti-
ficial separation between the campaign and the Oval Office. My

colleagues on the press bus live in an environment of verifiable fact. They chronicle the sights and sounds of campaign rallies, delve into the biographies of the candidates and detail the intricacies of their policy positions. The resulting dispatches from the front portray the candidates in two temporal spheres: how they are now and how they were in the past when clambering up the ladder of political success. But missing is that all-important future tense—how a candidate will handle the strains and stresses, the pressures and the pitfalls, if the voters elevate him to the highest office on the planet.

It isn't enough for reporters to assess the merits of a candidate's budget plan or to highlight the inconsistencies in his foreign-policy pronouncements. When I was covering Bill Clinton for *Time* magazine in 1992, I spent the requisite long hours huddled with campaign aides and independent experts trying to calculate the costs and the trade-offs involved in the candidate's pledge to provide health insurance for all Americans. What a recondite and ridiculous enterprise. Nothing that the Arkansas governor said on the campaign trail prepared the nation for the Rube Goldberg complexity of the White House plan that eventually emerged from the secret conclaves of Hillary Clinton's health-care task force. As a result, I and my equally fact-driven journalistic counterparts missed the real story, which was the vast policy-making powers that were soon to be ceded to an unelected First Lady.

I keep thinking of a scene that is endlessly repeated on press buses during a presidential campaign. A half dozen reporters huddle together, each with a tape recorder, trying to decipher a candidate's precise language in a just completed speech. Did he say "America's greatness" or "American greatness" before he was drowned out by applause? I say "spinach" to this kind of mind-numbing literalness. Somehow there has to be a vehicle for campaign coverage to get at larger truths. Yes, I understand and appreciate the canons of journalistic objectivity. But we lose something valuable in limiting our horizons to verifiable truths that are based on tape-recorded speeches, quotes from a campaign spokesman or even nasty put-downs uttered by consultants on a not-for-attribution basis. Somewhere amid the endless spools of TV tape and the gigabytes of text devoted to chronicling the 2004 campaign, we desperately need to find a way to make the daring leap from the realm of fact into the admittedly speculative world of presidential possibility.

I write this keenly aware of my own deficiencies as a prophet of presidencies. As a *USA Today* columnist covering the 2000 race, I was gulled by Bush's bland public pronouncements and his moderate record as Texas governor into badly misreading the far-reaching extent of his unswerving conservatism. I also neglected to fully appreciate the way that his Harvard MBA training and his post–drinking-life sense of discipline would contribute to what is unquestionably the most orderly, leak-proof and on-message White House in modern history. But my errors as an oracle have been bipartisan. Back in 1992, I was so impressed by Clinton's wildly improvisational style that I failed to foresee how this let's-pull-an-all-nighter freneticism would produce the debilitating chaos that marred his first years in the White House.

Okay, no campaign reporter or columnist can be a seer without peer. Walter Lippmann, after all, backed Richard Nixon in 1968 because he was convinced that Tricky Dick would end the Vietnam War. But the root of my errors in forecasting the contours of future presidencies was that I placed too much emphasis on the lessons of the campaign trail and spent too little time speculating about the essence of the candidates. As I have belatedly discovered, a slavish fidelity to so-called journalistic truth is ultimately little help in predicting how any new president will weather the transition from the confetti-cannon exuberance of campaign rallies to the sobering rigors of the Oval Office.

A presidential campaign is the dreamscape of democracy. Candidates, when allowed a moment of quiet contemplation, see themselves inscribed in the history books under the heading "A Return to Peace and Prosperity." Campaign aides picture themselves walking in the White House Rose Garden with the president's hand resting lightly on their shoulders as they offer sage advice on everything from Hezbollah to health care. Reporters, although we are loath to admit it, nurture the illusion that this will be the president who takes us into his confidence with so much access to the Oval Office that we will have our own Secret Service code name. But these private visions do not compare to the shimmering air castles built by Democratic voters.

Democrats have long been beguiled by the fantasy of the white knight president, the FDR-like leader who will somehow uplift the nation, inspire us to something greater than the next war or the next tax cut, and yet never lose his easygoing sense of authenticity. For sixty years, longer than most of us have been alive, the Democratic Party has been waiting for that transcendent next president. John Kennedy, for all the myth that has come to surround his memory, was too much a creature of muscular Cold War verities to measure up to this august standard when he was alive. Lyndon Johnson and Bill Clinton, such enormous talents in such flawed containers. And yet for all the disappointments and the undelivered promises, there is the enduring hope that maybe the next election will somehow fulfill these idealistic dreams.

In that optimistic spirit, let us jump over the hard-fought presidential primaries and the bruising general election campaign against Bush. Imagine instead that we have been transported to early 2005 and there is again a Democrat in the White House. Through the mists of time, we see . . .

As he strides into the Oval Office for the first time, the new president allows himself a moment of private celebration. "I still got the gift," he muses. "I had them going during the Inaugural Address, I really had them going. When I did that whole riff on equality, I almost expected Clarence Thomas to rise up shouting, 'Amen, brother!' When I was really rolling, I thought I even saw a flicker of a smile on old Dick Cheney's stone face."

The Leader of the Free World slowly circles the room, his

hand fondly stroking the silk of the sofas, as he says half aloud, "So this is the Oval Office. It's smaller than I imagined. Of course, if Bush had any grace he'd have invited me over for a chat during transition. But Republicans, they just have no manners when it comes to losing an election, especially when they were whomped by a Democrat like me. Well, Bush is now on the flight path back to the Texas two-step and—guess what?—I'm here in the big house."

He walks to the desk and peeks at the single sheet of paper resting on it—his schedule, embossed with the seal of the President of the United States. "Looks like it's time for a sit-down with my national security adviser," he observes. "Something about reassuring the allies. They should feel reassured already, since I'm the one president who's not about to bomb anybody. Except with love. You know, it would have been a hoot to keep Condi around. But despite certain affinities, there were, as they say, grave policy differences."

His reverie is interrupted by a soft knock on the Oval Office door. The president pauses, not knowing whether to shout "Come in" or open it with a flourish. The door opens a crack as a White House secretary announces, "Your national security adviser is here, President Sharpton."

THE SCENE: The Oval Office late on a January afternoon with a hint of sunset visible over the snow-covered South Lawn. Seated on couches are the president, his congressional relations chief and the four top Democratic leaders of Congress. Two other presidential aides stand awkwardly against the wall. The White House photographer, with an equipment bag at his feet, is recording the scene.

THE PRESIDENT: I've got to tell you—and you know this Tom, especially—how many times we've been over here as supplicants. Begging Bush for crumbs and Clinton for a bit more of a slice. It feels different now that I'm, I guess, the host.

TOM DASCHLE: It makes me feel proud, too, Dick ... er, Mr. President.

THE PRESIDENT: I'm not used to it either, Tom. I just wish my mother were here to see it. But we've got to get down to business. I have the Canadian prime minister coming in at 5:30. (Turning to the aide on the sofa.) Steve, could you bring us up to speed.

CONGRESSIONAL RELATIONS ADVISER: Mr. President, the White House task force will have your health-care plan ready to submit to Congress by mid-February. As you know, we have to phase it in more slowly than we'd like for cost reasons. Our thinking is that you should formally unveil it with a prime-time address to the Congress. That would set up a great "triumphant return to Capitol Hill" angle with the press.

NANCY PELOSI: President Gephardt, I hate to say this, but we don't have the votes to even get a shell of a bill out of committee in the House. It's not just the Republicans. Some of the Democrats on Ways and Means are also balking at the cost.

THE PRESIDENT: Tom, can we move it through the Senate?

DASCHLE: Not this year, I'm afraid. Maybe in early 2006, if some of those moderate Republicans start to get antsy about re-election.

THE PRESIDENT: I appreciate the honesty. But I've gotta tell you, I thought things would be different when I was president. But here I am, back at the same old stand, wishing and hoping and praying that someday the Democrats will win back the House. The French, I think, have got an expression for it: The more things change, the more they remain the same.

FADE OUT as a lone spotlight outlines the care-worn face of the new president.

"John Kerry. President John Kerry. Testing. Is this damn thing working? [Pause] Sitting here in the Oval Office speaking into a tape recorder, even a miniature one, I can't help feeling like Richard Nixon. God, I hated that man. I remember standing at the gates of the White House, must have been late '71, a VVAW [Vietnam Veterans Against the War] demonstration shouting—No, maybe the historical record doesn't need to know the precise twelve-letter epithet that the future forty-fourth president of the United States screamed at the thirty-seventh in this august line.

"For the record, it's shortly after 8:00 P.M. on February 16, 2005. Teresa insisted that I make these recordings, and she's probably right. I'd like to keep a written journal every day I'm here, but there isn't time or sometimes energy. Still, it's strange to be talking to yourself, president or no president.

"Where to start? What surprised me the most about this job is how constrained I feel by the Secret Service. Far more than in the campaign, you really feel like you're the man in the glass cage, a pampered zoo animal. Security, terrorism, staffing problems, the answer from the Service is always the same. A permanent and unalterable no to the Harley anywhere but Camp David. The closest I can ever get to the cockpit of a plane is to wander forward on Air Force One. And I'm not looking forward to the fight over ski trails when we finally go to Sun Valley next weekend. Maybe I'll feel differently when winter's finally over. I can't help getting a bit depressed, well, downcast over the way it gets dark so early.

"Still, we're making real progress. Dick Holbrooke and I have been working hard on the proposals to revamp the U.N. peacekeeping and decision-making mechanisms. That's been the problem with Democrats and foreign policy. We keep talking about the U.N. as if it's the Holy Grail, but we turn a blind eye to all its structural faults. But there doesn't have to be anything weak-kneed about working with, rather than against, the international community to deal with threats to peace.

"Now for the part that probably shouldn't be transcribed for a long, long time. It's John Edwards. I just wish I felt more comfortable with him. Okay, of course, it was political necessity to put him on the ticket. But often I sense he resents me in some deep social-class, Yale, son-of-a-diplomat way. No way I could make him understand the dynamics in the family or how lonely I felt being packed off to school and camp. John's always smiling, competent, hard-working. I wish I could add loyal, but I'm not sure. I wonder if he's still talking regularly to Clinton. At least, Hillary's on board with the high-speed rail. But with both of them—actually three of them if you count Clinton as well—I keep having to watch my back.

"Enough for tonight. John Kerry. President John Kerry, signing off."

REMARKS BY PRESIDENT AT PRESS AVAILABILITY

Winter White House
Burlington, Vermont
March 5, 2005

THE PRESIDENT: As thrilled as I am to be president, I have to tell you that it's great to be back in Vermont. The fresh air, the beauty, the snow. It's just not the same in Washington. Later today, Judy and I intend to do a little cross-country skiing. I better apologize in advance for any inconvenience this might cause my neighbors. Now I'll be happy to take your questions.

Q: Mr. President, North Korean radio today called your recent comments warning of aggressive action against their nuclear weapons program a "missile-rattling that could lead to war." Do you rule out using military force against North Korea?

THE PRESIDENT: No, I do not. I am not a pacifist, as some foolishly suggested during the recent campaign. I am deeply concerned about the proliferation of nuclear weapons and have always said that I would move forcefully to prevent it. My standard has always been: Is there an imminent threat to the United States? I fear that the conduct of North Korea is fast approaching that threshold.

Q: Mr. President, I don't know if you've yet seen the full-page advertisement in today's *New York Times* protesting your policies toward North Korea. It's signed by more than six hundred of your early supporters and it says, and I quote, "President Dean promised to uphold 'the Democratic wing of the Democratic Party.' Instead, he is upholding the Bush-Cheney wing." Any comment?

THE PRESIDENT: As a doctor, I must say that they're a little quick to accuse me of malpractice. In all seriousness, I am sure I'll take positions as president that will disappoint some of my supporters. But I'm not a rubber stamp, I'm the president. Perhaps if they had listened a little more closely to what I said in the campaign, they wouldn't be so surprised now.

Q: Sir, Senator Kerry said in a Senate speech yesterday ...

THE PRESIDENT: Next question.

3–12–05
Bob Graham
The White House

6:30—Awoke. Light rap on door from steward. Miss alarm clock.

6:45—Shower, shave, dress. Finished Colgate. Gray suit.

7:00—Breakfast at desk. Toast, Florida OJ, coffee.

7:15—Read overnight CIA material. Syria? Hezbollah again!

7:30—CIA-FBI terrorism briefing. Same old. Counted "Mr. President's." 47! 4 in one sentence.

8:00—COS [Chief of staff]. Work day—oil rig? SS [Secret Service] objects. Fear: small plane/bomb. Miss Senate.

8:48—Gwen [daughter] calls. Kids: flu. Repeats Leno monologue. Not funny!!

9:00—OMB director. Deficit up: $97 b. Delay Medicare plan??? What to cut?

9:30—Interior Secy. Everglades. Progress!

10:00—President of Chile. Talks much, says little. More coffee.

10:30—Girl Scouts. East Room. Need better talking points.

11:07—Dollar plunging. Phone George Soros. Deficit!

11:30—Press secretary, before his briefing. Next work day: no comment. Dollar: no comment. Medicare plan: no comment. Don't envy his job.

11:57—Adele stops by. Dinner: Suzanne [daughter]? Yes!

12:00—Daschle calls. GOP filibuster. Don't miss Senate.

12:15—Lunch at desk. Turkey/white toast/mayo. (Don't tell cardiologist re: mayo.) Wonder: what's Bush doing. Does he miss it?

From *Friday the President Stayed Home: The White House Journals of President Joseph I. Lieberman*:

... It is interesting what causes controversy for a president. During the transition period before the inauguration, I will admit that I worried that my decision to include three Republicans in the cabinet might cause difficulties for my party. But I believed then, as I do now, that it was important to send a strong signal that the days of poisonous partisanship in Washington were over. Speaking frankly, some members of my staff and some senior Democrats in the Congress expressed their concerns to me in advance. But I had what I called "the perfect squelch" when I asked each of them, "Can you name an American more qualified to serve as secretary of defense than John McCain?" Gratifying my hopes rather than feeding my fears, both the press and the public reacted well to what I called "a government of inclusion."

But what I never imagined were the difficulties that could be caused by my need for a second set of White House china. My branch of the Jewish faith requires separate sets of dishes so that you never violate the biblical injunction not to mix meat and milk. For a nation that has been so understanding of my obligation to respect the Sabbath and the other aspects of my religion, the extra tableware seemed a minor and easily surmountable problem. If I had it to do over again, Hadassah and I would have paid for the second set of dishes out of our personal bank accounts. But I had received an opinion from the White House counsel's office that it was permissible to solicit private donations to fulfill what I called our "two-china policy." Perhaps, in hindsight, I should have taken more care to scrutinize the backgrounds of the donors.

The press flap that some were to call "Plate-gate" erupted suddenly when ...

The Family-Friendly White House
Time magazine
March 22, 2005

Not since the early 1960s, when a young tyke named John-John hid under his father's desk in the Oval Office, have the excited shrieks of small children filled the most exalted workspace in the nation. But in the little more than two months that the Edwards family has been in residence at 1600 Pennsylvania Avenue, presidential visitors have grown accustomed to dodging racing tricycles and discovering half-eaten cookies buried in the White House furniture. The cookie culprit is generally four-year-old Jack, while his six-year-old sister, Emma Claire, is reputed to be hell on three wheels.

"When President Edwards promised an 'open administration,' even I didn't expect that it would be this open," confessed White House press secretary Jennifer Palmieri, who has learned the hard way the damage that stray Legos can do to pantyhose. Not all of President Edwards' staffers have adjusted as well to the child-centered White House. "It's hard to have a serious policy discussion with the president when Jack keeps wandering in with his juice bottle," grumped one aide whose attitudes toward children were seemingly influenced by the films of W. C. Fields. "Sometimes it's hard to remember that it's the White House and not a play school."

First Lady Elizabeth Edwards, in an exclusive interview with *Time*, explained, "John and I decided that we would do our best to replicate in the White House the way we lived as a family when he was in the Senate. And that means that we will not wall our children off from the rest of our lives." During the campaign, the family's two young children provided frequent distractions during strategy sessions at Chez Edwards. On one occasion, Jack scrambled off unnoticed with the only copy of pollster Harrison Hickman's latest survey and the slick-fingered lad was later discovered happily coloring over the numbers.

Jack and Emma Claire are, in a sense, the First Family's second family. Both were brought into the world as a testament of faith after the Edwardses' oldest child, Wade, perished in a car crash in 1996. Asked about the role that Wade's memory plays in the family's permissive approach to child rearing, the First Lady said bluntly, "That's something I'd prefer not to discuss." The Edwards' elder daughter, Cate, 21, is a senior at Princeton, who quietly slips into the White House on weekends . . .

Having traveled so many miles with so many Democratic hopefuls, it is strange to finish this report so far from the end of the journey. Well, almost finished. Every reporter who has ever ventured north of Manhattan or west of the Beltway in campaign season returns home to be confronted with the inevitable dinner party query: "What did you really think?"

That insistent question triggers one of those awkward social moments that are difficult to finesse. There is always the danger of lapsing into the blowhard bromides of TV talk shows: "The challenge for Kucinich is whether he can move to the center . . . Sharpton must win New Hampshire . . . Moseley Braun faces a daunting map after Iowa . . ." But the alternative seems either fatuous certainty or facile calumny. No one at a dinner party, after downing three glasses of chardonnay, wants to hear a judicious answer that begins, "To be honest, they're all good men with their own strengths and weaknesses."

So what do I think? Really?

Howard Dean is simultaneously beguiling and exasperating. Just as I was taken with a maverick named John McCain in 2000, I was impressed by Dean's self-confident disdain for the tremulous trimmers in Washington. But the intemperate style that has carried Dean so far, so fast is a double-edged sword: Too often he prefers to slice rather than splice, and every unneeded slash invites a backlash. If Dean were in the White House, Hallmark would probably rush out a new line of presidential apology notes.

John Kerry is the candidate with whom I would most enjoy going out for a beer. But then I have a weakness for cerebral guys who talk in complex sentences, get caught up in the nuances of policy, remember Vietnam and seem just depressed enough to be interesting.

Joe Lieberman, despite his Rumsfeld-Lite foreign-policy views, has the balanced temperament befitting a man who wants to be entrusted with the codes for nuclear weapons. He would be a good companion in a comedy club, though I would feel embarrassed for him if the performers were working blue.

Wesley Clark leaves me perplexed. I can't decide whether his surprise mid-September dive into the presidential scrum reflected naivete about the demands of running for president or disdain for the political calling. Either way, his initial shaky, learning-curve months on the campaign trail have undermined the purported electability that was the rationale for his candidacy in the first place.

Dick Gephardt reminds me about what I always liked about the never flashy Midwest. He may lack bandwidth, but his stout-hearted solidity, his good spirits and his loyalty to longtime advisers are all Old Economy virtues.

John Edwards is the presidential contender who is far more compelling in person than he is in theory. From afar, it is easy to dismiss his short résumé, his impetuous ambition and his over-dependence on trial lawyers for funding. But watching him in public settings or talking with him privately serves as a reminder that some politicians are simply blessed with The Gift. Edwards, the ultimate cockeyed optimist, never needs to buy a Hallmark card—he is a Hallmark card.

The coda to this chronicle is not designed to drape any of the 2004 Democrats in the mantle of greatness or to issue dire warnings about the deficiencies of a particular presidential contender. For I take seriously the hallowed journalistic dictum: No cheering in the press box. But my year-long odyssey along the back roads of Iowa and New Hampshire was never about just the 2004 Democrats and their campaigns. It was also about myself in midlife and my gnawing unease with the sound-bite superficiality of most political reporting. At this early date, there is no way of knowing whether I caught an early-bird glimpse of the man who will be taking the oath of office in January 2005. (And I was damned if I was going to visit the sun-parched soil of Crawford, Texas, to cover my bets.) But regardless of the outcome of the 2004 campaign, I have already found the object of my personal quest. Once again, I have come alive to the wonder of presidential politics and see the glory of my chosen calling. Once again, I understand what propelled me down this career path so many years ago when I first picked up my parents' Book-of-the-Month Club edition of *The Making of the President 1960*.

In a word, it's idealism—the belief that no matter how repetitive the rituals and Byzantine the process, there is an inherent majesty to bearing witness to a free people selecting its leader. Shared idealism is also, in a way, the true bond linking reporters with the candidates they cover. Every one of the Democrats I have followed, despite human flaws and foibles, sincerely believes that he can successfully lead this nation through the remainder of this arduous and anguish-filled decade. If there is a charlatan or a chiseler among them, then he has certainly evaded

my reportorial wiles. Far more likely, they are all good men seeking an unforgiving office in difficult times. Yes, some halos will
be dented and some images soiled along the way, for presidential
politics is not for the fainthearted. But these questers, these seek-
ers, these dreamers, with whom I have shared the romance of the
road, have won my admiration for daring to follow their ambitions as far and as high as fate will carry them.

Now let's lean back and enjoy the rest of the show.

And what a show it turned out to be.

When I wrote the passage above in late summer 2003 to conclude the hardcover edition of this book, I was akin to a carnival
barker promising gullible bystanders Siamese triplets and a Ger-
man shepherd who could recite Goethe. There was no way to
know for certain that the coming campaign drama I was shamelessly hawking would turn out to be the political equivalent of
The Producers—a box-office smash that would rejuvenate the
Democratic Party, restore the luster of the Iowa caucuses and
reward jaded campaign reporters like myself with enough goose-
bump thrills to require a defibrillator.

In early May 2004, two months after the Democratic primary
race was over, I ran into the beaten-but-unbowed Howard Dean at
the White House Correspondents Dinner. Awash in instant nostalgia, I suggested to Dean that forty years from now toothless
campaign veterans and jejune political science students would
still be reliving the roller-coaster ride of the final few weeks
before the Iowa caucuses. A momentary look of pain crossed
Dean's face as he said, "I certainly hope not."

Tough luck. It will probably be Dean's cruel and somewhat
unfair fate to be immortalized as the Democratic Party's answer
to Thomas E. Dewey—the candidate who, as the saying goes,
snatched defeat from the jaws of victory. But the home stretch of
the 2004 race featured more than a nuclear meltdown on par
with Chernobyl. John Kerry's gritty determination and John

Edwards's late-breaking surge ended up creating the perfectly balanced, North-South, old-new, solemn-and-sunny Democratic ticket. The presidential also-rans added intriguing subplots to the drama, especially the enigmatic Wesley Clark. The general's surprise candidacy, announced in mid-September, was like a comet streaking across the primary skies, an other-worldly apparition provoking media-driven fascination before flaming out into a handful of moon dust. And finally, there was the quiet dignity, tinged with sadness, as the perpetually star-crossed Dick Gephardt and the politically miscast Joe Lieberman met their pre-ordained destinies.

I stand by my prediction to Dean: As long as there are caucuses and primaries, as long as weary campaign aides and sleep-deprived reporters gather in late-night bars to revel in their shared political calling, they will still be harking back to those wintry 2004 days in Iowa and New Hampshire. So, to borrow a trademark line from the age-old radio broadcaster Paul Harvey, "Here's the rest of the story."

CHAPTER 12

Dateline: Des Moines

Around midnight on caucus night, January 19, I wandered into the bedlam of the lobby of the Hotel Fort Des Moines, where Mardi Gras revelry co-existed side-by-side with the alcohol-fueled lamentations of an Irish wake. For the Kerry cadres this was now Paradise Island, while the downcast Deaniacs regarded the same turf as the Heartbreak Hotel. The first person I spied was Mark Mellman, John Kerry's bearded and beaming pollster. I felt obligated to recall for Mellman's benefit, "A month ago when you told me that Kerry's strategy for a comeback in New Hampshire was to first win Iowa, I laughed uproariously."

My homing-pigeon instinct to head for the bar was tempered by an alert from David Wade, Kerry's steadfastly loyal press secretary, who had been along back in 2002 on my first adventures aloft with the now high-flying candidate. "Don't move from this spot," Wade urged. "Kerry's coming down any second." The traveling press corps, who were accompanying Kerry on a late-night charter flight to New Hampshire, had already been herded onto buses idling in front of the hotel. So I became the sole reporter poised to stake out Kerry, until, in a selfless gesture of journalistic camaraderie, I arranged to share my privileged position with my wife Meryl, who had written for *New York* the only magazine profile of Kerry to appear during his prior six months in political purgatory.

Meryl spotted Kerry first, and was rewarded with a hug. But that was his only outward sign of exuberance. Instead of "I'm King of the World" jubilation, Kerry radiated surprised satisfaction, curiously reminiscent of Oscar-winning Sally Field marveling, "You like me. You really like me." His first words to me were an acknowledgment of our shared journey, as he said, "You're going to go flying again with me, buddy?"

During post-game moments like this, TV sportscasters invariably burble, "Now that you've hit three home runs, and you're MVP of the World Series, and you're about to sign a $90-million contract, how does it feel?" Although my precise comments to Kerry immediately vanished into the mists of memory, I'm pretty sure that I didn't ask if he was going to Disney World. The candidate, who could now rightfully challenge Bill Clinton for ownership of the sobriquet of "The Comeback Kid," did admit, "There were some bleak moments, but we kept plodding through." But Kerry insisted that his prospects were never as dire as the polls and his press clippings had suggested. "I felt things begin to move at the end of the summer [of 2003]," he recalled. "But it was really hard to break through to get attention."

What stays with me from that lobby encounter was the mellowness of Kerry's mood on the night that, in retrospect, vaulted him to the nomination. Teresa Heinz, chatting with Meryl just a few feet away, was still firing off vituperative comments about Howard Dean, who had limped home a weak third in the caucuses. But Kerry, not normally apt to follow the Biblical admonition about turning the other cheek, was in a different place that night. It would be an overstatement to suggest that Kerry, like the protagonist of a Greek tragedy if I recall my college literature courses correctly, had achieved wisdom through suffering. But Kerry's ordeal along the road to Iowa—his mother's death, his prostate cancer, the disarray of his campaign, his collapse in the polls—had tested his inner resources in a raw and wrenching fashion. Rarely has there been a recent presidential candidate more deserving of such a moment of quiet vindication.

That was my last real glimpse of Kerry before he vanished behind a protective cordon of handlers, West Wing hopefuls and hard-eyed Secret Service agents. Ever since my first forays with the Democratic dreamers, I knew this transformation would be inevitable. In presidential politics, losers are liberated; winners are winched to their own success. Kerry, like every presidential nominee, has been forced, by necessity, to place his personality into a blind trust. The stakes are too enormous, the risks are too obvious, to dare traffic in spontaneity and to reveal honest emotion. With every off-the-cuff sentence parsed by the press and public, with every natural gesture turned into fodder for the late-night comics, a nominee retreats in the empire of the ersatz. Under the omnipresent eyes of the TV cameras, the only security lies in the sound-bite sentiments and polished platitudes of that learned language called "Candidate Speak." So by the strange and self-defeating dictates of our media age, the more familiar John Kerry appears to the voters, the more impenetrable he becomes behind his public veneer.

Now that the hurly-burly's done, now that the battle's lost and won, caucus night in Iowa still shimmers in memory. Since we know the outcome, it is nearly impossible to replicate the uncertainty that filled the anxious hours before 6:30 P.M. when 124,331 Iowa Democrats assembled at 1,993 caucus sites. (Adding to the suspense was the blissful absence of mid-day exit-poll numbers, which always cuts into the drama of primary nights). Never in my years of covering presidential politics can I recall a pivotal contest in which it seemed like any of four candidates could plausibly finish first or fourth. David Yepsen, the *Des Moines Register*'s widely respected political columnist, confidently predicted on caucus morning that Dean would win because he had assembled "the best get-out-the-vote operation ever seen in state." Even John Norris, Kerry's unflappably confident Iowa coordinator, thought that the order of finish would be Kerry, Dean, Dick Gephardt and then John Edwards. (The final numbers were Kerry 38 percent, Edwards 32 percent, Dean 18 percent, Gephardt 11 percent and Dennis Kucinich 1 percent).

Okay, I owe Iowa Democrats an apology. For all my persnickety comments earlier in this book about the undue political importance of this demographically unrepresentative state, for all my complaints about the paltry turnout for the 2000 Al Gore–Bill Bradley showdown, the 2004 caucuses more than justified the continued survival of this peculiar institution. Not only was participation double 2000 levels, not only did Iowans replicate the we-want-a-winner-in-November sentiments of national Democrats, but the caucuses also reminded me that they provide a flesh-and-blood reality that exists nowhere else in national politics. We have all absorbed the paeans to the secret ballot in our high-schools civics classes, but there is also an unmatched voyeuristic thrill in watching caucus-goers declare their allegiance in public.

At the recommendation of Edwards Iowa coordinator Rob Bernsten, I staked out Precinct 46 in Des Moines, which met at Mason Elementary School, near Drake University, in a neighborhood filled with young professionals in starter homes. My hunch that Edwards was surging panned out: I lucked into a caucus that came close to replicating the statewide results. On the sign-in line, I met first-time caucus-goer Ann Reinhart, a landscape architect in her early thirties, who was the embodiment of Indecision 2004. Even though she was clutching a Kerry sticker in her right hand, she was still attracted to Edwards, a candidate whom she only knew from his upbeat TV commercials, such as the one in which he stood in front of the modest house in which he grew up and declared "when you remember where you came from, you'll always know where you're going." Reinhart stressed that she didn't have a "hot-button issue" like the war in Iraq; she was just questing after the candidate with the best chance of beating George W. Bush.

Precinct 46 had initially been assigned to the school cafeteria, but when more than 250 Democrats turned out, the caucus was moved to the gymnasium. While some caucuses feature speeches on behalf of each candidate, veteran precinct chairman James Peterson was proud of his record of making the votes run on time. "I've been doing this for sixteen years," he announced standing on a chair in the middle of the gym. "And I've never been here after 9:00 P.M." Then Peterson instructed the supporters of each of the five candidates contesting the caucuses to move to different areas of the room.

This migration provided the first visible manifestation of the collapse of Gephardt and Dean. David Efron, an attorney who was precinct chairman for Gephardt as he had been in 1988, stood by a table decorated with a triangular cardboard placard for his candidate. Even though Efron was holding a four-page sheet of names, only sixteen Democrats rallied around the Gephardt banner, not nearly enough to meet the 15-percent threshold to win a delegate. "In this building we're dead meat," Efron declared, before leading his dejected band out of the caucus. Meanwhile, the forty-three members of the smaller-than-expected Dean brigade were nervously counting heads to make sure they were still in the game (called "being viable" in caucus lingo) and sadly wondering where all the momentum had gone.

On the other side of the gym, the Kerry and Edwards contingents were so large that they spilled into one another. Standing on the boundary line, like a refugee unsure whether to cross the border, was the still undecided Reinhart. Finally, she impulsively took a step to her left to caucus with Edwards. "I've got my heart over here and my head over there," she said, gesturing toward the Kerry camp. "Edwards just inspires me. I'm voting with my heart."

There was a brief intermission as supporters of the three surviving viable candidates vied for the allegiance of the nineteen anti-war, anti-globalism zealots who had backed Kucinich. This second-chance re-vote is one of the hallowed traditions of the caucuses, and, in practice, the brief bidding war combines the huckersterism of a Middle Eastern souk with the childish antics of "Red Rover, Come Over." Edwards and Kucinich had worked out a secret arrangement to urge their supporters, if the group was not viable in a particular caucus, to back the other candidate in the second-round balloting—a maneuver that may have added a few percentage points to Edwards's statewide total. But here at Mason Elementary School this odd-couple alliance was not visible: the Kucinich vote split three ways. The final totals from Precinct 46 were, for those keeping score at home, Edwards 97, Kerry 95 and Dean 50.

Back at the Hotel Fort Des Moines later that night, a rueful Kerry staffer described to Teresa Heinz a similar surge to Edwards at another caucus location. Deeply aware of the threat posed by the telegenic Southerner, she had only one question about the caucus-goers who joined the last-minute Edwards stampede: "Were they women?"

Any account of caucus night that doesn't mention Dean's "I have a scream" speech is like a retelling of Noah's life story entirely set on dry land. Replayed on cable TV more often than the O. J. Simpson Bronco chase, Dean's overwrought rhetorical style transformed a routine caucus-night concession speech into what seemed like the before-therapy portion of a public-service advertisement for psychological counseling. Speaking to 3,500 distraught supporters in a Des Moines ballroom, Dean, his voice rising to a feverish crescendo, rattled off a list of upcoming primary and caucus states—"We're going to South Carolina and Oklahoma and Arizona and North Dakota and New Mexico"—punctuated by a final "Yahoo!" that sounded like the growl that Dr. Jekyll uttered before he turned into Mr. Hyde.

What this outburst appeared to prove was that Dean was too unhinged to ever be trusted with the family car, let alone the nation's nuclear codes. What this incident actually demonstrated is that while cameras may never lie, microphones certainly do. As Steve McMahon, Dean's media consultant, explained to me later, "I could tell immediately that Howard was overcompensating for the PA system being down in the room." In other words, the decibel level heard at the rally was significantly lower than the sound that was going directly from Dean's microphone into the television feed. This interpretation is in line with a report by ABC's Diane Sawyer for *Good Morning America* that pointed out that Dean had been using a hand-held microphone designed to filter out background noise. Unfortunately for Dean, Sawyer's revisionist history was broadcast ten days after the caucuses and two days after the New Hampshire primary, at a time when his spavined candidacy was pointed toward the glue factory.

For me, the Dean concession speech illustrated a cardinal rule of journalism: You can mouth off on TV or you can cover events, but you can't do both. While Dean was self-destructing, I was fair and balanced on a stool in the scenic Iowa state senate chamber providing caucus-night commentary for Fox News. The impromptu set-up lacked a TV monitor, so while I could hear what the cable network was telecasting, I couldn't see it. So when Fox played the tape of Dean's rant several times during the one-hour show, I wondered if this was an exaggerated attack by the conservative network on a leading Democratic presidential hopeful. Only in my hotel room at 2:00 in the morning, when I finally watched a replay of the inflammatory speech on C-Span, did I grasp the full horror of the TV version of Dean's performance.

Months later, when I sat down with Dean to review the Icarus-like saga of his presidential campaign, I asked him about the event that had launched a thousand parodies. "The truth is—and I think the media knows this—that the scream speech was a media concoction," he said. "It wasn't that bad. It certainly didn't cost me the race; I had already lost Iowa. The bad thing about the scream speech was not the 'Yahoo!' The bad thing about the scream speech was that we should have been talking to the nation."

In a prior chapter, I argued that reporters should not try to shrink-wrap presidential contenders in an effort to conjure up some amateur-hour psycho-analytic theory of their essence. I drew a distinction between these fatally flawed attempts at pop psychology and the observable aspects of a candidate's temperament and personality. But the national demonization of Dean because of the deceptive TV tape left me troubled. Has the hyper-kinetic news cycle created a culture of mix-master mockery that reduces all would-be presidents to caricatures? Have the Personality Police of the press corps now joined forces with the old-time Character Cops who hounded Gary Hart and Bill Clinton?

Looking back on the campaign now, I find myself struggling to understand the harshness of the standard press-bus put-downs of Dean. Yes, political reporters are too gushy about candidates on the way up (warbling about Dean's fund-raising and his endorsements by Al Gore and Tom Harkin) and too vicious on the way down (sneering at his accurate-in-hindsight assessment that Saddam Hussein's capture did not make America safer). But the animus toward Dean seemed to reflect something deeper than the normal bio-rhythms of journalism. I got the sense, though I cannot prove it with specific examples, that many reporters privately felt that the tart-tongued former governor of a bed-and-breakfast state should not be elevated to the Oval Office in an era of terrorism. If my tentative theory is correct, this negative pre-disposition meant that when times got tough, Dean did not have the built-in reservoir of good will to catch a break from the press.

Tricia Enright, Dean's communications director, offered a dream-like metaphor to describe the death throes of her candidate. "After the scream," she said, "I pictured Howard Dean on the ground and the national press corps standing around him in a circle. The reporters are looking at Dean's unmoving body, and they're looking at each other, and they're saying, 'Just give him a little kick. Or prop his head up.' Finally they realize, 'Maybe we hit him too hard that last time.' It's that moment of disbelief, that belated recognition, that Howard Dean was not going to get up anymore."

Judged by book-shelf space alone, the Dean crusade is fast on its way to becoming the political equivalent of the Bloomsbury Group. Not since the 1972 McGovern debacle have veterans of a losing campaign been so inspired by their muse. Private citizen Dean was barely back in Burlington, cleaning out the gubernatorial memorabilia from his garage, when his pollster Paul Maslin published a withering campaign memoir in the *Atlantic*. (A sample sentence: "Our candidate's erratic judgment, loose tongue and overall stubbornness wore our spirits down"). By early summer, defrocked campaign manager Joe Trippi, who had become the James Carville of the Internet era, hit the bookstores with his even-handed, more-in-sorrow assessment, *The Revolution Will Not Be Televised*. Dean volunteer Dana Dunnan rushed into print with his bottoms-up account, *Burning at the Grassroots*. And the candidate's own recollections will be published this fall. Before this literary renaissance is over, we will probably be treated to such enduring works as *Van Driver: The Free-Wheeling Story of a Memorable Afternoon in the Dean Campaign* and *A Collector's Guide to Dean Lawn Signs*.

The fascination with this Lost Cause is understandable, since, to update Tolstoy: All winning campaigns are alike, all losing campaigns are dysfunctional in their own way. But the public back-biting over the internal dynamics of the Dean team (traveling aide Kate O'Connor's fierce over-protectiveness of the candidate; Trippi's inability to win control over the campaign budget; the organizational disarray in Iowa) obscures larger truths. Ever since Jimmy Carter in 1976, insurgent candidates—Gary Hart, Paul Tsongas, John McCain—have aroused passion with their outsider messages, but ultimately were thwarted by the party establishment. When I posed this interpretation to Dean, he snapped, "There hasn't been anybody who came as close as we did since Carter."

Dean's proud claim can be challenged, since, after all, he never won a contested primary. But unlike his fellow mavericks, Dean was anointed as the unquestioned favorite for the nomination months before the Iowa caucuses. As early as the first week in

August, both *Time* ("The Dean Factor") and *Newsweek* ("Howard Dean: Destiny or Disaster?") splashed his photograph on their covers in the same week. These portrayals of Dean's strength and the others that followed were probably exaggerated. Once again, the political community was snookered by the seemingly objective measurements of money and polling numbers. When Dean amassed a jaw-dropping $15 million in the third quarter of 2003 and surged toward the lead in the volatile and imprecise Iowa polls, it was akin to a triumphant Napoleon arriving at the gates of Moscow. Who would have dared prophesize the brutal winter that awaited Dean, the compact political general who commanded such a mighty Internet army?

If there was a moment that captured both Dean's brash confidence and the brutal confluence of events that lay ahead, it was the secret summit in early September between the governor and the general. This was the now-famous meeting at which Dean, although he still denies it, almost certainly dangled the vice presidency in front of Wesley Clark. Even today, the story remains a Rashomon-like tale in which the truth depends on the teller's perspective. This account—based on the recollections of Dean, Clark, Trippi and Dean political director Paul Blank—is my reconstruction of what probably happened.

For Dean, Clark represented both opportunity and danger. It must have been beguiling for Dean to imagine forging an alliance with an anti-war general who would instantly compensate for his lack of national-security credentials. But Clark, who was rapidly being seduced by an Internet-based draft movement, also posed an obvious threat to Dean's outsider image and his fund-raising prowess. The two men had already held several discussions, mostly about foreign policy. By chance, Dean and Clark were both in Los Angeles on September 6; the go-for-broke governor was playing to adoring crowds in what had become his fifty-state campaign and the still wavering general was covering his bets by wooing fund-raisers from the Left Coast.

The hush-hush Dean–Clark pow-wow was slated for a conference room right off the lobby at the Sheraton Hotel at LAX. But

Dean had also impetuously decided to hold a press conference in the hotel immediately afterwards to endorse beleaguered Governor Gray Davis in the California recall election. As a result, many of the national political press corps were already camped in the Sheraton lobby awaiting the Dean–Davis joint appearance, unaware that they were about to miss a far more intriguing face-off unfolding behind closed doors just twenty feet away. To maintain the cloak-and-dagger secrecy, Blank and Trippi walled off the conference room with a portable drape, claiming it was a Dean holding room, and Clark took the scenic route to the meeting through the hotel's kitchen.

Waiting for Dean to come down from his hotel suite, Blank found himself chatting with the general, whom he had never met. "You're one of those political professionals, aren't you?" Clark asked the twenty-seven-year-old Blank by way of greeting. Blank admitted that, yes, he had been working on campaigns since he was literally twelve years old. "I don't have anybody like you," Clark mused. "I'm not a politician. I don't really have political people around me." Blank, puzzled by this conversational gambit that seemed to be veering close to a job offer, blandly observed that Clark would solve that staffing gap if he became a candidate. Then, in a tone that radiated command presence, Clark declared, "You know, I've never done anything that I can't win."

Like a duel, the actual meeting was limited to the principals and their seconds, Trippi and Mark Nichols, Clark's chief of staff. The two aides quickly departed, leaving Dean and Clark alone. The general's account of the crucial moments of their private conversation is convincing, largely because the dialogue that he quoted to me sounded so plausible:

CLARK: Howard, I'm trying to decide whether to run or not to run.
DEAN: Don't you want to know the alternative?
CLARK: Okay, what's the alternative?
DEAN: You can be my vice president, but you'd have to be vetted.

There is no indication that Clark was ever seriously tempted. In fact, a half an hour later when Trippi re-entered the room,

Clark was confiding to Dean, his putative rival, about his wife's reluctance: "Gert doesn't want me to run." To Trippi's shock, Dean responded with words closer in spirit to a men's support group than to brass-knuckle politics. "It's not that bad," Dean said. "Judy had the same type of feelings initially. But now that I'm out there running, she thinks it's great. I'll be glad to have Judy call Gert." Trippi found Dean's c'mon-in-the-water's-fine offer to be bizarre, since the overriding purpose of the meeting was to convince Clark not to run. But as Dean later explained to me, "I figured if he was going to run, he's going to run. It was not my business to talk him out of running for president, so I didn't even try."

Judy Steinberg never called Gert Clark for girl talk about what to do when your man thinks he's got to run ... for president. But just eleven days after Dean offered his wife as a character witness for the joys of being a campaign spouse, Clark declared his candidacy for president in his home town of Little Rock. His eleven-minute speech was spare on specifics and brimming with banalities: "We're going to run a campaign that will move this country forward, not back." The fledgling candidate quickly moved up, not down, in the polls: A USA Today/CNN/Gallup national survey, conducted a few days after the roll-out, found Clark leading the Democratic pack with 21-percent support. These polling numbers, of course, were as ephemeral as a cloud formation and probably were inflated by the halo effect from the honorific "general" in front of Clark's name in the question. But they helped create the fiction that a modern-day Cincinnatus was about to rescue the Democratic Party, a hero motif that was magnified when *Newsweek* immediately rewarded Clark with a cover—recognition not offered Kerry until after he won the Iowa caucuses.

Despite his glittering press clips, Clark immediately paid a price for his temerity in seeking the presidency without ever deigning to go through basic training. Chatting with reporters on a charter flight from Little Rock to Florida a day after he tossed his brass hat into the ring, Clark undermined the anti-war rationale for his candidacy by stumbling over the simple question of whether he would have voted for the congressional resolution authorizing the invasion of Iraq. With every tortured sentence, the general appeared to shift his position on whether he ever supported the war. Finally, as recounted by Adam Nagourney in the *New York Times*, Clark begged for assistance from his new (and short-lived) press secretary Mary Jacoby, crying out, "Mary, help!" During the same airborne interview, the ill-prepared candidate described his initial forays on the campaign trail using this idiosyncratic simile: "It's like what we did in the military when we went to the motor pool and talked to the troops—only better."

There was always a tinge of cynicism to the notion that the only way that the Democrats could win would be to nominate a retired general who, as Joe Lieberman tartly put it, "had been a registered lobbyist before he was a registered Democrat." But Clark himself projected a cheerful innocence about the rigors and rituals of running for president. What other would-be candidate would have chosen to spend a chunk of summer 2003 mulling his future at the Aspen Institute rather than shaking hands in Keokuk, Iowa?

Unprovoked surrender is not standard military doctrine. But, in effect, that's what Clark did in mid-October by acceding to the recommendation of his top advisers that he abandon the Iowa caucuses. Veteran Democratic strategist Eli Segal, who served as Clark's national chairman, explained later, "It seemed to me and the others that for us to compete in Iowa—at a point when we did not know that we'd have the money and we didn't have the organization—was an impossible task." The Clark high command realized that hoisting the white flag over Iowa would probably cost them the endorsement of Gerald McEntee, the president of the public employee union, AFSCME. But the general's field officers did not understand (nor, for that matter, did most of the press) that the only route to the winner's circle at the Boston Convention began in Des Moines on caucus night. Lieberman—last

seen bravely chomping down on a deep-fried Twinkie at the Iowa
State Fair—also pulled up stakes and headed for New Hampshire
at the same time. But the hawkish Connecticut senator was
always culturally and ideologically out of place in the Hawkeye
State. Lieberman's withdrawal from the caucuses brought to
mind Dorothy Parker's crack on hearing about the death of Calvin
Coolidge: "How can they tell?"

Most of the political season consists of jousting, jamming and
jabbering about trivia—TV ads that are ignored by voters, over-
rehearsed ad libs that go unnoticed in campaign debates. But
every once in a while, a candidate and his advisers make a decision that matters far more than they could have ever imagined.
Which brings us to the story of the most important strategic
choice in the entire 2004 campaign—a bold move by Dean that
inadvertently handed Kerry the nomination and, perhaps more
important for Democrats, the wherewithal to aggressively challenge Bush.

Back in late 2002 when I began chronicling the money chase at
closed-door candidate auditions in Park Avenue board rooms and
at fund-raisers in palatial Fifth Avenue apartments, I could never
have envisioned the Democrats' strange fiscal landscape in the fall
of 2003. All the Dean team had to do was to project a new fund-
raising graphic onto their web page and enough small-donor contributions would roll in effortlessly to create the illusion of a
perpetual-motion money machine. Right before Halloween, the
Dean webmasters came up with a holiday version of their fabled
(baseball) bat—black flying animals purportedly designed to scare
George W. Bush. This childish gimmick alone raised $355,000 in
four days from more than 6,000 supporters.

In contrast, most of Dean's rivals were reduced to searching
for loose change on Iowa sidewalks. Fund-raising woes had
forced Bob Graham from the race in October, and his dedicated
daughter Gwen, who displayed a hereditary knack for politics,

soon signed on as Dean's southern coordinator. Gephardt was back where he had been in 1988, scratching for every dollar to keep his last-hurrah candidacy alive. Instead of gruel, Lieberman was subsisting on the bread of affliction. Even Edwards, who had struggled so hard to set the early fund-raising pace, was beginning to fail to cover his bimonthly payroll, which is usually the final stage before putting up a big "Going Out of Business" sign in the headquarters window. Then there was Kerry, who was now trailing Dean by a double-digit margin in the polls from what was supposed to be his safe haven of New Hampshire. I knew things were bad on the cash-and-Kerry front, but I did not realize how dire the fiscal situation was until I attended a Manhattan dinner party in early November where three of the candidate's top money mavens spent the evening sharing shell-shocked stories about how their candidate was tapped out in New York. "I just can't get anyone excited about him," lamented a woman of legendary prowess in fund-raising circles. The Massachusetts senator's stock was so low that a $2,000 contribution might well have put the donor on the short list for a European embassy in a then-hard-to-imagine Kerry administration.

This was the backdrop for the heart-pounding, spine-tingling adventure yarn of how Dean busted the caps. Okay, the political phrase "busting the caps" does not convey the appropriate blare-of-trumpets sense of drama; it sounds like it refers to a broken shift lever on a computer keyboard. What the phrase actually means is that a presidential candidate gives up federal matching funds in order to be liberated from the overall $45-million limit (the so-called "cap") that otherwise applies to all spending until the convention. This free-market approach to becoming president was pioneered, so to speak, by Bush in 2000, who used the fund-raising prowess of his "Pioneers" to corral more than $100 million, then an unprecedented figure for politics. This time around, the Bush campaign was well on its way to raising a daunting $200 million, a figure that would have made the Democratic nominee akin to a Monopoly player with a single house on low-rent Baltic Avenue while his GOP rival erected hotels on Board-walk and Park Place.

Joe Trippi first began toying with the notion of busting the caps in June when he grasped the fund-raising prowess of the Internet for a cause-driven candidate like Dean. But Trippi, who had an uneasy personal relationship with his candidate and faced continual internal opposition from Dean loyalists like Kate O'Connor, did not rule by decree. Only in September, as Dean was raising a Democratic-record $15 million for the quarter, did the campaign manager dare propose such a high-risk gambit, arguing, "Guys, you've got to do this. It's our only chance against Bush." Dean was resistant, but raised two practical questions: What if we can't replace the $19 million in public financing that we would be giving up? And how can I get away with being the first Democrat ever to abandon the matching-funds program without looking like I'm out to scuttle campaign reform?

The first question required faith, but the answer to the second came wrapped in the Confederate flag. Touching off one of those silly campaign flaps that helps explain why front-running candidates tend to equate reporters with hand grenades, Dean maladroitly told the *Des Moines Register* in late October, "I still want to be the candidate for guys with Confederate flags in their pickup trucks." It was easy to mock Dean's claim, since his supporters were infinitely more apt to drive BMW's than be called "Bubba." At a Boston debate sponsored by Rock the Vote, Dean came under withering fire from Edwards (the Confederate flag line was demeaning to Southerners) and Al Sharpton (hey, don't forget the racial context). Desperate to divert attention from the Stars and Bars, Trippi convinced Dean to use a November 5 speech at Cooper Union in New York to announce that he would conduct an on-line referendum to ask his donors if he should reject matching funds. This participatory ploy worked, albeit temporarily: More than 80 percent of the Deaniacs voted in favor of busting the caps and the Confederate flag abruptly disappeared from newspaper cartoons about Dean.

The overall Dean strategy, as Trippi later explained, was "to spend Kerry into the dust." But the decision to reject public financing had the opposite effect: It provided Kerry with political cover to partially pay for his own campaign with a $6.4 million cash injection from assets (the townhouse on Louisberg Square) he jointly held with his wife Teresa. Without the loan, Kerry's top staffers now freely concede, the campaign would have failed to cover its mid-December payroll. While Edwards inspired such intense loyalty that unpaid staffers kept their fiscal plight a secret, the news that the fractious Kerry campaign was broke would have immediately been ballyhooed on the front page of the *Washington Post*. Without the loan, Kerry would have gone into the final weeks before the Iowa caucuses enveloped in the sweet smell of defeat.

Dean stressed during our post-primary interview that he had always assumed that Kerry would reach for his personal checkbook when money became tight, since that was what he had done in his scorched-earth 1996 Senate reelection battle against Bill Weld. "I told John that to his face," Dean said, referring to a recent conversation with the Democratic nominee. That may be a self-protective view on Dean's part, since it spares him from additional strategic regrets. But everyone on the Kerry side of the equation, both current and former staffers, have convincingly argued that the cautious senator would not have taken out the loan without being able to claim that Dean made him do it. So without the Dean difference, Kerry probably would have gone broke instead of going for broke.

I was reviewing Dean's decision to reject public financing over lunch in Washington with Trippi in early July. Just that morning the papers had announced that Kerry had raised a staggering-for-a-Democrat $182 million through the first half of 2004, putting the nominee on virtually even footing with Bush. "Howard Dean made that happen," Trippi said proudly. "Without busting the caps, there was no way that Kerry would have a shot."

*

Kerry's resurrection began with a mid-October conversation on the Senate floor, one of those collegial huddles that can be glimpsed, but not heard, from the press balcony. Kerry wandered over to Ted Kennedy, the liberal patriarch with whom he had an uneasy history, to make a request: Can I borrow Mary Beth Cahill and Stephanie Cutter for my campaign? The forty-nine-year-old Cahill, whose prematurely white hair suggests a steady maturity rather than a volatile temperament, was Kennedy's chief of staff. She had made her political reputation in a series of hard-fought New England campaigns and at the feminist political action committee, Emily's List. Cutter, normally Kennedy's communications director, was already on loan to direct media strategies for the Boston Convention. Kennedy, playing a role midway between the Godfather and the father of the bride, gave his assent and promptly told Cahill about the conversation. But it all remained amorphous, Cahill recalled, "since I didn't hear anything for a month."

Jim Jordan, Kerry's beleaguered campaign manager, was in the precarious position of a South American leader who could see the tanks lining up in front of the presidential palace for a coup. Kerry, in the middle of what should have been his triumphant announcement tour in early September, was forced to respond to rumors that Jordan had been ousted. The candidate's initial remarks—delivered while holding several fast-melting ice-cream cones at a Des Moines photo-op—were far from a ringing vote of confidence: "You always leave windows open. If something isn't working properly, you do something."

But three weeks later Jordan thought he had been saved from defenestration when former New Hampshire Governor Jeanne Shaheen signed on to chair the national campaign. I was drinking with Jordan in the bar of Boston's Parker House the night before Kerry's New Hampshire press conference heralding Shaheen's new post. Jordan made no secret of being constantly undermined by back-channel cell-phone calls to Kerry from Boston-based strategists with long ties to the candidate. Shaheen, Jordan believed, would be an honest broker, refereeing between the campaign, the Boston Mafia and sharp-elbowed imagemaker Bob Shrum. What Jordan didn't know was that he was, in effect, being papered over. As Cam Kerry, the candidate's brother and Jordan critic, later told me, "We tried to work around it"—the campaign manager's fragile authority—"for a while, but it didn't work."

Not until Friday night, November 7, did Cahill get the summons that she had been awaiting. As Cahill recalled, Kerry told her by phone that "he needed someone to run this thing, so that he could get back to being a candidate." She soon called Cutter to announce, "I think it's happening." But, as is so often the case in politics, the campaign manager was the last to know.

Early Sunday evening Jordan and Shaheen conferred with Kerry in the basement den of his townhouse on Louisberg Square. There was a curious what-elephant-in-the-corner flavor to the meeting, since Jordan spent the first hour going over a cash-flow chart that showed that the campaign would soon be insolvent unless Kerry was willing to play Daddy Warbucks and take out a loan. "It was a hard decision," Jordan recounted, "but we finally worked it through. One of the things that held it up was that John had never told anyone what his financial capacity was. He never said, 'I can borrow X, Y or Z.' He would just mumble something like 'Maybe I can do that.' Finally that night he said, 'I can and I'm going to.'"

Having dealt with money, it was time for mayhem. Kerry announced, according to Jordan, "We have something else to discuss. We've decided to make a change—we don't think it's working." Kerry spent the next few minutes alternating between praising the ever-loyal Jordan for his accomplishments and lamenting that there was no other way to end the tensions within the faction-ridden campaign. Then the candidate, maybe insincerely and certainly unrealistically, suggested that Jordan could stay on in a diminished role: either working out of the office of media consultant Jim Margolis to frame the campaign's message or even becoming communications director. Jordan quickly dismissed these face-saving notions as unworkable. The defrocked campaign manager's five-year association with the senator was coming to its inevitable conclusion when Kerry made a final demand that turned a harmonious exit into a rancorous departure. Kerry insisted that Jordan announce to his staff and the press that he was quitting voluntarily. "I'm not inclined to lie for you about this," Jordan responded angrily. "And nobody in the press would believe that I would bug out on you seventy days before Iowa." Voices were raised, harsh words were exchanged before Jordan stormed out of the townhouse to catch a flight back to Washington. At the Cheers bar at Logan Airport—a comically inappropriate locale—Jordan made by cell phone a final emotional speech to his former staff.

These days, the Kerry comeback has become as mythologized as the French Resistance. Not surprisingly, the instant historians have followed the traditional allocation formula: To the victors belong the credit. In truth, by early November many of the planks had already been nailed down that would provide Kerry with a platform to rise above his rivals as the most credible alternative to Dean. Margolis, an ad maker brought into the campaign by Jordan, and later squeezed out by Shrum, had already filmed the most powerful positive commercial of the primary season: Kerry's Vietnam crew-mate Del Sandusky testifying that "the decisions that he made saved our lives." The high-risk Iowa-or-bust gambit had first been discussed during the campaign's July 2003 retreat on Nantucket. True, the final decision was not made until mid-December and Cahill insisted to me that when she took over, "The banking-on-Iowa strategy was nowhere." But you did not have to be on the distribution list for promising Iowa polls by Mark Mellman (a Jordan hire) or dire New Hampshire surveys by Tom Kiley (a Boston Kerry crony) to grasp the inevitability of the choice. As Iowa coordinator John Norris, who later became Kerry's national field director, put it, "I don't think it was a brilliant strategic decision by anyone. It was a reality decision."

None of this is to minimize the mid-season firing of Kerry's campaign manager, a political drama that might be called, "There Goes Mr. Jordan." But what this staff shakeup fostered was not so much Clauswitzian maneuvers on the political game board as a transformation in the candidate's psyche. Even though Kerry helped produce decision-making paralysis with his incessant cell-phone calls to Boston from the road, he simultaneously could not abide the chaos. Cam Kerry best explained the virtues of replacing Jordan with Cahill: "Above all, it harmonized the campaign and it harmonized John Kerry."

Dick Gephardt was reminiscing about Iowa, sitting with his legs crossed in a side chair in his congressional office. The setting was not his former palatial leadership suite in the Capitol, but the ordinary chambers in the Longworth Building that now were the bounds of his empire during these last months in the House. He was wearing—c'mon take a wild guess—a crisp white shirt, a blue tie and a relaxed all-the-time-in-the-world expression. In a few hours on this Wednesday afternoon in mid-June, he was to meet with Kerry to discuss the vice presidency. But after twenty-seven years on the national stage, after four Sisyphean struggles to win back a House majority and become speaker, after two failed presidential campaigns, Gephardt radiated a well-deserved fatalism about all matters relating to ambition.

"I don't have any beefs," he said, referring to his fourth-place Iowa finish that drove him from the race. "I'm happy. I did the best I could. It was important to me to do it. I have no second thoughts." During our half-hour formal interview, followed by a 30-minute off-the-record conversation—just two guys, who have been around the track more than once, chatting about politics and fate—he never voiced any regrets. Gephardt had waged a disciplined campaign based on a determination not to repeat the mistakes of 1988. During that bygone campaign, he banked everything on his victory in the caucuses and—in sharp contrast to

Kerry this time—ended up with nothing to show for his Iowa-only obsession.

The closest to an if-only moment came when Gephardt said, "The only thing we failed to do very well, and it wasn't anybody's fault, is that I didn't get to spend the time on the ground in Iowa that I had in '88. And I really needed to in '04. That was because"—and here he allowed himself a rueful chuckle—"we were cursed and blessed with Iowa." The easy familiarity of the caucus state created front-runner expectations that Gephardt had neither the time, the money, nor enough labor-union support to meet. He worked to establish beach-heads in New Hampshire and South Carolina, where he earned the backing of Congressman Jim Clyburn, the most influential black political leader in the state. Out-of-state fund-raising trips also took a constant toll. "So I couldn't get to every county in Iowa," he explained. "I couldn't weld those relationships. It's so personal and so intense personally."

Gephardt always carried with him on his presidential quests a personal divining rod attuned to intimations of political doom. He knew it was over in 1988 when, flipping channels in a Texas hotel room, he was unable to find any of his own commercials amid a sea of spots for Michael Dukakis and Al Gore. This time around, "Taps" sounded a week before the caucuses when Dean broadcast an attack ad featuring a picture of Gephardt with Bush at the White House endorsing the 2002 Iraqi war resolution. The commercial—which began with the ominous question, "Where did the Washington Democrats stand on the war?"—also took brief shots at Kerry and Edwards before coming back to zap Gephardt again for his consistency in voting for $87 billion in appropriations for Iraq. "When that ad came on," Gephardt recalled, "I knew we were in trouble."

That killer spot prompted a vicious counterattack from Gephardt: a commercial that, taking words out of context, slammed Dean for calling Medicare "one of the worst federal programs ever." The two ads are now immortalized in campaign legend as the "Murder-Suicide Pact," which left both Gephardt and Dean awaiting a coroner's inquiry. While this shootout violated the obvious strategic doctrine of not firing at just one rival in a multi-candidate race, it is hard to envision how either Dean or Gephardt would have triumphed even if they had limited their ad buys to rebroadcasting excerpts from *Teletubbies*.

Dean, at least, made a cursory effort to include Kerry and Edwards in his broad-brush indictment. But why did Gephardt respond with a Medicare assault aimed solely at Dean? I have heard uncorroborated theories that range from ill-considered revenge in the heat of battle to a calculated ploy by Gephardt forces to throw the caucuses to Kerry. Gephardt strategist Steve Elmendorf, who is now Kerry's deputy campaign manager, insisted to me, "We didn't think we could maintain an attack on more than one candidate." Gephardt himself, who also cited limited resources, said that he worried about appearing too negative and jeopardizing a Democratic victory in November if he had tried to wage a three-front war in the waning hours before the caucuses. As he put it, "How do you come out of this if you're going after everybody?"

While Gephardt and Dean were demonstrating the folly of mutual assured destruction, the little-noticed Edwards was humming, "Put on a Happy Face." Ever since William Jennings Bryan stampeded the 1896 Convention with his "Cross of Gold" address, candidates have nurtured the fantasy that they could win a presidential nomination with a transcendent burst of oratory. Edwards, of course, didn't go all the way, but he did talk himself onto the Democratic ticket with his "Two Americas" stump speech that electrified Iowa and almost carried him to a stunning victory in the caucuses.

I had been anticipating the Edwards Moment ever since my first trip to New Hampshire in June 2002, when I witnessed the North Carolina senator's natural rapport with voters in Katie

Paine's living room in Durham. But by the end of 2003, with Edwards mired in single digits in the Iowa polls, I had begun to conclude that his still inchoate campaign was the political version of *Waiting for Godot*. Every month or two, in a journalistic triumph of hope over experience, I would devote a day to following Edwards on the road. Each trip, I would see Iowans nod with approval as he spoke, but then hesitate to take the final step of filling out a caucus pledge card. Talking with Democrats afterwards, I would hear explanations like "He's too young" or "He's rehearsing for 2008" or "He'd make a great vice president for Dean."

Finally on December 29, I saw it all come together. The campaign day began at the Creative Visions community center in Des Moines where the normally extemporaneously glib candidate took the unusual step of reading flatly from a prepared text. This, it turned out, was the formal unveiling of "Two Americas." But as the candidate's motorcade hit the road, traveling northeast to Newton, Vinton, Toledo and Waterloo, I watched Edwards transform these words that had begun on a printed page into a new stump speech all his own. Part of it was counter-programming as he ridiculed the negativism of his opponents as small-minded in Newton: "We can't lose sight of what's important with this day-to-day sniping about 'Look what so-and-so said yesterday' and 'Didn't so-and-so say something seven years ago?' Who cares? This is about the future, about what you and I together can do for the country."

But the essence of the stump speech was a smiling populism, an appeal to eliminate unfairness based on social class, delivered without a hint of pitchfork-waving anger. This argument has now been honed to a fine edge and broadcast to the nation in Edwards's speech to the Boston Convention. But like a veteran traveler who loudly complains that mass tourism and jumbo jets have ruined Marrakech, I prefer the off-the-cuff version that I first heard in Waterloo: "I'm here to tell you—we still live in two

Americas. We have one America for the privileged and one America for everybody else. We have two tax systems, one for Americans who can afford to take big tax breaks and big tax cuts. And then we have you, who pay your taxes every year and carry the tax burdens. We have two health care systems ... In a lot of America, we have two school systems. One for the haves, the affluent, and one for everybody else."

As a connoisseur of campaign rhetoric and a long-ago White House wordsmith, I instantly recognized that Edwards was finally making a lasting connection with Iowa Democrats through the most primitive instrument available in a media age: the human voice. Yes, there were other factors that helped power Edwards's closing kick in the caucuses. His surprise endorsement by the *Des Moines Register* gave the first-term senator instant credibility as ready-to-serve White House material. Kerry won the respect of caucus-goers hungry for a challenger with the national-security credentials to go head-to-head with Bush. Edwards, in contrast, won the backing of Iowa Democrats desperate to fall in love with their candidate.

My wife spent part of the day before the caucuses with Elizabeth Edwards. Meryl was on the campaign bus waiting at the airport when the candidate returned to Des Moines after his final fly-around the state. Even though staffers were pantingly eager to confer about last-minute tactics, Edwards's first move was to scoop up three-year-old Jack into his arms and ask, "Would you rather be on a plane or a bus?" Like any small boy with a passion for big machines, Jack opted for the plane. In his parental role, Edwards explained that he preferred the bus "because I can be with you and Emma Claire." What quickly became apparent was that Edwards was still high on the applause, his adrenaline surging, as it seemed after all those lonely months in the wilderness he was finally in sight of the Promised Land. Offering his own pre-caucus analysis, Edwards said that Iowa Democrats were moving away from Dean and, as a result, taking a long look at Kerry and himself. Kerry was running a strong campaign, his rival and future running-mate conceded. But Edwards (surprise!) remained optimistic about his chances.

At that moment, the bus arrived at Drake University and Edwards got a chance to demonstrate natural incandescence. As he stepped off the bus, he was mobbed by photographers and ordinary voters who had been lining up to shoehorn their way into the crowded college gymnasium. What was striking at that moment was that Iowans didn't just want to see the candidate or cheer him—they wanted to touch him as if that small act of physical connection somehow elevated the transaction from politics into something intensely personal. Okay, okay, you had to have been there to fully appreciate what was happening to this candidate who was nearly broke, who had no major constituency group like labor supporting him and whose statewide caucus organization had been assembled out of tin foil and chewing gum.

Five months later, I recalled that anticipatory moment on the eve of the caucuses when I interviewed Edwards in his Senate office. It was late June, just two weeks before the once-and-future candidate was rescued by Kerry from potential political oblivion as a prematurely retired senator. As I had with Gephardt, I asked Edwards if he had a list of if-onlys about the late, lamented campaign. "Yeah," he said with a laugh, "If only I started doing better in Iowa earlier. If I started earlier with the 'One America-Two Americas' message. Because it only came together at the end of December, the beginning of January. That meant only three weeks in Iowa. And it's clear that message resonated with caucus-goers. If I had more time to get traction, if I had come up with it myself earlier, it would have made some difference."

Jeani Murray, Dean's Iowa coordinator, estimates that the third-place candidate spent about $9 million on the caucuses. That ballpark calculation will have to suffice, since a precise number cannot be derived from the Federal Election Commission reports.

On caucus night, about 22,000 Iowans declared their allegiance to Dean. Let's stipulate that half this group would have backed Dean anyway because of his anti-war stance even if his spending had been curtailed to Dennis Kucinich levels. This arithmetic suggests that the campaign squandered more than $800, roughly the cost of a new refrigerator with an automatic ice-maker, for each Democrat who was persuaded by TV ads and paid staffers to caucus for Dean. That is a staggering amount for a Michael Bloomberg, let alone for a frugal former governor who once angrily objected to Vermont spending $50,000 for rock chipping to artificially beautify new highway construction.

Everyone who covered the caucuses or worked on a campaign has their own set of vivid examples to illustrate how Dean for America became *Rebel Without a Cause*. What lingers in my memory is a focus group I attended in Des Moines on the Thursday night before the caucuses that was arranged by Republican pollster Frank Luntz for telecast on MSNBC. During an off-camera interlude, Luntz asked the twenty likely Democratic caucus-goers if they or anyone close to them had been for Dean a month ago, but were no longer backing the candidate. Every single hand went up. Focus groups do not provide a scientific sample, but it was hard to ignore that degree of unanimity.

The next day I drove to Marshalltown and saw further evidence of the looming Dean debacle. Two busloads of reporters and photographers were trailing the candidate, but at this wan rally the press corps and the Dean entourage outnumbered the roughly eighty would-be caucus-goers in attendance. As Dean pointedly reminded the scant crowd of his early opposition to both the Iraq war and the No Child Left Behind education program, he seemed like an aging rock star reduced to reprising his greatest hits in smaller and smaller clubs.

A few days before the caucuses, I received an e-mail from Rick Ridder, Dean's first campaign manager, who had returned to Iowa in an ego-less gesture to help organize Davenport and the surrounding Mississippi River counties. Using standard campaign lingo that refers to hard-core, walk-through-fire supporters as "1's", Ridder wrote, "I'm worried since 65 percent of our 1's have never been to a caucus before." The morning after Dean became the Incredible Shrinking Candidate, I called Ridder to get his interpretation of the caucus results. "You know what," Ridder said, "65 percent of our 1's still haven't been to a caucus."

CHAPTER 13

To Boston and Beyond

Disappointment and defeated dreams are usually endured behind closed doors and drawn drapes with the only solace to be found in a vodka bottle or a bag of Oreos. But in presidential primaries, it is the triumphant candidate and his closest advisers who revel in seclusion, swapping high fives and bear hugs in hotel suites, as they wait for the proper TV moment to swoop down into the bedlam of their rapturous supporters to proclaim victory before a national audience. At life-changing moments like this, it is the vanquished who cannot endure solitude. They are too restless to hide; too eager for company as they pore over the early exit polls, searching for a glimmer of hope amid these statistical portents of doom. On primary days, the hotel lobbies belong to the losers.

In my mind's eye, I can still see a bone-weary Joe Trippi and Tricia Enright, looking like flood victims at a Red Cross shelter, bravely clinging to the fantasy that Howard Dean had roared back with a screaming finish in the New Hampshire primary. It is late afternoon on January 27, and they are hunched over a table, normally used for a breakfast buffet by cost-conscious business travelers, on the ground floor of the Homewood Suites at the

Manchester airport. What animates them are the first wave of network exit polls, which show Dean within just 5 percentage points of Kerry, with Wesley Clark, John Edwards and Joe Lieberman badly trailing. And the *Los Angeles Times*, which conducts its own survey, actually has Dean with a one-point lead. Enright is quizzing anyone who crosses the lobby—reporters, staffers and probably even hotel maids—searching for a Deaniac equivalent to Bill Clinton's famous 1992 claim, after a death-defying second-place finish in New Hampshire, that he was now "the Comeback Kid." At one point, Trippi jokingly suggests, "We've been defibrillated." But Enright's quest for a primary-night sobriquet soon proved as unnecessary as trying to concoct a Secret Service code name for President Dean. The actual returns heralded a second breakthrough victory for Kerry (38 percent), followed by Dean (just 26 percent), Clark (12 percent), Edwards (fewer than a thousand votes back, also with 12 percent) and finally Lieberman (9 percent).

Another primary afternoon, another lobby. John Edwards is asleep in his suite at Milwaukee's jewel-like Hotel Pfister, Emma Claire and Jack are back home in Washington, and Elizabeth Edwards is nervously prowling the hotel. There are no exit-poll numbers yet for the February 17 Wisconsin primary, but the pre-election surveys auger a rout: Kerry is trouncing Edwards by more than a two-to-one margin with Dean, the other surviving major candidate, third. Meryl and I are lingering over a late lunch in a Pfister coffee-shop booth when we spot the wandering Elizabeth, who joins us, eager for distraction and news. The news soon arrives with a roar (actually, it was my cell phone tinkling, "Take Me Out to the Ball Game")—Edwards is within a half dozen percentage points of Kerry in the exit polls. For the next three hours, Elizabeth stays rooted in the coffee shop with Meryl, while I return to my room to write my column. What I miss is a scene that any old-time wardheeler would appreciate: the presidential candidate's wife passionately urging her waitress, a waiter and the coffee-shop hostess to vote in the primary. Elizabeth even sets up an impromptu phone bank, convincing the hostess to call home so that she could make a please-rush-out-and-vote-for-my-husband pitch to a family member. This coffee-shop mobilization only ends when the candidate arrives, in his jogging clothes, searching for Elizabeth. Then, following the same regimen as on primary day in New Hampshire, Edwards sets out on a loneliness-of-the-long-distance-runner journey. The hopes that ran with Edwards that afternoon through the bitterly cold streets of Milwaukee were never realized. Although the actual Wisconsin results came in as advertised (Kerry received 40 percent of the vote, Edwards 34 percent and Dean 18 percent), the 2004 Democratic race was effectively over, just twenty-nine days after the Iowa caucuses.

It is probably possible to create a computer simulation to test whether, in an alternate universe, Kerry could have been stopped after Iowa. Maybe my imagination has become stunted by the reality of Kerry as the nominee, but it is difficult for me to construct another plausible scenario. Dean, who rallied from a post-scream nadir of 12 percent in his own internal tracking polls, did all he could in New Hampshire, even bringing out the reclusive Judy Steinberg for a winning primetime ABC interview with Diane Sawyer. And it wasn't enough. Clark, having mistakenly skipped Iowa, needed Dean—the contender with the shakiest national-security credentials—as his foil. The save-the-party-from-disaster rationale behind Clark's ungainly candidacy collapsed when it was Kerry, a Vietnam veteran and a traditional Democrat, who was crowned king of the caucuses. Lieberman, who never lost his good humor amid his campaign-trail humiliations, was always running for the nomination of a centrist political party that didn't exist. And Edwards, well, let him speak for himself. After Iowa, he said during our June interview, "The die was cast. I think it was very hard—though we proved in Wisconsin it wasn't impos-sible—to change the dynamic after that point. I think Iowa created the dynamic. I think the winner of the Iowa caucuses had it been Kerry, as it was, or me would have been the likely nominee."

Having come this far together, dear reader, indulge me in one final image from the primaries. On the final Saturday afternoon before New Hampshire voted, frost-bitten volunteers for all the candidates waved signs to impress motorists in the parking lot of Concord's largest shopping center. The Lieberman forces, such as they were, had deployed a two-person operation proclaiming the theoretical doctrine of "JOE-MENTUM." But the young stalwart, entrusted with the "JOE" placard, had rationally chosen warmth over politics. Left behind was a brave and lonely volunteer trying to sway voters with his cryptic battle cry of "MENTUM."

Mentum, as now inscribed in my personal lexicon, is momentum with half the enthusiasm missing. And that, in this strange and memorable campaign year, was enough to propel Kerry's swift boat through the primaries. Kerry emerged victorious from Iowa, in part, because he was a war hero. And then, aided by the hyper-drive political calendar, Kerry kept winning against weakened opposition largely because he had already won. Fewer than 50,000 Iowa Democrats caucused for Kerry on the never-to-be-forgotten evening of January 19. But that was enough mentum to anoint Kerry as the Democratic nominee who may well win more than 50 million votes on November 2.

My first Democratic convention was the Lyndon Johnson coronation in 1964 when, along with three high-school buddies from Connecticut, I set out for Atlantic City, innocently unaware of such minor logistical details as the need for gallery passes. Arriving in the salt-water-taffy tawdriness of this pre-gambling beach resort gone to seed, we quickly discovered that our tenuous ties to local Connecticut Democratic dignitaries did not give us the clout to get into the convention hall.

Then in one of those youthful moments when you suddenly decipher how the adult world works, I realized that a far-away state like Idaho probably had more tickets than it could use. So I called the number listed for the Idaho delegation and somehow found myself talking to Verda Barnes, Senator Frank Church's longtime administrative assistant. Displaying what I thought was the guile of a confidence man, I explained with a breathless string of implausible whoppers that after my parents divorced, my father moved to Boise, and while, yes, it was true that I was going to school in Connecticut, my heart belonged to Idaho. Probably barely able to restrain her giggles, this nice woman gave me four tickets for each night of the convention. So I was in the hall when the Mississippi Freedom Democrats struggled to be seated, when Robert Kennedy delivered his emotional tribute to his slain brother and when vice-presidential nominee Hubert Humphrey brought down the galleries with his withering assault on the GOP nominee's nay-saying Senate voting record, punctuated by the refrain, "But not Senator Goldwater."

This forty-year-old personal history may explain my grumpiness as the Democrats assembled in Boston to rubberstamp the nominations of Kerry and Edwards. Having experienced the earthy excess of the real thing, I was saddened by the message-of-the-moment manipulation and homogenized hoopla of a twenty-first-century convention. I'm too much of a traditionalist to enjoy watching the once-brawling, boisterous Democrats emulate corporatized Republican politics by putting on a show with all the spontaneity of a Stepford Wives reunion. And even if the convention concluded the dramatic arc of this narrative, I will confess that more than once, as I searched for a story amid the sanitized serenity of Boston, I found myself thinking, "How I wish I were back in Iowa."

I watched Kerry's acceptance speech in my hotel room at a Holiday Inn, following the philosophy that made-for-TV moments should be witnessed on the screen rather than in the hall with the studio audience. So I was alone—and therefore free from the constraint of never revealing genuine political sentiment in front of press-box colleagues—when I was surprised to find myself moved by this passage in Kerry's address: "John Kennedy called my generation to service. It was the beginning of a great journey, a time to march for civil rights, for voting rights, for the environment, for women and for peace. We believed we could change the world. And you know what? We did. But we're not finished. The journey isn't complete. The march isn't over. The promise isn't perfected. Tonight, we're setting out again."

Those words brought back a memory from my first trip to New Hampshire with Kerry, then a fledgling presidential candidate. Two years earlier, almost to the day, Kerry stood on a rock at sunset in a backyard in Londonderry and conjured up the idealism of the 1960s as personified by Gene McCarthy's presidential campaign. He spoke about a crusade against an ill-conceived war and about the roots of the environmental movement. His phrases that day were not polished and his syntax was rough, but his emotion seemed heartfelt as this sad-eyed senator in late middle age struggled to express his passion to recapture the idealism of his youth.

Kerry was the same person standing on that rock as daylight faded in Londonderry as he was on the stage of the Fleet Center bathed in a halo of light. The atmospherics were different as he was now addressing the nation instead of 150 New Hampshire Democrats. But there was an inescapable sense of continuity as John Kerry's journey had come full circle. If Kerry can go on to redeem those dreams in the White House, I will always remember with pride that I was there with him in New Hampshire on that August 2002 day when it all began.

Acknowledgments

For the casual reader, this section is of primarily voyeuristic interest, the addendum from which you learn that Paris Hilton did the fact checking and Kim Jong Il provided the original inspiration for the book during a boozy lunch in Pyongyang. For the writer—especially one not used to brandishing statuettes over his head and shouting, "I'm King of the World"—this is a tricky moment, not from lack of gratitude but because our culture tends to ridicule those who breathlessly burble thanks to their nutritionist, their feng-shui consultant and their favorite barista at Starbucks.

Still, having had more than my share of failed book projects over the past two decades, I come to this moment brimming with appreciation and keenly aware of my indebtedness to enough people to fill the Des Moines phone book. In my effort to achieve some sense of brevity and to gracefully leave the stage before my microphone is cut off, I apologize in advance for the inadvertent omissions in the list that follows. And, of course, despite the assistance that I have received from so many, errors in the text are solely my own responsibility.

My publisher, Peter Osnos, deserves garlands for the trust that he has displayed over nearly twenty years—in a modern-day triumph of hope over experience, clinging to the belief that somehow, someday I would produce a book for him. Now that we have finally reached that moment, I am humbled by his persistent faith. Lisa Kaufman, who took over editing the manuscript at the midway point, has been a writer's dream with her insight, her graceful appreciation of language and structure and her enthusiasm for the project. Paul Golob, now the editorial director at Times Books, had the genius to envision the contours of this book during a lunch in early July 2002 and the patience to guide a fledgling author through the thicket of his first chapter outline. Everyone else at PublicAffairs has more than earned my unflagging gratitude. I would also like to raise a toast to my agent, Flip Brophy, who was there whenever I needed her.

As a writer with a demanding day job as columnist for *USA Today,* I want to thank my colleagues for the understanding and support that they gave me during this year-long project. In particular, I want to express my indebtedness to Karen Jurgensen, the editor of the paper, Hal Ritter, the managing editor for news, and Bill Sternberg, who is my editor on the "Hype & Glory" column. I also benefited, as always, from the assistance of my *USA Today* compatriots on the campaign trail, especially Jill Lawrence and Susan Page.

No list is more encyclopedic than the roster of campaign staffers and political insiders who have enthusiastically given me their time, their insights and their assistance with this project. One of the joys of covering presidential campaigns is the companionship of these practitioners of the political trade. Obviously not all of them will thrill to every paragraph and interpretation in this book, which is why I have decided not to include the lengthy roll call of my interview subjects. But there is a special category of staffers who made this book possible—the first person associated with every major candidate who grasped what I was trying to accomplish with this chronicle of the Invisible Primary. So a grateful tip of the hat to Kate O'Connor (Howard Dean), Mike Briggs (John Edwards), Erik Smith (Dick Gephardt), Buddy Menn